AF540506

Economic Development and Planning in India

By the same author

- Urbanization, Urban Development and Metropolitan Cities in India
  Edited by S.K. Aggarwal
- Regional Development and Planning in India
  Edited by S.K. Aggarwal
- Economic Development and Planning in India
  By V. Nath
- *Rural Development and Planning in India*
  By V. Nath in press

About the Author

Dr. Vishwambhar Nath was one of the leading development economists of India. After getting degree in Geography from Government College, Lahore in 1946, he received his Ph.D. from the University of Maryland in 1949. Returning to India, Dr. Nath joined the Planning Commission of India from 1950-1966 with a break from 1960-63 when he was posted as Collector in two districts of Rajasthan where he got opportunities for intensive studies in socio-economic changes in village India and in creation of other country's best known Tiger reserve—the Ranthambor Sanctuary. In the Planning Commission, he led the Project Evaluation Organization (PEO) and later was Chief of its Natural Resources and Urban Planning Divisions was involved with and assisted in preparing the plan for the Calcutta Metropolitan Region.

In 1966, Dr. Nath was deputed to the United Nations Development Programme and began his UN service as a Professor at the Training Institute of Economic and Social Development Planning for the Middle East in Kuwait. Later assignments included Development Planning positions in Sierra Leone and Gambia. He spent a year as a Visiting Professor of Geography at the University of Kentucky, and spent two years as a Visiting Scholar at Boston University. Returning to India in 1986, Dr. Nath was attached to the Centre for Policy Research in Delhi and continued his writing and scholarly work until his passing on September 10, 2002.

Economic Development and Planning in India

Dr. V. Nath

CONCEPT PUBLISHING COMPANY PVT. LTD.,
NEW DELHI-110059

ISBN-13: 978-81-8069-658-9 **ISBN-10: 81-8069-658-8**

First Published 2010

Published and Printed by

Concept Publishing Company Pvt. Ltd.
Regd. Office:
A/15-16, Commercial Block, Mohan Garden
New Delhi-110059 (India)
Phones : 25351460, 25351794, *Fax* : 091-11-25357109
Email : publishing@conceptpub.com,
Website: www.conceptpub.com

Editorial Office:
H-13, Bali Nagar, New Delhi-110 015, India.

Cataloging in Publication Data-- *Courtesy:* D.K. Agencies (P) Ltd. <docinfo@dkagencies.com>

Nath, Viswambhar, 1923-2002.
Economic development and planning in India / V. Nath.
p. cm.
Includes bibliographical references.
Includes index.
ISBN 13: 9788180696589 ISBN 10: 8180696588

1. Economic development--India. 2. India--Economic policy--1947- 3. India--Economic conditions--1947- I. Title.

DDC 338.954 22

Preface

Since Independence of the country planning for economic and social development has been the main instrument to forge India from an underdeveloped/ developing to a developed country. Pandit Nehru the first Prime Minister of India was a great believer in economic and social development through planned development; he was much impressed by the progress made by USSR in this direction since it started centralized development planning. India however had to start this endeavour within its political ideology of a socialist democracy adopted by the Constitution in 1950.

Infrastructure needed and created by the Government of India, since the launch of planned development, are detailed in another volume by the author, 'Administration and Development Planning in India' (forthcoming). The author was a witness to the creation and growth of such infrastructures as well as links established between the central planning agency — The Planning Commission - and the implementation agencies at the center, state and local levels over a period of more than half a century.

Besides the existing and new structures, several semi-autonomous and autonomous institutes have collaborated in providing basic data and monitoring of the progress and assess the development needs of the country in view of the targets set by the Planning Commission. Data on natural resources, land use, growth of population, production, productivity, incomes, investment, consumption and cost of living is continuously updated, analyzed and presented to the users. Innumerable academicians and researchers - Indian and foreigners – have been analyzing the data and give their opinions on policy issues.

Planning exercise in India, however, has been burdened with imbibing contradictory ideologies from socialist democracy when most of the basic needs of development – production of basic materials, and social infrastructure – were planned to be undertaken in the public sector (PSUs) and private sector development was licensed including nationalization of banks, to liberalization of the productive sectors including sale and disinvestment of the loss making PSU and even privatization of health care, education and insurance etc.

Development resources – man, material, capital and technology – for planned development have mainly been tapped from within the country. However, help from multinational and international agencies has been forthcoming whenever needed and requested.

India has emerged one of the few countries where central economic planning is being practiced without centralized controls. Efforts have been made to replicate the Indian model for development planning in several countries of Africa. Under assistance from United Nations several countries have set up development planning agencies and have produced five year development plans. Their implementation in these countries, however, is a different story.

The author had life long sustained inquisitive interest in studying the planning process in India even when, after 18 years of association with the Planning Commission, his career interest with the United Nations led him to focus on teaching and preparation of five year plans in Middle East and West Africa. He kept on writing on planning and development in India as is evident from his collection of writings, mostly published but some unpublished, contained in the five volumes that have been/being published.

In this volume the author has made significant contribution to the process of development planning through his thoughtful writings on various aspects of planning through analysis of available data on natural resources, land use, agricultural, industrial, rural and urban development and goals and strategies of development during half a century of development planning and prospects for 2020.

He reminisces in the last chapter of this book that in 1950 the 'country needed a plan' and there was much excitement when the Draft of the First Five Year Plan was released. However by 2001 while planning still is needed and serves a very central and useful purpose, fascination with Five Year Plan is over!

June 2009 Kamla Nath

Acknowledgements

As mentioned in earlier two volumes, I have undertaken the task to bring into FIVE volumes academic writings on India by my husband Dr. Vishwambhar Nath. This, 'Economic Development and Planning in India', is the third volume. The earlier two volumes, 'Urbanization, Urban Development and Metropolitan Cities in India' and 'Regional Development and Planning in India' were published in 2007 and 2008 respectively. The remaining two volumes, 'Rural Development and Planning in India' and 'Administration and Development Planning in India' will be published soon.

Dr. Nath had a life long interest in economic development of developing countries in which he was engrossed, initially with the Indian Planning Commission and later during his tenure with the United Nations Development Programme, which took him to work on Planning and Economic Development in West Africa—Sierra Leone and the Gambia. Major part of his writings and working life, however, was devoted to work on development and planning in India.

He was one of the first two officers hired by the Planning Commission soon after it was set up in 1950. He had the privilege to head the Programme Evaluation Organization (PEO) as its Director and Chief of the Natural Resources and Urban Planning Divisions of the Planning Commission.

An interlude with the Indian Administrative Service (IAS) enabled him not only to study socio-economic impact of planned development in rural India but also the role of administration in development planning and implementation of development programmes at the district and lower levels. His teaching assignment with Economic and Social Development Training Institute for the Middle East in Kuwait led him to write about the importance of Administration and Administrative structures in planning for economic development and social change.

Articles written on various aspects of Economic Deveopment and Planning in India have been collated in this volume. I am thankful to Mrs. Suhasini Ramaswamy who sustained her interest in this work and has put in enormous amount of time in giving shape to this volume and for editorial and proof reading work. I am thankful also to Mr. Ranjan Sasmal who spent hours typing for the book.

The publisher, Mr. Ashok Kumar Mittal has kept me encouraged by promising to publish all the five volumes. I am thankful to Mr. Mittal for this.

Last but not the least I am thankful to my three children Virendra, Arvind and Jyotsna whose sustained emotional support sustained me in keep going with the work. I have been lucky in sharing a deep love and companionship with my husband which was the main inspiration to start this project. As I have gone on to reading the interesting contents of the articles, I am today much better informed person than I was before I started work on his writings. Nath was not only my husband in many ways, he was also my teacher. He seems to have left these notes to teach me what he knew best. This has been a blessing in disguise in an otherwise very time consuming task.

December 2008 **Kamla Nath**

Contents

1

Economic Development and Planning in India

The Meaning of Development: Developed and Underdeveloped

'Development' is a mental construct, based on collective value judgements of social scientists (economists and others) and of practical people, such as political leaders and administrators. Acceptance of 'development' as an objective of national/group endeavour involves further value judgement that it is desirable and attainable. The judgement was made in the post-war period by the leaders of the newly independent countries of Asia and Africa and other relatively poor and backward countries, and 'development' is the most significant process in them at present. Development planning is a body of techniques and procedures designed for greater efficiency in achievement of the objectives of development. The basic tools of planning are: clearer definition of goals and objectives, closer relation of goals and objectives to resources, and more efficient allocation and utilization of the resources.

The basic technique for measurement of level of development, and for classifying countries (regions, groups) into 'developed' or 'under-developed', is to set up a scale, based on an individual indicator, or a group of indicators, and place the different units on it. The terms, 'developed' and 'developing' are quite recent, in fact, their usage derives partly from the sensitivity of the Asian, African and other poor and backward countries to be designated as such. This had been the case in the pre-war period.

The most popular measure of the level of development, used by economists and increasingly by others, is 'per capita gross national product (GNP) or per capita income'. Various other indicators, such as per capita energy consumption; the proportion of population living in the urban areas;

the proportion of labour force engaged in non-primary activities; literacy rate (or other measures of the spread of education); numbers of doctors or hospital beds per million of population; vital rates; per capita calorie intake or consumption of proteins etc. are also widely used. But there is a growing trend towards replacing them with composite indicators, such as 'the level of living index'. One example of the latter is the index, based on about 40 indicators (divided into 7 groups), and developed by the United Nations Institute of Social Research, Geneva.

Deriving from per capita income as a measure of the level of economic development is the most commonly used measure of economic progress—the rate of economic growth, or annual increase in per capita income. Furthermore, since underdeveloped countries are characterized by relatively static per capita incomes, while the developed countries have continuously increasing incomes, the rate of economic growth itself becomes a basis for distinguishing between underdeveloped and developed countries. Finally, the term 'economic development' is reserved by some economists for the relatively brief, but most important, period in the development process in which the transformation from static to continuously increasing per capita income takes place. Rostow's concept of the "take-off into self-sustaining growth" is similar.

Development planners follow development economists in accepting per capita income as the principal measure of the level of economic development, and of the rate of economic growth as the principal measure of economic progress. But, with increasing realization of the limitations of per capita income as a measure, there is progressive acceptance of the 'level of living index' as another measure of economic development or economic welfare. The most important target in a typical development plan relates to the rate of economic growth; but many plans contain specific targets relating to raising the 'level of living' in general, or selected specific indicators of it such as the literacy rate, the calorie or protein intake and the doctor/population ratio. However, increase in economic growth/levels of living during the past fifty years have led to ecological and social problems and the concept of per capita income and consumption as indicators of development are prone to value judgement leading to a further corollary that the judgement can change over a finite period. It recalls, moreover, the question raised by W. Arthur Lewis, in the early 1950s, "Is economic growth desirable?" We have all decided that it is desirable, but we may soon have to add the proviso "up to a point".

The Development Process

Development leads to a multi-faceted change process. The principal changes relate to:

(i) Use of natural resources;
(ii) Organization and technology of production;
(iii) Consumption patterns;
(iv) Social values, attitudes, patterns of relationships and institutions;
(v) Political behaviour patterns and institutions; and
(vi) Motivations of individuals and groups.

Consistent with the acceptance of development as a multi-faceted process, the decision-models (on projects etc.) have also to be modified and made more adequate, so as to take into account the needs of social, political and other non-economic aspects of development which may hinder or propel the development process. Of particular importance are the:

(i) Social structure,
(ii) Political structure, and
(iii) External assistance/foreign aid.

Social Structure

The centre piece of India's in-egalitarian social structure is the caste system, which indicates a prescribed occupation for each caste and determines the social, political, and economic power of people of different caste groups. At the top of the social structure are the high castes—Brahmins, Rajputs and Mahajans (or traders). They own most of the wealth and land in rural areas and property in urban areas. At the bottom of the structure are the scheduled castes and the scheduled tribes. They are the poorer quarter of the population and have besides very low social status. The traditional occupation of the scheduled castes was labour on lands owned by the high castes. Furthermore, they performed tasks, such as flaying of hides and skins of dead animals, dressing them to make leather goods for shoes and for some operations on farms and scavenging which are considered 'dirty' by the high caste Hindus. To add insult to injury, they were considered untouchables, i.e. their touch was considered polluting by the high castes. In the villages, they could not draw water from the wells used by the high castes or worship in the temples of the high castes.

They had their own drinking water wells and temples. In most parts of the country, they lived in hamlets spread around a central inhabited area, in which the people of the high castes lived and which gave the habitat its name. In states such as Punjab, Haryana, Rajasthan, Gujarat and western U.P. in which the relatively large, tightly nucleated village is the norm, they lived in a separate quarter of the village so that their physical contact with residents of these high castes was minimal.

All this has changed during the last half a century of development planning and practice of democracy. Untouchability has been abolished by a directive principle of the Constitution—its practice is a cognizable offence—and is slowly disappearing in practice in both the rural and the urban areas.

The owner of a tea shop located in a small town, a few miles from the village, does not ask the caste of his or her customers. And people of the high castes, who would never allow the village well to be used by the scheduled castes, do not have any hesitation in taking tea from the same shop as men of the scheduled castes. Similarly, the priests of the biggest temples in metropolitan cities do not ask the castes of the devotees.

More important, as a result of the land reforms introduced in most of the states during the early 1950s, large areas of cultivable lands which were lying fallow have been allotted to landless agricultural labourers most of whom belong to the scheduled castes in order to raise their social and economic status. Large areas of cultivable lands became available also as a result of the abolition of exploitative intermediary tenures such as *zamindari* and *jagirdari*. Most of the croplands held by the *zamindars* in the former British provinces and their counterparts the *jagirdars* in the princely states were taken away from them and allotted to their tenants who used to cultivate the land and who belonged to the scheduled castes or other backward castes. The former *zamindars* and *jagirdars* have accepted the change as inevitable as a result of the political change to a democratic society. It is only in parts of Bihar and of the Telugu speaking part of the former dominions of the Nizam of Hyderabad that there are cases of burning of scheduled caste villagers by their former high caste landowners or of the killing of individual landowners by their former tenants.

The revolutionary social change has produced great social tensions, one symptom of which is widespread monetary corruption among the political elite, a significant proportion of which have been elected to their high office by the use of money and muscle power. Monetary corruption has percolated also to the middle and lower rungs of the bureaucracy so that the citizen has to pay a bribe to the official who is to give him a piece of land for housing, connections for water or electricity in urban areas or the right to cultivable land in the rural areas conferred on him by the land reforms.

Political change has been so great that the Chief Ministers in most of the states belong to the dominant cultivating castes or other backward castes. The Constitution provides for reservation of one-fourth of the seats in Parliament and legislative bodies in the states for members of the scheduled castes and the scheduled tribes. Similarly ministers in most state cabinets belong to these formerly depressed castes.

Fifty years ago the position was radically different. The Prime Minister of India and Chief Ministers of most of the states belonged to the high castes. The proportion of ministers of the scheduled castes and the scheduled tribes was similar or lower than their proportion in the population. Furthermore, ministers belonging to the high castes took most of the ministries responsible for making the major decisions on governance of the state. Ministers belonging to the scheduled castes and the scheduled tribes were responsible for decisions which affected only the welfare of members of their own castes.

Political Structure: Pluralist or Competitive Democracy

Although the concept of planning for economic development was successfully practiced by countries run by the Communist Party—the USSR, Yugoslavia etc., India selected the system of parliamentary democracy for governance of the people. This means that different political parties compete for control of the government. The party, which has the maximum number of legislators in these bodies, forms the government and carries out development and other programmes following its party manifesto. As soon as a party loses its majority, after an election or earlier at times, it goes out of office and is succeeded by a party or a coalition of parties which can muster a majority of seats.

Although the majority of the electorate are poor and illiterate they have exercised their votes with ultimate care. They consider this a valuable gift of independence from the British.

Fourteen elections have been fought since the Constitution of India was enforced in 1950, without too much violence. The present government, which came into power in 2004, is the fifteenth since Independence. It expects to complete its term of office of five years and may thereafter be either re-elected or form the opposition.

It is significant that most elected governments formed so far have followed the same economic and fiscal policies that were introduced by the government led by the Congress Party in 1991 in order to avert the balance of payment crisis that the country faced in that year because it felt that these are in the best interests of the country. Certain important factors of foreign policy of all governments formed so far, i.e. relations with the neighbouring and other countries are not too different from the policies initiated by Pandit Nehru in 1952 or earlier. Thus, there is both continuity and comprehensiveness in India's parliamentary system of government.

In addition to the Parliament and State Governments, the democratic system of elections has also been introduced for governance at the local level—from village to district—through the introduction of the Panchayati Raj Institutions which were intended to be apolitical institutions of governance but in practice the elections to these institutions are fought and supported by local political parties which may be branches of national or state level parties.

The Role of Foreign Aid and Foreign Direct Investment in India's Economic Development

When the former colonies of Britain, France and the Netherlands became independent in the 1950s and the 1960s, there was much discussion of aid by the former colonial powers and by the U.S.A. to help their economic development.

This was based on the American experience of aid towards rebuilding quickly the industries, agriculture and cities of its allies—France and Britain and former enemies Germany, Italy and Japan which had suffered severe damage or had been destroyed during, Second World War. American aid had within 15 years, i.e. by the beginning of the 1960s rebuilt these war-ravaged economies so well that their traditional exports were flooding the markets of the world. The Japanese had, with American aid, built such state of the art steel plants and shipyards that import of their steel led to closure of many steel mills in the U.S.A. and Britain, and import of their ships led to closure of some American shipyards. Furthermore, Japanese T.V. receivers and music systems were the rage in the U.S.A., Britain and west European countries.

Motives of Aid

The motives of giving aid to the developing countries were mixed. The former colonial countries, Britain, France and the Netherlands, wanted that their influence should remain strong in their former colonies and dependencies. The British, the Dutch and the French wanted that the ruling elites of newly independent Malaysia, Indonesia and former colonies in Africa and Asia should not nationalize the plantations of oil palm and coffee or mines of tin and other minerals but should be partners with the erstwhile colonial planters and mining companies to exploit these resources.

All these countries wanted also that they should be free to exploit the newly discovered oil fields of Nigeria and the Republic of Congo in Africa and Malaysia and Indonesia in Asia. The British and the French succeeded in their efforts. The newly independent elites of African countries retained English as the language of communication with foreigners and adopted parliamentary democracy as their mode of government. However, the plantations of oil palm, cocoa and coffee in Ghana, tea and coffee in Kenya, Uganda and Tanzania were nationalized. The Nigerians invited all the seven oil potential major African countries to explore their oil fields.

The newly independent elites of the former French colonies similarly retained French as the language of communication with foreigners, shopped in Paris during the summer and patterned their legislatures after the Chamber of Deputies in Paris. They did not nationalize the mines but ensured that a part of the profits went into supporting their French mode of living, building approach roads, and to finance essential consumer goods.

The Kenyans quickly decided that they had better retain the British as managers of plantations, but the Ghananias, the Ugandans and Tanzanians decided otherwise. They were all victims of grinding poverty and a succession of *coups d' etat* in Ghana and Uganda and it was years before their economies reverted to the position at Independence. Furthermore, improvement of communications in all African countries brought to the cities, millions of young men and women who wanted jobs as domestic servants and other unskilled workers, because they no longer wanted to do the backbreaking work in subsistence agriculture.

Moreover the amounts given in aid were too small to have any tangible effect on the economies of these countries and were mostly absorbed in salaries and perquisites of the technical assistance experts and expenditure on equipment bought in the aid giving country. Aid with such mixed motives was severely criticized as evinced by Sameer Amin an Egyptian economist and many other political economists. They described it as neo-colonialism in another form.

Foreign aid and foreign direct investment has been too small to assist India's economic development after its initial role in establishing India's basic industries. Most of the amounts given as 'aid' have had to be repaid over the decades. Foreign aid and foreign direct investment in less developed countries of sub-Saharan Africa has only brought to them the serious problems of over-urbanization and political instability due to too rapid migration of youth to cities where there were no jobs for them.

The ruling elites of the resource rich countries are cooperating with the former colonial power to build their cities and provide education and health to their populations. They have also made peace on their own terms with the Chinese who provide most of the skilled labour force for the mines and plantations.

2

Natural Resources and Economic Development: A Survey*

Natural resources are materials available in nature which man utilizes for economic activity, e.g. land, forests, minerals, falling water, an estuary which contains a harbour and the climate etc. The concept of natural resources is culture-bound and depends upon such cultural factors as the state of technology, the nature of demand, prices and socio-economic institutions. In India, while very small numbers of primitive shifting cultivators can obtain only a precarious living from vast areas of forest, large populations of settled cultivators live next to them on small areas but at much higher levels of living. The advance from hunting and food gathering or primitive, shifting cultivation to settled agriculture is accompanied by an enormous increase in the efficiency of resource use and in the range of natural materials used. Similar changes take place with industrialization. Per capita consumption of natural materials is much higher in developed countries than in the underdeveloped countries which are predominantly agricultural or pastoral. The U.S.A. with only six per cent of the world's population is estimated to account for more than half of the total annual world consumption of natural materials.

Efficiency of resource use is also much higher in the developed countries than in the underdeveloped countries: this is reflected in the higher productivity of agricultural land and of labour employed in natural resource exploitation activities in the former. An indication of the higher productivity of agricultural land is given by the data on yields of wheat and rice in selected developed and underdeveloped countries (Table 2.1). Crop yields have been increasing in the developed countries for a century

* Published in "Economic Structure and Activities", *The Gazetteer of India*, Editor: Dr. P.N. Chopra, 10 March, 1975, Vol. III, pp. 39-74.

Table 2.1: Yields of Rice and Wheat—Developed and Underdeveloped Countries

(kg. per hectare)

Paddy Rice (Average 1966-68)		*Wheat (Average 1966-68)*	
Developed Countries			
Italy	46.4	United Kingdom	38.5
U.S.A.	49.6	U.S.A.	18.1
Japan	55.3	France	33.8
U.S.S.R.	31.7	U.S.S.R.	13.3
Underdeveloped Countries			
India	14.9	India	9.5
Burma	15.8	Pakistan	8.9
Thailand	16.8	Turkey	12.0
Brazil	15.0	Argentina	11.4
U.A.R.	49.8	U.A.R.	25.8

or more as a result of improvements in techniques and management practices—use of improved, higher-yielding seeds, chemical fertilizers and pesticides. Similar increases in crop yields with the application of modern technology are now taking place in the underdeveloped countries. Yields of most crops have risen slowly in India during the last 15 years (Table 2.2). The yield of rice increased from 874 kg. per hectare in 1955-56 to an average of 1,054 kg. per hectare during 1967-69. The increase was greater in the case of wheat, from 708 kg. to 1,137 kg. in the same period, because the new, high-yielding varieties, introduced since 1966, have proved very successful in the wheat growing areas of northern India.

Table 2.2: India—Trends in Yields of Selected Crops

(kg. per hectare) (Average)

	1955-56	*1961-62*	*1967-69*
Rice (Cleaned)	874	1,028	1,054
Wheat	708	823	1,137
Cotton	88	103	123
Jute	1,082	1,248	1,210
Sugar cane (*Gur*)	3,289	4,303	4,834

Differences in labour productivity in the natural resources sectors of the developed and the underdeveloped countries are much greater than differences in productivity of land; average productivity per agricultural worker, as measured by value of output, is nearly 34 times greater in the U.S.A. than in India.

Technological Advance

Besides raising productivity of land and labour used in the natural resource sectors, technological advance has been responsible, especially in recent years, for (i) development of synthetic substitutes for natural materials, ranging from metals to fibres, and (ii) an enormous increase in the spatial range of the exploitation of natural resources. The most notable example of the latter is provided by extension of exploitation of oil and natural gas resources to the offshore areas. Offshore production of both has increased rapidly during the last decade and the recent discoveries in a number of regions, from the North Sea and the Mediterranean to various parts of the Western Pacific, especially the South China Sea, indicate that significant proportions of the world output of oil and natural gas will come in future from offshore sources. Exploitation has been confined so far to shallow, continental shelf areas; but the technology is advanced enough for development of resources located at greater depths. The sea floors may become important sources of other minerals also in the not so distant future.

Technological advance is often triggered off by shortages resulting from interruption of supplies, as during a war, or from progressive depletion of supply sources. Development of synthetic rubber, nitrogenous fertilizers and fibres like nylon has all resulted from war-time shortages of natural materials. Exploitation of offshore petroleum sources is a response to progressive depletion of on-shore oil-fields in major producing countries, such as the U.S.A., and the failure of new discoveries to keep pace with the rapid growth of demand—seven to eight per cent a year during the post-war period. On the other hand, there are innumerable examples of mineral deposits ceasing to be worked or crops or other natural products not being produced because of the discovery of new, richer deposits, or availability of better or cheaper substitutes. The coal industries of the U.S.A. and Western Europe have been depressed during most of the post-war period because of progressive increase in the proportion of energy derived from oil and natural gas in these countries. Cultivation of indigo stopped in India after the development of aniline dyes.

Abundance or scarcities of natural resources are relative terms which describe the demand-supply relationship. The latter depends in turn, on such factors as the size of the population and its level of living (demand) and the levels of technology and organization (supply). The expression, 'high pressure of population' on land, used so frequently for India, merely indicates that at the present levels of technology and organization, agriculture does not provide to the population of the country, food and other agricultural products, commensurate with its demands. A significant change in anyone of the variables will change the relationship. Thus, the recent success of the high-yielding varieties of cereals (change in technology) has not merely relieved food shortage but has also changed the long-term outlook for increasing the food output to meet the increases in demand resulting from growth of population and rise in per capita consumption with increase in income. Accordingly, the natural resources of India have been viewed here in relation to the size of the population (547 million in 1971); its rate of growth (2.3% a year during the 1960s); the present levels of production and consumption of primary products, and projections of these to 1980-81, contained in the Fourth Five Year Plan.

Natural Resources in the Indian Economy

As in most other underdeveloped countries, most of the population of India is dependent upon agriculture and other primary activities which consist in direct exploitation of natural resources. Nearly three-fourths of the labour force is engaged in primary activities, with 70 per cent in agriculture alone. Agriculture contributes about half of the gross national product; forestry and mining contribute about one per cent each, and fishing accounts for about 0.5 per cent. But in contrast to most other underdeveloped countries in which primary products are the major source of export revenues, India is a net importer of these products. In 1968-69, the value of agricultural and mineral imports was nearly 50 per cent higher than that of exports (Table 2.3). Furthermore, according to current projections, the values of agricultural and mineral exports and imports will just balance by 1980-81, despite rapid expansion of the exports and stoppage, during the 1970s, of imports of food grains. As the following survey indicates, the natural resources of India are varied and provide an adequate basis for building a diversified modern economy. But they are not of such magnitude that exports of primary products could finance economic development in a significant way. The high pressure of population on land limits prospects of exports of agricultural products and deficiencies of petroleum and metallic and non-metallic minerals have necessitated sharply rising imports of these with industrial development.

Table 2.3: Contribution of Agricultural and Mineral Products to Exports and Imports in 1968-69 and Projections for 1973-74 and 1980-81

(*Value figures in Rs. million*)

	1968-69		1973-74		1980-81	
A. **Export:** Total	13,600	100.0	19,000	100.0	30,200	100.0
1. Agricultural and allied products:	4,500	33.1	6,050	31.8	9,580	31.7
■ Tea	1,560	11.5	1,700	8.9	1,900	6.3
■ Marine Products	230	1.7	480	2.5	1,160	3.8
2. Minerals:	1,320	9.7	2,030	6.8	3,160	10.5
■ Iron ore	880	5.9	1,550	8.2	2,520	8.3
3. Manufactures	7,040	51.8	10,100	53.2	16,390	54.3
B. **Imports:** Total	19,040	100.0	22,000	100.0	29,500	100.0
1. Food grains	3,370	17.7	300	1.4	–	–
2. Metals including metalliferous ores and scrap	1,810	9.5	3,550	16.1	4,500	15.3
3. Crude oil and petroleum products	1,330	7.0	1,800	8.2	3,300	11.2
4. Fertilizers and raw materials	1,850	9.7	3,100	14.1	4,300	14.6

Knowledge of Natural Resources

Knowledge of natural resources is much better in the case of India than in most underdeveloped countries. Basic resource survey agencies have been in existence for a century or more and systematic surveys and investigations of resources have been undertaken by them. The Trigonometric Survey of India was started in 1802, although the beginning of the Survey of India goes back further to the Survey of Bengal by James Rennel in 1767. During the nineteenth century, the Survey of India covered the entire country and several adjacent countries with topographic maps. The maps were periodically revised, but the work fell into arrears during Second World War and the post-Independence period, because of other urgent demands on the resources of the survey. Cadastral surveys formed an integral part of the system of land revenue administration which was established by the British. Large scale maps were prepared for all 'settled' villages in all the British provinces and in a number of princely states. In addition, detailed data on topography, climate, soils, drainage and the local social and economic conditions were collected during the periodic 'settlement and survey' operations that were undertaken in all areas of 'temporary settlement' (of land revenue) and were incorporated in the Settlement Reports and in the records maintained by the Land Revenue Department. These reports and records have few equals in the world for the wealth of local data that they contain. The field-by-field inspection, conducted by the village accountant (known as *patwari* in North India, *talati* in Maharashtra and by other local terms in other regions) during every crop season, still forms the basis of data on land utilization and crop production. Surveys of forests were undertaken similarly as part of the system of forest administration. Forest areas were mapped and detailed information on forest types, nature and density of vegetal cover, species of plants and wild life, which is of great scientific value, was collected. The Geological Survey of India, established in 1848, had prepared the first geological map of India as early as 1877. The map was revised in 1911 and again in 1933. Systematic geological mapping had been completed for one-fourth of the area of India by the time of Independence and smaller scale maps had been prepared for another one-eighth. Important mineral-bearing areas, such as coal-fields, had been surveyed in greater detail.

Besides surveys by the established survey agencies, valuable work on assessment of specific natural resources was done by various commissions and committees that were set up from time-to-time. The Irrigation Commission and the Electricity Commission made in the early years of this century detailed estimates of the irrigation and hydro-electric potentials respectively. Perhaps the principal deficiency in the pre-Independence system of surveys was in respect of survey of soils. Systematic soil surveys were undertaken only for small areas, mainly areas of irrigation projects, in which they were needed for crop planning or correction of soil defects such as salinity or alkalinity. For the remaining agricultural areas, general qualitative descriptions of soils were contained in the Settlement Reports. They were useful for administrative purposes, but did not have systematic data on fertility characteristics or chemical composition of soils. Moreover, since a scientific scheme of classification of soils was not evolved, the descriptive data had limited value for a systematic survey of soils.

Work on mapping and surveys of natural resources have been expanded greatly under the five-year plans. The older survey agencies, such as the Survey of India and the Geological Survey, have been expanded in order to enable them to undertake larger programmes of work, and new agencies have been created to undertake specialized tasks or surveys in fields which had not been covered earlier. The Survey of India, which has had to undertake, in addition to its normal work of revision of topographic maps, topographic surveys in areas of various irrigation and other projects to provide base maps for them, has been greatly expanded and use of modern survey techniques, such as aerial photography, has increased greatly in its work. The Geological Survey has been similarly expanded in order to enable it to undertake detailed surveys and assessment of reserves of coal, iron ore and other minerals. The groundwater survey work of the GSI has also increased and is supplemented by groundwater investigations by the Exploratory Tubewell Organization of the Ministry of Agriculture as well as by the State Governments. The Indian Bureau of Mines was established in 1950 to undertake economic assessment of mineral resources and to formulate programmes of development. The Oil and Natural Gas Commission, established in the late 1950s to undertake exploration and development of petroleum resources, has been responsible for major discoveries of oil and natural gas in Assam and Gujarat. The Central Water and Power Commission, established in 1945, has the responsibility for co-ordination of hydrological investigations and assessment of water resources. It has revised the estimates of irrigation and hydro-electric potentials made earlier by the Irrigation Commission and the Electricity Commission respectively. A Soil and Land Use Survey has been established under the Indian Council of Agricultural Research and systematic soil surveys are being undertaken by it in co-operation with the State Departments of Agriculture. The country-wide fertilizer trials, undertaken since the early 1950s under the direction of the Indian Council of Agricultural Research, are yet another noteworthy aspect of work on soils. The national laboratories and institutes of scientific research also undertake studies relating to evaluation or utilization of natural resources. The work of the National Metallurgical Laboratory on metals and of the Central Fuel Research Institute on coal deserves particular mention. The areas covered by the different natural resource surveys by the end of the Second Five Year Plan are shown in Table 2.4.

But experience under the Plans has demonstrated the need for further expansion or acceleration of work in some directions, greater use of modern survey and mapping techniques and more adequate economic assessment of natural resources. Investigations of soil fertility and of groundwater will need to be expanded and improved further in order to provide data for intensive use of chemical fertilizers and efficient water management which are essential for the successful use of the new high-yielding varieties of cereals or other programmes of intensive cultivation. Modern survey techniques, such as aerial photography, aero-magnetic survey and remote sensing, which have advanced very rapidly in recent years but which are not used adequately by the Indian survey agencies, will need to be used much more. The use of these techniques reduces the time requirements of surveys and preparation of maps, makes possible surveys of inaccessible areas and aids location or estimation of reserves of minerals and other natural resources. Precise estimation of coal and iron ore resources began to be undertaken when large programmes of expanding production of these minerals were initiated under the Second Plan. Similar surveys of other important minerals, such as bauxite, are an important part of the national resource inventory and should be undertaken. Another essential activity is illustrated by the work of the Energy Survey of India Committee (1965) which made an overall assessment of energy resources of the country and projections of demand up to 1986. The projections are being constantly revised on the basis of new discoveries or more precise estimation of the known energy resources and trends in demand.

Land, Topography and Climate

Forty-three per cent of the geographical area of India is plain, another 28 per cent is plateau and less than 30 per cent is under hills and mountains (Table 2.5). It has been estimated that 62 per cent of the total area is

Table 2.4: Areas Covered by Surveys

1. Topographic Survey (By Survey of India up to 1960)	
Area surveyed on 1″- 1 mile or larger scales	2,294,214 sq. km.
Area surveyed on smaller scales	668,688 sq. km.
2. Cadastral Survey	
Surveyed areas:	
(a) With reporting agency which maintains land records and also reports agricultural statistics	223.97 mn. hectares
(b) With no reporting agency maintaining records but for which statistics are reported by the States	23.52 mn. hectares
Unsurveyed areas:	
(a) With no reporting agency but for which statistics are reported by the States	43.68 mn. hectares
(b) With no reporting agency and no statistics	35.22 mn. hectares
3. Soil Surveys (up to 1961)	
(a) Surveys in areas of irrigation projects	9.77 mn. hectares
(b) Detailed or reconnaissance surveys by the Soil and Land Use Survey	6.07 mn. hectares
(c) Surveys by State Governments	10.28 mn. hectares
4. Forest Surveys (up to 1957)	
Total area under forests	783,962 sq. km.
Surveyed	353,711 sq. km.
Unsurveyed	430,251 sq. km.
5. Geological Survey (up to 1961)	
Area surveyed on scale of 1″ - 1 mile	1,135,520 sq. km.
Area surveyed on smaller scales	4,30,743 sq. km.

topographically usable. The distribution of temperature and rainfall is also favourable for utilization of a large proportion of the area for agriculture or other productive purposes. Temperatures over the whole of India, except above certain altitudes in the Himalayas, are high enough to permit crop production throughout the year. The distribution of the geographical area by zones of annual rainfall (Table 2.5) indicates that more than two-thirds of the total area is in zones with rainfall of 750 mm and above, and only two per cent is in the zone with rainfall below 250 mm. But, in most parts of India, rainfall is concentrated in the brief monsoon period of three to four months—the period extends to nearly six months in Kerala and parts of Eastern India—and the rest of the year is practically dry. This means that, except where irrigation facilities are available, or the dry season crop can be sustained by sub-soil moisture, supplemented by the minimum rainfall during the dry season, crop production has to be confined to the monsoon period. As a result, only a small proportion of the cultivated area, about 15 per cent, grows more than one crop in the year. Moreover, since there is great variation in the monsoonal and the dry season flows of rivers, large storage reservoirs have to be built for irrigation, generation of hydro-electricity or other purposes, and most rivers are not suitable for navigation.

Table 2.5: India—Classification of Total Area by Topography and Annual Rainfall

I. Topography Per cent of total land area classified as:		
Plain	43.05	
Plateau	27.67	
Hill	18.53	
Mountain	10.74	
Topographically usable area*	62.08	
II. Annual Rainfall Per cent of gross sown area in zone of average annual rainfall:		
Assured	Above 1,875 mm	11.1
	1,250 mm—1,875 mm	22.3
Medium	750 mm—1,250 mm	33.8
	375 mm—750 mm	25.0
Low	250 mm—375 mm	5.6
	Below 250 mm	2.0

* Topographically usable area has been calculated as follows:

Plain	95%
Plateau	75%
Hill	25%
Mountain	5%

Soils

In the soil map of India, prepared by the Indian Agricultural Research Institute, 27 broad soil classes, besides glaciers, have been distinguished. The areas under the classes are given in Table 2.6. The agriculturally important soils are generally grouped into three major groups—alluvial, black and red and yellow. Their distribution is as follows:

Soil Group	*Area (Million hectares)*	*Per cent of total area*
Alluvial including coastal and deltaic	142.50	43.7
Black including mixed black and red	60.31	18.5
Red and yellow, including laterites	61.93	19.0

Table 2.6: India—Classification of Area by Broad Soil Classes

(Approx. area in million hectares)

1.	Alluvial soil	101.21
2.	Alluvial soil, highly calcareous	8.91
3.	Coastal alluvium	8.50
4.	Deltaic alluvium (occasionally saline)	17.00
5.	Alluvial soil, affected by salinity and alkalinity	6.88
6.	Desert soil	14.57
7.	Deep black soil	6.88
8.	Medium black soil	18.62
9.	Shallow black soil	4.86
10.	Black soil affected by salinity and alkalinity	6.88
11.	Black soil undifferentiated	12.55
12.	Mixed red and black soil	10.52
13.	Red soil	30.36
14.	Red gravelly soil	1.62
15.	Red and yellow soil	17.81
16.	Laterite	10.12
17.	Laterite and lateritic soil	2.02
18.	Brown soil under deciduous	1.62
19.	Gray and brown soil	3.64
20.	Hill soil	2.43
21.	Podsolic soil	3.64
22.	Forest soil laterised	6.48
23.	Foot hill/Terai hill	5.67
24.	Mountain Meadow soil	11.74
25.	Mountainous soil undifferentiated	6.48
26.	Skeletal soil	2.43
27.	Peat muck, very humus and humus soil, also called bog soils, organic soils and half bog soils	0.24
28.	Glaciers and eternal snow	4.05
	Total:	**326.15**

Note: Figures, given in acres in the original, have been converted into hectares.

Alluvial soils are found in the Northern Plain, the Plains of the East and the West Coast and in river valleys in the Peninsula. The largest area of black soils is in the western part of the Peninsula and is underlain by basaltic lavas, although the soils are found also, pure or mixed with red soils, in other parts of the Peninsula. Red and yellow soils are found mainly in the eastern and southern parts of the Peninsula which are underlain by ancient crystalline rocks. The structure, depth and texture of soils in different areas vary greatly with variations in the nature of the underlying rocks, topography, rainfall, drainage and other factors. In general, the black soils tend to be heavy, clayey and moisture-retentive—they have a tendency to fissure in the dry season; the alluvial soils are clayey or sandy loams while the red and yellow soils are light sandy loams. The alluvial soils and the black soils have higher natural fertility than most red and yellow soils. But all soils of India are low in nitrogen and organic matter and respond well to applications of nitrogenous fertilizers and organic manure.

Land Utilization

Data on land utilization in 1950-51, 1960-61 and 1966-67 given in Table 2.7, bring out the trends in utilization of land for agriculture and other purposes during the period of the first three Five Year Plans. The projections of the cropped area and the irrigated area to 1980-81, (Tables 2.8 and 2.9), indicate the likely trends in agricultural land use during the present decade. Taken together, the Tables provide a synoptic view of agricultural land use over a 30-year period.

Agricultural Land

This is defined here to include 'net area sown', 'current fallows' and 'land under miscellaneous tree crops and groves' (Lines 9, 8b and 6 in Table 2.7). The total area of agricultural land was 154.4 million hectares in 1966-67. Arable land, defined somewhat differently by the Food and Agriculture Organization (FAO) of the United Nations, totalled 163 million hectares in 1968, or just over 50 per cent of the total geographical area (Table 2.10). The latter figure is the highest among the large or medium-sized countries of the world, indicating (i) the influence of favourable physical factors such as large areas, extent of plains and plateaus and very small extent of arid area (annual rainfall below 250 mm), and (ii) extension of cultivation to a large proportion of the cultivable land. But, because of the large population of the country, arable land per capita is

Table 2.7: India—Land Utilization and Irrigation, 1950-51 to 1966-67

('000 Hectares)

	1950-51	*1960-61*	*1966-67*
1. Geographical area	326,809	326,809	326,809
2. Reporting area	284,315	298,458	305,610
3. Forest	40,482	54,032	62,335
4. Not available for cultivation	47,517	50,751	48,293
4a. Land put to non-agricultural uses	9,358	14,840	15,534
4b. Barren and uncultivable land	38,159	35,911	32,759
5. Permanent pastures and grazing lands	6,675	13,966	14,085
6. Land under miscellaneous tree crops and groves (Not included in net area sown)	19,828	4,459	4,110
7. Cultivable waste	22,943	19,212	17,101
8. Fallow land:			
8a. Other than current	17,445	11,180	9,357
8b. Current	10,679	11,639	13,282
Cultivation and Irrigation			
9. Net area sown	118,746	133,199	137,047
10. Area sown more than once	13,147	19,573	19,520
11. Gross cropped area	131,893	152,772	156,567
12. Net irrigated area	20,853	24,661	27,478
13. Gross irrigated area	22,563	27,980	32,754

Table 2.8: Growth Rates of Agricultural Areas, Production and Productivity—Trends and Projections, 1949-50 to 1980-81

(Per cent per year)

	Gross cropped area	*Productivity*	*Production*	*Gross Irrigated area*	*Area sown more than once*
1949-50 to 1968-69	1.4	1.5	2.9	2.4*	2.6*
First Plan: 1951-52 to 1955-56	2.6	1.4	4.1	2.6	6.7
Second Plan: 1956-57 to 1960-61	1.3	1.8	3.1	1.8	1.5
Third Plan: 1961-62 to 1964-65	0.6	2.7	3.3	2.2	1.9
1969-70 to 1980-81 (Projection)	1.2	3.7	5.0	4.2**	4.6**

* 1950-51 to 1966-67.

** Calculated from figures given in Table 2.9.

I t high; the figure of 0.3 hectares is lower than the average for the world a d is only one-third of the U.S. figure. About 15 per cent of the sown a a is multi-cropped (sown more than once in the year), while a fifth of th gross cropped areas (20.9% in 1966-67) is irrigated. Irrigation makes pc ssible extension of cultivation to dry lands which would not be cultivated

Table 2.9: Agricultural Areas, 1950-51 to 1966-67 and Projection for 1980-81

(Million hectares)

	1950-51	1955-56	1960-61	1964-65	1966-67	1980-81 (Projection)
1. Total reporting area	284.3	291.9	298.5	305.3	305.6	n.a.
2. Net sown area	118.7	129.2	133.2	138.1	137.0	151
3. Area sown more than once	13.1	18.2	19.6	21.1	19.6	37
4. Gross cropped area (Lines 2+3)	131.8	147.4	152.8	159.2	156.6	188
5. Gross irrigated area	22.6	25.6	28.0	30.7	32.8	58
6. Cropping intensity (Lines 4/2) per cent	111.2	114.1	114.7	115.3	114.3	124.5
7. Irrigation percentage (Lines 5/4)	17.1	17.4	18.3	19.3	20.9	30.9

Table 2.10: Arable Land in Selected Countries

	Arable land/ Geographical area (Per cent)	*Arable land per capita (hectares)*
World	10.5	0.42
U.S.A.	18.8	0.87
Canada	4.4	2.06
Brazil	3.5	0.33
United Kingdom	30.2	0.13
France	36.2	0.38
India	50.1	0.30
Japan	15.4	0.06
Sudan	2.8	0.47

otherwise. More important, it raises productivity of croplands through increases in the intensity of cropping and in crop yields. Most of the multi-cropped area is irrigated, and the security provided by irrigation facilities is a major factor in intensive application of labour and other inputs to obtain high yields. The influence of irrigation on crop yields is indicated by the following data on yields of rice and wheat taken from the National Sample Survey, 16th Round (1960-61):

Crop		*Yield (Lbs, Per Acre)*
	Irrigated	*Un-irrigated*
Rice	1,204	761
Wheat	985	545

Figures are not available for later years, but the yield differentials between irrigated and unirrigated lands have probably increased after adoption of the high-yielding varieties, which are confined, almost, to irrigated lands. The yield of wheat in Punjab-Haryana, where most of the crop is irrigated, was in 1961-62 81 per cent higher than the yield in Madhya Pradesh where most of the crop is unirrigated; by 1970-71 it was more than three times as high:

State	*Proportion of cropped area irrigated (Per cent)*	*Yield (kg. per hectare)*		*Increase in yield 1970-71 over 1961-62 (Per cent)*
		1961-62	*1970-71*	
Punjab-Haryana	71.1	1,243	2,173	75.0
Uttar Pradesh	59.1	1,013	1,286	27.0
Madhya Pradesh	10.4	685	657*	–4.0*
India	37.9	890	1,299	46.0

*1968-69.

Moreover, since increases in output through use of modern technology (high-yielding seeds, chemical fertilizers, pesticides etc.) will continue to be concentrated in areas with assured, adequate and well regulated water supplies (mainly irrigated lands), the productivity differentials between irrigated and unirrigated lands will continue to increase.

Non-Agricultural Land

This includes land under forests, permanent pastures and other non-agricultural uses (towns, villages, roads, railways etc.); land classified as 'culturable waste' and 'fallows other than current', as well as barren and uncultivable land of mountain and desert areas. The total area of non-agricultural land was 172 million hectares in 1966-67. The classification of non-agricultural land has been improved considerably during the period of the Plans: a more detailed scheme of classification was adopted in the early 1950s, and there is more careful recording of actual land use. Even so, the figures of different classes of non-agricultural land do not give an accurate idea of the nature of vegetal cover on them, or actual land use or the land use capability. In the areas classified as 'forests', the nature of vegetal cover varies all the way from dense forest through open woodland to poor scrub. On the other hand, some areas classified as 'culturable waste' are wooded. Grazing of livestock is not confined to the small areas, classified as 'permanent pasture'. It is permitted in most forest areas and most of the 'culturable waste', fallow lands (current and other than current) and vacant cultivated fields are also used. The large livestock population of India—228.9 million bovine animals and 96.5 million sheep and goats in 1966—is supported in this way. Finally, not all the areas classified as 'culturable waste', are suitable for cultivation. The Working Group on Land Use Policy of the Union Ministry of Agriculture had stated, after a reconnaissance survey of these lands in 1960, that "Ten million acres might be the upper limit of the additional areas that might become available for arable farming out of the existing culturable waste during the period of about fifteen years beyond 1960-61."

An adequate inventory of the land resource will involve:

(i) further improvement in classification of land;
(ii) specifying the nature of vegetal cover on all non-agricultural lands;
(iii) indicating the land use capability of all lands, agricultural and non-agricultural, and the measures needed to effect changes from present to capability uses in lands in which such changes are required; and
(iv) approximate estimates of the costs involved.

The inventory will require surveys of land use and land use capability over large areas and feasibility studies for reclamation and other land development projects in selected areas. The changes in land use will include both extension of cultivation to suitable waste and fallow lands and retirement from cultivation of agricultural lands of very low productivity, those suffering from severe erosion or located in erosion-prone areas, such as steep hill slopes. It may be mentioned that large areas of waste and fallow land remain uncultivated only because they suffer from defects, such as severe soil erosion, infestation with weeds, salinity or alkalinity. The total extent of such areas; the extent of the areas which can be reclaimed economically and the costs of reclamation should be indicated by the surveys and studies.

Trends in Land Utilization

The changes in land utilization between 1950-51 and 1966-67 (Table 2.7) represent the combined effects of extension of reporting to the areas which were non-reporting earlier; improvements in classification and actual changes in land use. The three effects can be separated only by examining district-level data, particularly for States like Rajasthan and Madhya Pradesh in which extension of reporting was the maximum. However, the data of Table 2.7 bring out (i) the progressive reduction in the areas classified as 'culturable waste' and 'fallows other than current' and increase in the 'net sown area'; (ii) significant increase in the 'area sown more than once'; and (iii) a large, 45 per cent, increase in the irrigated area. Reclamation of waste and fallow lands was relatively rapid during the 1950s following land reforms, such as abolition of *Zamindari* and *Jagirdari*. The dispossessed *Zamindars* and *Jagirdars* reclaimed lands which had been left to them for 'personal cultivation', while their former tenants reclaimed waste and fallow lands to which they had acquired rights. The process was aided by loans and subsidies from the State Governments. The increase in the irrigated areas was due primarily to the plan programmes of major, medium and minor irrigation. The programmes had created a total potential of about 18.5 million hectares by 1968-69, of which about 17 million hectares had been utilized.

Agricultural output increased at an average rate of 2.9 per cent a year during the period 1949-50 to 1968-69 (Table 2.8). About half of the increase was due to increase in the cropped area, while the remainder was the result of improvement in productivity. Increase in the cropped area was most rapid during the early 1950s and slowed down later, while improvement in productivity had the opposite trend. The rate of growth of agricultural output, projected by the Planning Commission for the period 1968-69 to 1980-81 is much higher than the rate achieved in any earlier plan period; achievement of the projected high rate is considered essential for meeting the increases in demand for food and other agricultural products resulting from increases in population and per capita consumption. The rate of population increase, estimated at 2.5 per cent a year for 1968-69, is expected to decline to 1.7 per cent by 1980-81 with decline in the birth rate under the impact of the family planning programme. But the decline will be more than compensated by increase in per capita consumption; the rate of economic growth is expected to go up from 5.5 per cent during the period of the Fourth Plan (1969-70 to 1973-74) to 6 per cent in the remaining period.

Three-fourths of the projected increase in agricultural output is expected to come from improvement in productivity, the rate of which is expected to go up from 2.7 per cent a year during the Third Plan period to 3.7 per cent during 1969-70 to 1980-81. The projected rate of increase in the cropped area is also quite high, 1.2 per cent a year, or twice the actual rate of the Third Plan period. But less than half of the projected increase will be through extension of cultivation (increase in the 'net area sown'); the balance is expected to be contributed by increase in the 'area sown more than once' (Table 2.7). The intensity of cropping is projected to increase from 114.3 in 1966-67 to 124.5 in 1980-81, but to be as high as 150 on the irrigated lands. Gross irrigated area is also expected to increase rapidly by 4.2 per cent a year, to reach a total of 58 million hectares by 1980-81.

The projected increases in both productivity and the intensity of cropping are closely related to use of the new high-yielding varieties of cereals. Use of the varieties has been the major factor in the increase in food output experienced during recent years—from an average of 82.5 million tonnes during 1961-62 to 1964-65 to an average of 99 million tonnes during 1967-68 to 1970-71, and it is expected to contribute two-thirds of the projected increase in food grain output during the period of the Fourth Plan. Secondly, since the varieties have shorter growing seasons than the old varieties, multi-cropping becomes more feasible. But successful cultivation of the new varieties requires intensive use of chemical fertilizers, careful preparation of land and efficient water management. The last is best achieved in irrigated lands in which water supplies are adequate and assured, and can be effectively regulated to suit the requirements of individual crops. The emphasis on extension of irrigation and on improvement in the quality of irrigation in the Fourth Plan derive primarily from the water requirements of the new varieties. The principal programmes for improving the quality of irrigation are construction of wells and tubewells and installation of electric pumps on them. The programmes, initiated along with introduction of the new varieties in 1966, are being continued under the Fourth Plan and later through the 1970s. The emphasis on exploitation of ground-water is due partly to the large unexploited potential of the resource in some regions, but even more to the fact that water supplies from wells and tubewells can be regulated much more effectively than supplies from canals or tanks. In Punjab-Haryana and Uttar Pradesh, where large areas are affected by salinity or water logging as a result of canal irrigation for several decades, the farmers have a preference for irrigation from wells and tubewells. Moreover, as experience during the recent drought years 1965-66 and 1966-67 demonstrated, water supplies from ground-water sources hold up better during a drought than those from surface sources, especially tanks.

Soil Erosion and Other Defects

Among the defects, such as soil erosion, infestation with weeds, salinity, alkalinity and water logging, which lead to deterioration or depletion of the land resource, soil erosion is the most serious, because it affects by far the largest areas. A detailed survey of soil erosion, estimating the total extent of erosion-affected areas and classifying the affected areas by type and severity of erosion, has yet to be made; but according to a preliminary estimate, about 200 million acres (80.8 million hectares) of land in the country require protection by soil conservation measures. The most serious damage is done by ravine erosion and erosion by *chos* (hill torrents). Ravine erosion is widespread in Madhya Pradesh, Uttar Pradesh, Rajasthan and Gujarat. It is estimated to have destroyed about 1.4 million hectares in Uttar Pradesh alone; while the total area affected by it and associated severe gully erosion may be as large as 10 million hectares in these four States. Erosion by *chos* occurs mainly in the sub-mountain area of Punjab-Haryana, where about 1,813 sq. km. are affected by it.

Soil erosion affects both agricultural and non-agricultural land. Large areas of agricultural land, especially in Peninsular India, are affected by gully erosion; the areas whose fertility is depleted by sheet erosion are much larger. But the most severely eroded lands are non-agricultural, in which erosion follows denudation of vegetation as a result of overgrazing and indiscriminate cutting of trees and bushes. Village pastures, 'cultivable waste' and 'fallows other than current' need particular mention in this context. Since grazing is free for all livestock belonging to the villagers, the numbers grazed are generally excessive. The consequent over-grazing and absence of any measures for improvement of pastures, lead to progressive denudation of vegetation, and in turn to soil erosion, which spreads frequently to the adjoining agricultural lands.

Programmes for control of erosion and conservation of soil and moisture have to be drawn up separately for agricultural and non-agricultural land and have to include in addition to agronomic and engineering measures, economic and socio-institutional measures. In agricultural land, the most needed measures are contour-bounding, contour-ploughing, terracing, planting of legumes and other soil-enriching crops, and changes in the cropping pattern, particularly reduction of fallow periods. They have to be accompanied by technical and financial assistance (loans and subsidies) to the cultivators. In some areas, tenancy reforms which give the cultivators security of tenure and provide them with adequate incentives to undertake the improvements may also be needed. Some agricultural land, located on steep slopes and other erosion-prone areas, may need to be taken out of cultivation and put under pastures or forests. In non-agricultural land, the most important measures are effective control over grazing and felling and gradual rehabilitation of the eroded areas through pasture improvement or plantation of trees. Engineering measures, such as terracing and construction of check dams are needed in severely eroded areas. The village *panchayats* have to be given technical and financial assistance for efficient management of the lands which are under their jurisdiction. But in critical areas, such as the watersheds of major irrigation or multi-purpose projects, if management by the panchayats does not result in adequate control over erosion, management by the Forest Departments should be undertaken.

Infestation with deep-rooted weeds such as *kans* is a serious problem in parts of Madhya Pradesh, Rajasthan and Bihar. An estimated 4 million hectares have been rendered uncultivable by it. A large programme of reclamation of these lands with heavy tractors was started in 1948 by the Government of India. But it had to be given up after some time because of the high cost of reclamation and various organizational difficulties. Reclamation by the tractor organizations of the State Governments and by individuals, however, continues.

Salinity or alkalinity of the soil and water logging are generally associated with irrigation from canals. They arise from seepage of water from canals and distributaries and faulty irrigation practices. The total area of saline and alkaline lands is estimated at 6 million hectares; most of it is located in Punjab-Haryana, Uttar Pradesh and Maharashtra. The area affected by water logging is estimated at 1 million hectares and is located mostly in Punjab-Haryana. The remedial measures include flooding of the land to remove excess salinity or alkalinity; providing efficient drainage, and lining of the canals and distributaries (generally drainage with brick masonry) to prevent seepage. The new canals of the Bhakra-Nangal and Rajasthan Canal projects have been or are being lined.

Programmes of soil conservation and correction of other soil defects have been undertaken since the First Five Year Plan and have been progressively expanded. The expansion of the former is indicated by the following figures relating to expenditures and the areas benefited during the first three plans, and the targets of the Fourth Plan:

Soil Conservation Programmes	*Plans*			
	First	*Second*	*Third*	*Fourth*
Expenditure (million rupees)	16	180	780	1,594
Area benefited* (million hectares)	0.3	0.8	4.0	6.9

* Figures for the First and the Second Plans relate only to areas benefited by contour-bunding.

Since the areas affected by soil erosion and the investment needs of erosion control and soil conservation programmes are very large, it has been necessary to select priority areas for the programmes. In the first three plans, priority was given to agricultural land, catchments areas of river valley projects and certain non-agricultural lands from which erosion spread to threaten large areas of agricultural land. The priorities remain unaltered under the Fourth Plan, but conservation measures in the catchment areas of the projects have been intensified, because sedimentation surveys have revealed that in a large number of projects, the actual rates of sedimentation are higher than the rates assumed at the time of construction.

Water

Assessment of water resources is required for development of irrigation and navigation, generation of hydro electricity and meeting the domestic and industrial needs for water. These uses may be complementary or competitive. Irrigation and generation of hydro electricity are largely complementary, but irrigation and domestic and industrial use of water are largely competitive. Assessment of the water resources must include both surface flows and ground-water supplies and should indicate, in addition to the total quantities available, their location, seasonal distribution and quality. In India as in many other countries, there is a hiatus between the geographical location of the areas and the seasons of the most urgent need for water and its availability in abundance, which limits possibilities of utilization of the available supplies of water and raises costs of utilization. A large proportion of the water supplies is located in zones with annual rainfall of 1,250 mm and above, but the need, particularly for irrigation, is greatest in the zones of medium or low rainfall (below 1,250 mm.) The concentration of rainfall in the monsoon season further limits the scope for economic utilization of the available water supplies. Defects in the quality of water also limit utilization in some areas; ground-water is brackish in large parts of Western Rajasthan. Pollution of river waters by discharge of urban and industrial wastes can affect their usability by communities or industries located downstream. The problem could become serious in the not too distant future in case of river systems, such as the Ganga-Yamuna, on which a large number of cities are located.

The annual water balance of India has been estimated as follows:

	Million Hectare Metres
Total precipitation	373
Evaporation	124
Surface flow	168
Seepage	80.9
Of which soil moisture	43.6
Annual enrichment of ground-water	37.3

One-third of the surface flow (56 m.h.m.) and 22 m.h.m. of ground-water are considered to be usable for irrigation. The ultimate potential of gross irrigated area had been estimated earlier at 70.85 million hectares; but the estimate has been recently revised to 82 million hectares. The increase is due mainly to the larger possibility of multi-cropping, with use of the new high-yielding, short duration varieties of cereals. The progress of utilization of the potential under the plans and projections to 1973-74 is as follows:

	Surface-water		*Ground-water*	
	Quantity (Million hectares mtrs.)	*Gross irrigated area (Million hectares)*	*Quantity (Million hectares mtrs.)*	*Gross irrigated area (Million hectares)*
Total Potential	56	60	22	22
Utilization:				
At beginning of First Plan (1950-51)	9.5	16.1	6.5	6.6
1968-69	20.5	25.0	10.9	10.9
1973-74 (Projections)	25.5	n.a.*	11.0	n.a.*
Projected time period for full utilization of the potential	—about 20 years		—about 20 years	

* The projection of gross irrigated area for 1980-81, from both surface and ground-water sources, is 58.0 million hectares.

The estimate of the ultimate irrigation potential is based on detailed investigation of the potential of irrigation projects on the different river systems and of the ground-water supplies in different regions. The earlier total of 70.85 million hectares had been made up of 40.50 million hectares from major and medium projects and 30.35 million hectares from minor irrigation works. The region-wise distribution of the potential of major and medium projects is shown in Table 2.11.

Table 2.11: Irrigation Potential of Major and Medium Projects

		Irrigation potential (Million hectares)
Zone 1:	West-flowing rivers (covering river basins in Kerala, Mysore and Maharashtra states and the basins of Tapti, Narmada and others)	4.05
Zone 2:	East-flowing rivers (covering the basins of Tambraparani, Vaigai, Cauvery, Mahanadi, Godavari, Krishna, Pennar and others)	13.35
Zone 3:	Indus basin	5.26
Zone 4:	Ganga basin (covering Chambal, Yamuna, Ramganga, Tons, Gomti, Sone, Ganga and its tributaries)	16.60
Zone 5:	Brahmaputra basin	1.21
	Total:	**40.47**

Sources of Irrigation

Somewhat over 40 per cent of the total irrigated area is served by canals; another one-third is served by wells and tubewells and the balance gets water from tanks and other sources. The areas irrigated by canals and wells have increased more rapidly during the period of the plans, than that irrigated by tanks, while the area irrigated by other sources has declined:

	1950-51		*1960-61*		*1966-67*	
Irrigation Source	*Area irrigated (m/hectares)*	*Per cent*	*Area irrigated (m/hectares)*	*Per cent*	*Area irrigated (m/hectares)*	*Per cent*
Canals	8.3	39.8	10.4	42.1	11.4	41.4
Wells and tubewells	6.0	28.7	7.3	29.6	9.5	34.5
Tanks	3.6	17.3	4.6	18.5	4.6	16.6
Others	3.0	14.2	2.4	9.8	2.1	7.5

The efficiency and dependability of irrigation from the different sources also vary considerably. In the areas irrigated by canals, supplies of water are generally more adequate and dependable for fields located at the head of an irrigation channel than for those located at the tail end. Supplies from tanks are less dependable than those from canals or wells during periods of drought, such as the two recent years 1965-66 and 1966-67. On the other hand, irrigation from wells can be regulated most efficiently to meet the requirements of crops because the irrigation source is entirely under the control of the individual farmer, and is also more dependable than from tanks or canals.

Water for Domestic and Industrial Uses

Estimates of domestic and industrial consumption of water and projections of growth of consumption have not been made so far. This is a serious lacuna in assessment of the water resource which will affect efficient allocation of water among its competitive uses in particular regions. The requirements of water for domestic and industrial uses are not large in comparison with those for irrigation, but they have increased rapidly in recent years, and will increase perhaps even more rapidly in future with acceleration of urban and industrial growth. The increases in supplies have not kept pace with increases in demand in most large cities of the country, so that water shortage has become chronic. In Bombay, where water shortage has persisted since Second World War, the demand was estimated at 350 million gallons a day in 1965, when the supply was only 210 mgd. In Kolkata, the water shortage had become so acute by the early 1960s that 'emergency' water supply schemes had to be undertaken to relieve it.

One reason for the failure of supplies to increase along with increases in demand is the high cost of storage, transport and distribution works.

The cost of the expansion programme for Bombay to meet the projected growth of demand up to 1980-81 was estimated at 1671 million rupees. In Chennai, the cost of increasing supplies from conventional sources was estimated to be so high, until investigations revealed suitable ground-water supplies near the city, that desalination of sea water was considered as a possible source of supply. The cost of desalination, although still high in comparison with water supplies from conventional sources, has fallen rapidly during the last two decades with advances in desalination techniques. It is still falling and desalination is beginning to be competitive with alternative sources of supply where the cost of the latter is high, or where desalination can be combined with generation of electricity and industrial development, such as manufacture of chemical fertilizers. Schemes for establishment of multiple desalination-power-fertilizers complexes, such as the one along the Saurashtra coast have been considered by the Government of India. A comprehensive survey of domestic and industrial water needs and formulation of a long-term programme for meeting them are urgently needed. The programme should also include measures to check pollution and maintain the quality of water at acceptable levels, especially in densely populated areas such as the Ganga-Yamuna basin.

Sources of Energy

Per capita consumption of energy is an important indicator of economic development; it is much higher in the developed countries than in the underdeveloped countries. Figures for selected countries (Table 2.12) indicate that consumption in the U.S.A. was more than 50 times that in India in 1969, while in Japan it was nearly 15 times. The Indian figure is itself nearly four times the figure for Burma. Moreover, per capita consumption of energy has increased in India with economic development; the 1969 figure of 193 kg. of coal equivalent was 75 per cent higher than the figure of 110 kg. for the early 1950s.

Table 2.12: Per Capita Consumption of Energy in Selected Countries in 1969

(Kilograms of coal equivalent)

World	1,804
U.S.A.	10,774
Canada	8,794
U.K.	5,139
W. Germany	4,850
France	3,518
Italy	2,431
Yugoslavia	1,243
U.S.S.R.	4,199
Japan	2,828
India	193
Burma	58
Ceylon	118
Taiwan	874

Coal, oil and natural gas, hydro-electricity and nuclear fuels are the principal sources of energy in the developed countries. Commercial use of nuclear energy began only in the 1960s, but its growth has been so rapid that nuclear power stations, now under construction, represent substantial proportions of the new power generating capacity in the western developed countries. The three Indian nuclear power stations, located at Tarapur, Kotah and Kalpakkam near (Chennai), will add more than 1 million kW of generating capacity by the early 1970s. Coal is the most important source of commercial energy in India. In 1960-61, it contributed a little more than 20 per cent of the total energy supply (Table 2.13). Oil is a close second, but hydro-electricity, which contributed less than 3 per cent of the total energy supply in that year, is of minor importance. But all the commercial sources of energy contributed only 40 per cent of the total energy supply in 1960-61, and the remaining 60 per cent came from non-commercial fuels, such as cow-dung, fire-wood and vegetable wastes. Use of commercial fuels is confined to the modern sectors of the economy and to the urban areas; the energy needs of the rural population, 80 per cent of the total, are met almost entirely by non-commercial fuels. A study of rural fuel consumption, conducted by the National Council for Applied Economic Research, revealed that in 1960-61 only 5 per cent of the energy needs of the rural population were met by commercial fuels. The preponderance of non-commercial fuels in rural energy supplies reflects the subsistence nature of the rural economy; the fuels are used because they do not have to be purchased. But it constitutes wasteful use of resources. Use of cow-dung for fuel is particularly wasteful because it deprives the soil of most valuable organic manure. Some of the vegetable wastes could also be used in more productive ways. *Bagasse* could be a very useful supplementary raw material for manufacture of paper. The demand for paper is increasing rapidly and the principal raw materials, bamboo and *sabai* grass, are in short supply. Supplies of fire-wood are dependent upon large areas being kept under fire-wood plantations. While this may be the optimum land use for some areas, for most others it is not. But progress in changing rural consumption patterns is not likely to be rapid; non-commercial fuels are expected to continue to meet most of the energy needs of the rural population, and their consumption is expected to increase. The Energy Survey of India Committee had estimated a 43 per cent increase in energy generation from non-commercial fuels by 1980-81, although its contribution to total energy supplies was expected to decline from 60.4 per cent in 1960-61 to 27.8 per cent by 1980-81, due to more rapid growth of energy generation from commercial fuels (Table 2.13). The Committee made three projections of growth of demand for energy, based on different assumptions relating to growth rates of national income and industrial production. The projected values of the index of energy consumption in 1980-81 (1960 = 100) varied from a low 264.2 to a high 368.3. The intermediate projection, based on annual growth rates of 6 per cent in national income and 8.5 per cent in industrial production, has been used in Table 2.12 and in this section. The estimates of reserves of energy sources, given in the following paragraphs, are also based on the report of the Committee.

Table 2.13: India—Energy Consumption in 1960-61 and Projection for 1980-81 (by Primary Sources, Expressed in Terms of Million Tonnes of Coal Replacement)

Energy Source	*Consumption in 1960-61*		*Projection for 1980-81**	
	Quantity	*Per cent*	*Quantity*	*Per cent*
Coal	49.9	20.6	208.9	27.8
Oil	39.1	16.2	279.9	37.2
Hydro power	6.8	2.8	38.4	5.2
Nuclear	–	–	15.4	2.0
Total commercial sources	**95.8**	**39.6**	**543.1**	**72.2**
Cow-dung	21.6	8.9	25.0	3.3
Fire-wood	95.3	39.4	125.0	16.6
Vegetable waste	29.2	12.1	59.0	7.8
Total non-commercial sources	146.1	60.4	209.0	27.8
Grand Total	**241.9**	**100.0**	**752.1**	**100.0**

* Intermediate projection, assumes annual growth rate of 6 per cent for national product and 8.5 per cent for industrial output.

Coal

The principal coal-fields of India are in the eastern and central States of Bihar, West Bengal and Madhya Pradesh. Outside of this area, there is only one important coal-field, the Singareni in the Godavari valley of Andhra Pradesh, although there are lignite deposits at Neyveli in Tamil Nadu, in the Assam Hills and at Palana in Rajasthan. The concentration of coal-fields in one region and absence of water transport facilities from it to the consumption centres are handicaps for industrial and economic development; the cost of transport of coal by rail to most points in Southern and Western India is very high.

The total reserves of coal are large, but most of the coal is of poor quality. It is high in ash and has low calorific value. The reserves of coking coal, suitable for metallurgical uses, are small, being limited to the coal-fields of Bihar and West Bengal, principally the Jharia fields of Bihar. But much of the coking coal also has high ash content and has to be washed before being used for metallurgical purposes.

The Energy Survey of India Committee estimated that out of the total reserve of 5,800 million tonnes of coking coal down to 610 metres in the Jharia coal-fields only about 1,800 million tonnes would become available for industrial use. Its calculation was as follows:

(million tonnes)

Seams IX/X to XVIII	*Proved*	*Indicated*	*Inferred*	*Total*
1. Down to 610 metres (2,000 ft.)	2,510	2,504	786	5,800
2. 610 to 1,220 metres. (2,000-4,000 feet)	11	406	1,820	2,237
3. Total 1,220 metres (4,000 ft.)	2,521	2,910	2,606	8,037
4. Mined coking coal 50% of 5,800*				2,900
5. Washery yield 50% of 2,900*				1,450
6. Addition of blendable 25% of 1,450*				360
Total Available for Industrial use (5+6)				1,810

The quantity of usable coal could in fact be larger. Mining losses could be considerably less than 50 per cent; the committee referred to a view of the Department of Mines and Metals of the Government of India according to which the losses could be reduced to 25 per cent, raising the recovery ratio to 75 per cent with stowing. Some production could also be expected from reserves below 610 metres, which have been entirely ignored by the committee. But these modifications do not alter materially the general picture of 30-40 years' supply of coking coal for an iron and steel industry of moderate size producing about 50 million tonnes of pig iron a year. The need for conserving coal has been recognized by the Government of India for a long time and a number of conservation measures have been taken. These include stowing, establishment of washeries, blending of weakly coking or non-coking coal with strongly coking coal, and substitution of coking coal by non-coking coal for non-metallurgical uses. The reserves of non-metallurgical coal, currently estimated at 115,000 million tonnes, are quite large. Recent advances in techniques of power generation from low quality coal and of transmission of power at high voltage over long distances favour construction of large, coal based power stations near the coal-fields and supply of power from them over large areas. These developments as well as advances in the technology of gasification of coal could reduce to a considerable extent the disadvantages of concentration of the coal-fields in one region of India.

Petroleum

The position regarding reserves of petroleum was summarized by the Energy Survey of India Committee as follows:

> "India possesses an area of about one million sq. km. of sedimentary rocks which theoretically represent an oil potential; this constitutes nearly one-third of the country's total area. As the available geological knowledge regarding several of these sedimentary basins is meagre and of a very general nature, it is for the moment impossible to make any firm assessment of possible petroleum reserves. Of the areas so far explored for oil, the most promising are those in Assam and Gujarat. The figures given for estimated reserves are constantly changing in the light of new knowledge. Recent guesses are that proved reserves in Assam may amount to 50 million tonnes and those in Gujarat to another 50 million tonnes—they can be little more. Both these areas are being intensively studied and it is too soon to be certain what the total reserves may be. There are approximately 100 million tonnes of proved reserves; including possible inferred reserves, the total may conceivably reach 175 million tonnes ... We are informed that the proved and inferred natural gas reserves, as estimated on the basis of present explorations, are 31.5 million cubic metres or only about 50 million tonnes of coal equivalent determined on a calorific equivalent basis."

There have been promising new discoveries in recent years, especially in the offshore area of the Gulf of Cambay. Estimates of petroleum reserves are liable to change continually with new discoveries, and further exploration in the Cambay area could lead to large oil finds, altering materially the above assessment. However, the Planning Commission has assumed only a modest increase in domestic production of petroleum—from 6 million tonnes in 1968-69 to 8.5 million tonnes in 1973-74—and continued dependence upon imports for the greater part of the petroleum needs. Consumption of petroleum has been projected to increase from 16.1 million tonnes in 1968-69 to 26 million tonnes in 1973-74.

Hydro-Electricity

The estimates of the hydel power potential, made in the early years of this century by the Electricity Commission, have been revised in recent years, after further surveys and more precise estimation, by the Central Water and Power Commission. The ultimate potential is now estimated at 41 million kW at 60 per cent load factor. Only 3.6 per cent of the potential had been developed by 1960-61. The total potential, the proportions of the potential developed and the demand for electricity in the different regions of India are given in Table 2.14. Both Southern India and Northern India, which are far from the coal-fields, have large potentials, while Eastern India in which most of the coal-fields are located, has only a limited potential. Relatively high percentages of development of the potential in Southern and Western India, mostly in stations located along the slopes of the Western Ghats, reflect the comparative advantage of development of hydel power in these regions. On the other hand, as much as 30 per cent of the total potential of the country is located in Assam, where the demand for electricity is very low, development is negligible at present and could remain limited. Other handicaps in development of the hydel potential are difficult communications; soft, unstable rocks in the Himalayan region and the susceptibility of the region to earthquakes; concentration of rainfall in the monsoon season, and fluctuations in rainfall from year to year. Because of these rainfall characteristics, storage works have to be large and thermal power stations have to be built alongside hydel stations, as standby power sources.

Table 2.14: Regional Distribution of Potential and Development of Hydel Power and Demand for Electricity

Region	*Potential**		*Development*	*Demand for electricity*
	Million twh	*Per cent*	*Per cent of potential developed by 1960-61*	*Per cent of All-India demand*
Eastern	14.2	6.5	5.6	26.4
Northern	36.6	16.9	2.8	9.6
Central	43.9	20.3	1.1	15.5
Western	13.6	6.3	10.0	21.5
Southern	42.6	19.7	9.7	26.1
Assam	65.5	30.3	0.03	0.9
All India	**216.4**	**100.0**	**3.6**	**100.0**

* The hydel power potential is estimated in aggregate at 41 million kW at 60 per cent load factor, which corresponds to 216.4 million twh annual output on a firm basis.

Nuclear Fuels

The nuclear fuels found in India are uranium and thorium. Deposits of uranium have been located in Bihar, Rajasthan and Tamil Nadu. The Bihar deposits have been investigated in some detail and 'indicated' and 'inferred' reserves in them are estimated to be in the neighbourhood of 10,000 tonnes. The reserves of thorium are much larger and it appears that, in the long run, development of nuclear energy will be with the use of thorium. "There are some 500,000 tonnes of thorium, mainly in two deposits. About 200,000 tonnes are contained in the very rich (9% concentration) monazite sands of Kerala ... An even larger deposit in the Ranchi Plateau, partly in the Bihar region and partly in Bengal ... contain some 300,000 tonnes of thorium in monazite of a concentration of 10 per cent. The 500,000 tonnes of thorium have been described as equivalent to the entire world's known uranium in ore containing 1 per cent and above." But the use of thorium for generation of energy awaits the solution of a number of technical problems, especially development of suitable breeder type reactors. When suitable breeder type reactors are commercially available, India will be richly endowed with nuclear fuels.

Non-Conventional Energy Sources

Coal, oil and natural gas are fossil fuels. Generation of energy from them only means using up past storages of energy. Much experimental work is in progress at present on utilization of currently produced energy—solar, wind, tidal, wave and geothermal. The problems relate mainly to reducing costs of obtaining energy from these sources to competitive levels. Work on solar energy is of particular interest to India because of the large number of sunny days during the year in most parts of the country. A technological breakthrough in this area could change the energy outlook for India significantly.

Minerals Other than Fuels

This collective term may be used to include ferrous and non-ferrous metals and the non-metallic minerals. The latter is a very diverse group, however, including minerals ranging from sulphur and common salt to building stones and clays. India has large resources of some of these minerals, but is deficient in others; an indication of the resources and deficiencies is given in Table 2.15, in which are included data on estimated reserves of about 20 selected minerals.

Table 2.15: India—Estimated Reserves of Selected Minerals

Mineral	*Unit*	*Quantity*	*Mineral*	*Unit*	*Quantity*
Coal	million tonnes	123,000	Bauxite (aluminium ore)	million tonnes	260
Petroleum	"	100-175	Mica	"	n.a.
Manganese ore	"	180	Asbestos	"	0.58
Iron ore	"	21,870	Gypsum	"	1,117
Chromites	"	2.3	Limestone	"	15,740
Vanadium ore	"	26.7	Magnetite	"	100
Limonite (Titanium ore)	"	350	Sulphur (element)	"	neg.
Copper ore	"	32.9	Pyrites (40 per cent)	"	384
Lead ore	"	10.7	Phosphoric nodules	"	2.0
Zinc			Appetite	"	0.87
Tin	"	neg.			

India's resources of iron ore are among the world's largest, are of high quality and are well distributed regionally. The largest deposits are in the eastern and central States of Bihar, Orissa and Madhya Pradesh but there are large deposits also in the South, in Tamil Nadu and Mysore, and in the West, in Goa and Maharashtra. India has large deposits also of high grade manganese ore and of limestone and dolomite and is thus well supplied with all the raw materials of the steel industry except coking coal.

But the situation is different in respect of non-ferrous metals, such as copper, lead, zinc and tin, and some non-metallic minerals, such as sulphur and rock phosphate. The known deposits of all of them are small and the demands are met mainly or entirely by imports. The principal deposits of copper are in Bihar, Rajasthan and Andhra Pradesh. Domestic production had until recently been only from the Ghatsila mine in Bihar but the Khetri deposit in Rajasthan has been developed and development of the Andhra Pradesh deposits is being considered. Production of lead and zinc is only from the Zawar mine in Rajasthan. There is no indigenous production of tin. The deficiency of copper is made up to some extent by the existence of large deposits of bauxite. Aluminium can be a substitute for copper in the electrical industry and has also a wide variety of other uses. It is a versatile metal, whose consumption has increased rapidly in recent decades. The bauxite deposits are of high grade and are well distributed regionally, being located in Bihar, Orissa, Madhya Pradesh, Maharashtra and several other States. The principal problem in their development is the high cost of power required in very large quantities for the conversion of alumina to metallic aluminium. The prospects of development appear most favourable in Bihar and Madhya Pradesh where large blocks of relatively cheap power could become available from thermal stations based on low-grade coal.

Among the non-metallic minerals, there are large deposits of mica, principally in Bihar and Rajasthan, which are worked mainly for export. The most notable deficiencies are those of sulphur and rock phosphate, raw materials of the chemical industry. There are no known deposits of elemental sulphur. There is a deposit of pyrites in Bihar, but production remains small because of the high cost of recovery of sulphur. Large deposits of high-grade limestone and dolomite are found both in Eastern India in the vicinity of the coalfields and the iron ore mines, and in other parts of the country. Building stones of great variety are found in different parts of Peninsular India. The white marble of Makrana in Rajasthan; the red and yellow sandstones of Rajasthan and Madhya Pradesh, and the granites of South India are the best known among them. Common salt is obtained by evaporation of sea water all along the coasts, and also from Sambhar Lake and salt wells in Rajasthan. The largest manufacture of sea salt is in Gujarat. The salt industry offers considerable scope for increasing recovery of by-products, such as potassium chloride.

Forests

There is a large variety of forest types in India—from the tropical evergreens of Kerala and Assam to the conifers of the Western Himalayan region, and from the tropical deciduous of Madhya Pradesh and Orissa to the thorny scrub of Rajasthan. The variety of species is even greater. This variety of forest types and species is often found within short distances. Thus one can see within a small area of the Himalayan region the entire range from the luxuriant sub-tropical vegetation of the *terrain* and the foothills to the conifers of the higher slopes. The variety of wild life matches the variety of vegetation; the two could be very valuable in the development of recreation industries.

The total area under forests was reported to be 62,335,000 hectares or 623,350 sq. km. in 1966-67 according to the statistics on 'Classification of Area', collected by the Revenue Departments of the State Governments (Table 2.7). But according to the 'Forest Statistics', which are collected by the Forest Departments of the State Governments, the total area was

752,982 sq. km. (Table 2.16). The discrepancy between the two figures is due to differences in the methods of classification of 'forest' adopted by the two departments. The distribution of the forest area, as reported in the 'Forest Statistics', by type of forest, ownership, management and economic value, is given in Table 2.16. Coniferous forests, which occupy 6 per cent of the total forest area, are confined to the Western Himalayan region—in Uttar Pradesh, Himachal Pradesh and Jammu and Kashmir. Among the other forests, the most valuable are those of *sal* and teak, which cover together 189,000 sq. km. or about one-fourth of the total forest area. Most of the area of 'miscellaneous forests' is covered by poor scrub. More than 90 per cent of the total forest area is under the ownership and management of the Forest Departments, the remainder being with the *panchayats* and individuals. But only the Reserved Forests of the Forest Departments are managed according to scientific management practices and have good stands of timber. These practices cannot be followed in the 'Protected Forests' because the local people have virtually unrestricted rights of felling of trees and of livestock grazing in them. Large areas of such 'Forests' suffer from severe soil erosion resulting from denudation of vegetation. The condition of most 'Unclassified Forests' is equally bad or worse. The classification of forest areas by economic value indicates that as much as one-fourth does not contain any merchantable timber.

Table 2.16: Classification of Forest Area as Reported by Forest Statistics, 1964-65

Area (in sq. kilometres)

1. Total forest area	752,982
2. Type:	
▪ Coniferous	46,144
▪ Broad-leaved: *Sal*	97,818
▪ Teak	91,222
▪ Miscellaneous	517,798
3. Ownership:	
▪ Forest Department	696,582
▪ Civil authorities	16,084
▪ Corporate bodies	24,573
▪ Private individuals	15,743
4. Legal status:	
▪ Reserved	327,181
▪ Protected	226,027
▪ Unclassified	179,412
5. Economic value:	
▪ Merchantable	590,064
▪ Unprofitable or inaccessible	162,918

Consumption of timber and other industrial wood was estimated at 11 million cu. m. in 1968-69 and was expected to increase by 1973-74 to 16-17 million cu. m. In order to meet the increasing demand for industrial wood, a massive programme of clearing the existing forests and planting the cleared areas with quick-growing species, suitable for industrial use, was initiated in 1961. The programme represented a significant departure from the earlier forest management practices, which had been based on the principle of sustained yield through natural regeneration. The new approach emphasized quicker growth and higher yields with the aid of modern plantation practices. By 1968-69, 0.65 million hectares had been covered by the programme. In order to extend coverage by it, a pre-investment survey of 75,000 sq. km. of forest area is being undertaken during the Fourth Plan period.

Pulp for paper and other products is manufactured in most other countries from coniferous softwoods. The area of coniferous forests being small in India, the pulp is manufactured from other materials. Paper pulp is manufactured mainly from bamboo, but the rayon industry depends upon imported pulp. The forest development programmes, included in the Fourth Plan, aim to achieve self-sufficiency as early as possible, in major forest-based products such as pulp, paper, newsprint, wood panel products and matches. Furthermore, sizeable exports of paper and wood panel have been projected.

The increasing demand for fire-wood—a 25 per cent increase between 1960-61 and 1980-81 had been projected by the Energy Survey of India Committee (Table 2.12)—can also be met efficiently by plantations, located in wastelands and other suitable areas, in the vicinity of towns and villages. The plantations can be managed directly by the Forest Departments, or by the village *panchayats* under the direction of the Forest Departments. The need for such plantations has been recognized for over a century—the first statement on the Indian Forest Policy, made in 1870, included their establishment as one of its principal objectives—and plantation programmes have been undertaken. But they have not been adequate, and a serious shortage of fire-wood is apprehended in rural areas. The Fourth Plan proposes an expansion of the programme and emphasizes the need for co-ordination of efforts among the various agencies concerned.

Forestation in critical areas forms an essential part of erosion control and soil conservation programmes. The obvious first priority areas for the programmes are the catchments of major irrigation and river valley projects, in which forestation is needed to prevent rapid silting of the reservoirs. Forestation programmes have been undertaken in several catchments areas, from the Second Plan period and, as mentioned earlier, have been progressively expanded.

Recreation and tourism industries are just beginning to develop in India, but they have a large potential for growth. In order that forest areas may be utilized adequately for these industries, access to them has to be improved by construction of good roads and suitable facilities have to be provided for the stay of visitors. At the same time, adequate steps have to be taken for protection of wild life and natural vegetation. National Parks and Wild Life Sanctuaries have been established in India as in most countries. To achieve the twin objectives of recreation and protection; and facilities for travel to, and stay in them are being progressively improved in India. The parks and sanctuaries are attracting considerable numbers of visitors, including foreign tourists, and can attract much larger numbers in future because they offer an opportunity to see wild animals—the tiger, elephant, bison and rhino,—and also to observe flora of great variety and beauty. However, in view of the serious threat to survival of the animals due to poaching, measures for protection of wild life and natural vegetation will need to be made much more effective, and soon, if the rich wild life and natural vegetation of the Indian forests are not to be lost irretrievably.

Fisheries and Resources of the Sea

India has a coastline of nearly 5,635 km. but exploitation of fisheries and other resources of the sea has remained an activity of minor economic importance. Consumption of fish, marine or fresh-water, is small—less than 3 kg. per capita in a year. Fish is a significant item in the diet only of the people of coastal areas, or of States such as West Bengal in which fresh water fish is plentiful. Limited development of marine fisheries is due partly to unfavourable physical conditions—narrow continental shelf and a straight coastline with few good harbours. But cultural and techno-economic factors have also hampered development. Fisheries along the coast of Gujarat were not exploited until recently because the local people are vegetarians. Secondly, since fishing has traditionally been done in small, non-power-driven boats, it had to be confined to a narrow zone of a few miles from the coast and had to be virtually suspended during the monsoon season and other stormy periods when the boats could not go out to sea.

The total catch of fish was estimated at 1.5 million tonnes for 1968-69. The Fourth Plan has indicated a target of production of 1.97 million tonnes, consisting of 1.4 million tonnes of marine fish and 0.57 million tonnes of inland fish for 1973-74. The bulk of the marine fish catch consists of mackerel and sardines, although in recent years there has been a rapid increase in the catch of prawns, mainly for export.

Fishery development programmes under the Five Year Plans have concentrated on the following:

(i) for marine fisheries, mechanization of fishing boats and use of improved tools by the fishermen; use of trawlers for deep sea fishing, and provision of facilities for storage and transport of fish from the coastal areas to the major cities; and

(ii) for inland fisheries, stocking of reservoirs, streams and other water bodies with fingerlings.

The use of mechanized fishing boats has increased progressively; the Indo-Norwegian Fishery Development Project, which began in Kerala in 1952, has made a major contribution to the increase. By 1968-69, a total of 7,800 mechanized boats were in operation, and the number is proposed to be increased by 5,500 during the period of the Fourth Plan. The plan programmes include also addition of 300 trawlers, construction of additional facilities for storage and transport of fish and expansion of the fish stocking programmes in inland waters. A noteworthy development of recent years has been rapid increase in exports of fish and other marine products, especially prawns. The value of the exports increased from Rs. 46 million in 1960-61 to Rs. 340 million in 1969-70.

Other Resources of the Sea

Reference has been made above to exploitation of offshore oil and natural gas resources, manufacture of common salt from sea-water and desalination of sea-water. These constitute, however, only the beginnings of exploitation of the resources of the sea. The sea floor is rich in minerals and technology is now sufficiently advanced to bring exploitation of these within the range of possibilities of the near future. Plant life of the sea also has immense potential for supplying food and raw materials. Marine algae are used for food in Japan and China and sea food can be processed for being added to cattle feed and for extraction of substances such as agar. The possibilities of economic exploitation of plant life of the sea are dependent, to a large degree, on technological advance.

Conclusion

This review has sought to relate the availability of natural resources of India to the present and projected near future (up to 1980-81) and demands on them. The picture that has emerged is one of high pressure of population on land and forests; adequacy (or abundance) of some minerals and energy sources, but deficiency of others. A somewhat longer perspective, say up to the year 2000, will indicate rapidly increasing demands on natural resources to meet the needs of population growth and economic development. The population of India may be anywhere between 0.89 billion and 1.1 billion in that year; the lower projection of the Planning Commission, is based on expectation of a significant decline in fertility from the early 1970s, while the higher projections of the United Nations is based on the assumption of later decline in fertility. National income will be more than seven times the 1968-69 figures, if the rates of growth of 5.5 to 6 per cent up to 1980-81 and at least 6.5 per cent thereafter, projected by the Planning Commission, are achieved. Estimating the magnitudes of demands on specific natural resources, or of specific primary products, is a complex undertaking, and the estimates have their limitations; the most recent estimates for the U.S.A., made in 1963, are already outdated because of rapid technological change. But absence of detailed estimates need not stand in the way of perception of the overall situation relating to the demands on natural resources, or of the measures needed to ensure that deficiencies of resources do not prove to be a serious impediment to economic development.

The growing demands for primary products will have to be met mainly from domestic production because, as experience during the drought years of the 1960s demonstrated, the need to import large quantities of primary products puts severe strains on the economy and the process of economic development is disrupted. But rapid enough expansion of domestic production will require, especially in agriculture, forestry and fishing, rapid modernization of production techniques; the slow rate of modernization of the period 1950-1965 will not be adequate. The high-yielding varieties programme in agriculture, the plantation programme in forestry, and mechanization of fishing constitute significant beginnings of the modernization process. In the mineral and energy sectors also, there is a very large potential for raising productivity and expansion of the usable resources through further modernization and technological advance. Productivity in coal mining can be greatly increased and the efficiency of utilization of coal can be greatly improved through these means. And, in the case of nuclear and solar energy, India has a vital interest in the development of new technology which would bring the large potential within the range of economic utilization.

Of course, modernization and technological advance are only one element of a comprehensive framework of policies on natural resources which must include, in addition, conservation, control over pollution and preservation of the natural environment. These elements have begun to receive considerable attention in recent years in the developed countries in which serious problems of depletion of natural resources, pollution and deterioration of the environment have arisen. These problems exist in varying degrees in India also and these elements must be important constituents of the policies on natural resources; references have been made earlier in this chapter to the needs for conservation and control over pollution. But if any aspect of these policies has to be singled out as being the most important at the present stage of India's economic development, it is unquestionably rapid modernization of production techniques.

Appendix 1

A Method to Indicate the Preference of Land Which Should be Under Forest: Some Comments

In his article to above title in the *Indian Forest*, the editor, had made some very useful suggestions on determinations of the proportions of land which should remain under forest in hilly and plain areas*. The method suggested by him for hilly areas would prove to be a useful guide for foresters, administrators and others who need to have an approximate idea of the areas which should be under forests and other uses in particular areas. The method, as the author has himself pointed out, can give only approximate results. But its value will be appreciated when it is borne in mind that data on soils and other characteristics by which land use capability may be accurately determined are very meagre (virtually non-existent in most areas), and it will take several years before the necessary surveys are conducted, and such data become available. Two observations on this method may, however, be made:

* Comments by Dr. V. Nath on Chopra's suggestion on determination of properties of land which should be under forest in hilly and plain areas.

(i) The method is designed to give an approximate idea, on *a regional basis*, of the proportions of land which should remain under forests. It is not meant to be, and should not be used to determine whether a particular piece of land should or should not be under forests. The method relies only upon determination of slopes. Slope is undoubtedly a very important factor in determining land use capability, and perhaps the most important on a regional basis. But where specific locations are concerned, and the most suitable land use for particular area is to be determined, one or more of the other factors determining land use capability like character of the underlying geologic formations, nature and depth of soils, drainage etc. may be of equal or even greater importance than slope.

(ii) The figure of 12 per cent slope which has been used in the article is merely illustrative. It should not be taken as a criterion on the basis of which one could demarcate forest and non-forest areas. The figures of 12 to 20 per cent are, as explained by the author, based upon American experience, and he has also explained why he has chosen the former figure. In case of India, the figures would most probably be lower than these. There are two main reasons for this. Firstly, in the tropical climates of India withering is more rapid than in the sub-tropical and temperate climates of U.S.A. Secondly, the monsoon rainfall of India is of a torrential character and is more erosive than rainfall in large parts of U.S.A. (especially Northern U.S.A.), which comes, in long, gentle showers. The critical percentages would vary also in different parts of India itself. They will have to be determined in different areas by actual tests. It will not do to apply figures derived under different conditions of another country.

Calculations on the area which should be mentioned under forests in the plains are most interesting. Here, the main consideration is supplying the needs of the population for forest products; physical consideration like slope is less important. According to the author, in areas having a population density of 500 persons per square mile, about 20 per cent of the land should be under forests in order that the needs of the population for fuel and other forest products may be adequately met. These calculations lead to one conclusion; the forests and tree lands (including village plantations) located within the densely populated plains can supply only a small proportion of the needs for forest produce; a large parts of needs must be met by imports from other areas (or by alternative fuels, in case of fuel needs), and the higher the population density, the greater this dependence upon the imports or alternative fuels. The reason for this conclusion is obvious. In most of the plain areas, where the density of population is 500 or above a very large part of the land is taken for cultivation (up to 80-90 per cent in many parts) and the balance is occupied mainly on grazing lands, fallows or non-agricultural uses like towns and villages, roads, canals, railways, industries etc; the area under forest is very small and under a well-planned system of land use. It can be increased only to a limited extent. Take West Bengal plain as an example. Population density is nearly 1,000 per square mile. On the basis of the above calculations, nearly 40 per cent of the land would be needed for forests. But the area at present reported under forests is only 6 per cent of the total. Sixty-one per cent of the land is under cultivation, 6 per cent is under fallows and the balance is waste or is occupied by non-agricultural uses. Obviously it is not possible to obtain anything like the requisite percentages of 40 per cent under forests in this area as the needs of agricultural, settlement, industries and transport are much more important. The situation in other densely populated areas, like Uttar Pradesh, Bihar and other plains of East and West Coast is essentially similar. Requirements of fuel and forests produce are very large because of the large population, but as very high proportions of land are occupied by agriculture and other uses, areas under forests are small and cannot be greatly increased.

This is not to deny the need for creation of tree plantation close to villages, or of bringing under forests all waste or idle lands in the plains. These measures are very necessary both for reducing dependence upon imports and of preservation of proper physical conditions and conservation of the resources of soil and water. But it must be recognized that these measures, necessary though they are, provide only a partial solution of the problem of supplies of fuel and other forest products in most densely populated plains.

It is but natural, that the demand for forest produce from the plains should impinge first and most heavily on forests in the marginal zones between the plains and the mountains or plateaus (the foot-hill zone of the Himalayas and the lower slopes of the plateaus and hills of Peninsular India), which are nearest the concentration of population. Forests in these zones would be the first to be exploited and would also be under constant pressure for larger and larger supplies, because supplies from such forests would be the cheapest. These forests would quickly disappear, as they have done in many parts of the country, unless exploitation is carefully regulated and constant vigilance is exercised for their protection. But preservation of forests in these areas is most urgent in order to protect the plains from soil erosion, floods, silting of streams and fertile croplands, desiccation etc. The problem is thus a complex one. The short-term interest of getting supplies at the lowest price possible and the long-term need for conservation of natural resources are in conflict in these marginal zones, and only with the most careful regulation can forests in such areas be protected from depletion.

The solution of problem of supplies of fuel and other forest produce has to be worked out separately for each region, depending upon the particular conditions in the region. In those regions, where large tracts of forested lands in the plateau or hilly areas are located close to the plains, these lands can supply the needs of the plains to a large extent. The plains and their adjoining plateau or hills lands can thus be visualized as composing one unit, the two parts of which are complementary to each other. The Malabar-Konkan Coastal Plain and the Western Ghats, the Chhota Nagpur plateau and the plains that surround it in North Bihar and West Bengal are examples of such complementary regions.

As the demand for fuel especially is very large, use of alternative fuels to supplement firewood appears to be necessary in most areas. In Bengal, Bihar, Uttar Pradesh, and other areas situated close to the coalfields, soft coke provides a suitable alternative fuel and its use should be encouraged as much as possible. In southern and western India, however, where distances from the coalfields are long and cost of transport of soft coke is very high, the problem is more difficult. Development of hydro-electricity and of locally available fuel deposits, like the South Arcot lignite, offer fruitful lines of approach for these areas.

3

Regional Development and Planning in India

Introduction

The previous chapter on Natural Resources, Planning and Development, focused on differences in topography, climate, type of soil, availability of subsoil water and potentials for irrigation of land, sources of energy and minerals, forests and access to sea water and fisheries etc. Based on these differences and land use possibilities, this chapter advocates that an analysis of regional differences in natural endowments should be identified and regional development and planning should form the basis for economic development planning in order to achieve balanced growth. The author identifies five macro regions of the country and analyses the differences in economic and social development between the regions which could have been minimized if balanced regional development had been the focus of planning and development during more than half a century of development planning in India.

A major problem in planning for every large country is that of development of its different regions. It raises questions of regional allocation of resources, location of major projects, and rates of growth of production, income and employment in different regions, and allied questions of inter-regional movements of goods and people. Planners in every country are concerned with these questions. Plans must contain clearly articulated policies in respect of them and appropriate programmes to implement the policies. In case of large countries, such as India, the national plan must be accompanied by regional plans for States and smaller areas.

However, regional planning problems had not until recently, received adequate attention from planners in many countries. National plans continued to be concerned primarily with overall growth of the economy and with sector-wise and project-wise allocations of investment and other resources. Regional allocations of investment, rates of growth of different regions or special measures needed to accelerate growth in the depressed or retarded regions received only secondary attention. One reason for inadequate interest in regional problems is that the issue of spatial location of economic activity has not received enough attention in economic analysis. Some economists have given attention to it from time to time; but it has not been in the mainstream of economic thought. This is due mainly to the fact that space and distance introduce a complicating factor in economic analysis. Most economists have chosen to ignore them and have been content to record that decisions relating to location of enterprises are made by entrepreneurs on the basis of available natural resources and markets. The influence of other factors, such as availability of capital, entrepreneurial skill and skilled labour in attracting industries to particular locations has been recognized and it is also admitted that some locations can only be explained on the basis of historical accident. The agglomerative tendency of industries is recognized in Marshall's concept of external economies. Alfred Weber, made an attempt to develop a systematic theory of location of economic activities; but his work had not received much attention until recently. A considerable advance has been made in this field in recent years, especially as a result of the work of Losch and Walter Isard; even so, the theory of location remains one of the less developed branches of economic thought.

The issue of development of regions began to engage the serious attention of planners, administrators and economists during the depression years of the 1930s, when there was acute economic distress in some regions. This distress, it was found, was not a temporary phenomenon but a semi-permanent state, caused either by chronic depression in the industries on which the regions had depended or by the fact that the regions had been by-passed in the economic development process.

In recent years the issues of location of economic activities and regional development have been brought to the attention of planners and economists from another direction—the phenomenal growth of metropolitan regions. The agglomerative tendency of economic activities has been seen in a particularly pronounced form in the post-war period of rapid economic growth: it has resulted in metropolitan cities and other major industrial regions of every country growing more rapidly than other areas. This trend, coupled with the trend towards dispersal of settlement from the central areas of cities to the suburbs, has created gigantic conurbations.

The issues of location of economic activities and of development of regions have considerable importance in developing countries, such as India. The disparities in levels of development within these countries, e.g. between the metropolitan cities and the hinterland areas are as great (if not greater) as in the developed and developing countries. Moreover, the tendency towards further concentration of modern economic activities in the metropolitan centres is very strong. The strength of this tendency is borne out in India, by the experience of industrial location during the period of the Plans. In this period, in spite of the preference of Government for dispersal of industries and of various measures taken by it to achieve this objective, about 70 per cent of all new factories or substantial additions to old factories have been located in the cities; 40 per cent in and around the 1 million (population) cities alone. Such concentration of modern activities in the metropolitan cities creates a growing cultural hiatus between them and the rest of the country. It creates what Lewis calls a drift towards a "polarized dual society" (Lewis, 1963, p. 178). Secondly, rapid growth of the cities, resulting from such concentration, has created difficult problems of housing, water supply, transport and other urban services. These problems have reached crisis proportions in the largest cities, such as Kolkata, Mumbai and Delhi; their solution requires large investments and major administrative and technological innovations.

The issues of location and regional development are important in India for another reason also. In a country of India's size and diversity of economic and social conditions, it is essential that people of different regions have a feeling of benefiting adequately from the development process. They must see that projects are located in their regions and that production, employment, income and levels of living go up. But concentration of economic activities in metropolitan cities or in a few other favoured regions can only create a feeling among people of the rest of the country that they are being asked to bear the burdens of economic development without benefiting adequately from it. This will lead, in a federal democracy, to increasing political pressures on location decisions, of which we have seen some evidence in recent years. Therefore, in order that location decisions do not become the subject of political pressures, but are guided by techno-economic considerations, it is important that the principles of spatial distribution of economic activities and the policies relating to development of regions are clearly defined. This requires, as a corollary, that regional science—the theories of location and of growth of regions, and the techniques of regional analysis—be developed rapidly.

References

John P. Lewis, *Quiet Crisis in India*, The Brookings Institution, Washington, 1962.

V. Nath, *Urbanization, Urban Development and Metropolitan Cities in India.* Concept Publishing Company, New Delhi, 2007.

4

Regional Disparities in Economic and Social Development in Five Macro Regions of India[1]

The author advances the hypothesis that there are five macro regions in India among which there are striking differences in physiographic and agro-climatic conditions, availability or otherwise of natural resources, economic motivations of the people and consequent differences in levels of economic and social development and per capita income. Each region covers more than one state. And that these differences are due in large part to trends in economic, industrial, agricultural and social development during the last half a century as a result of which some of the states which were backward earlier are now among the most developed. The differences have developed largely on account of the ways in which people of different regions have availed or failed to avail of the opportunities for economic development that have arisen on account of investment plans and economic or social policies of the Government of India and of the States and technological changes in agriculture, industries or services sector. The propensity to migrate to other parts of India or abroad in pursuit of higher income and policies of the State Governments to promote or fail to promote economic development or social change have also been factors in influencing the rates of economic development and social change in different states and regions.

All available data indicate that there is great disparity in levels of economic and/or social development among different states. They will increase further unless steps to reduce them are taken by the National and State Governments. Data on following indicators have been used in support of the hypothesis:

1. Population and growth rates 1971-81 and 1981-1991
2. Average and female literacy rates in 1991

3. Proportion of children in primary schools
4. Infant mortality rate, 1996
5. Proportion of workers in factory industries and proportion of population of all India in selected states and

5a. Electronics production profile

6. Per capita net state domestic product at factor cost (Current Prices in 1996-97)
7. Proportion of population below the poverty line, 1993-94
8. Net irrigated area as per cent of net cultivated area, 1993-94
9. Proportion of villages electrified.

Indicators of social, agriculture infrastructure and industries developments used and their data sources are as follows:

Indicators of Social Development

1. Adult and female literacy rates—major states (Census Paper, p. 72)
2. Life expectancy at birth (Census Paper, p. 72)

Agriculture

3. Principal crops and rates of growth of agricultural output (Proportion of cultivated area provided with irrigation) (State Outline, p. 63)

Infrastructure

4. Proportion of villages electrified (State Outline, p. 76)
   Proportion of villages within 2 km. of a motorable road
   Proportion of villages having safe and adequate drinking water

Industries

5 Principal industrial centres and industries

6. Population below poverty line (State Outline, p. 213)

The Six Macro Regions are:

1. *Southern India*: comprising the states of Tamil Nadu, Andhra Pradesh, Karnataka and Kerala and the Union Territory of Pondicherry.

2. *Western India*: comprising the states of Maharashtra, Gujarat and Goa and the Union Territories of Daman, Diu and Dadra-Nagar Haveli.
3. *North Western India*: comprising the states of Punjab and Haryana, the National Capital Territory of Delhi and a strip of land 100-150 km. in width extending from Dehra Doon in the north to Gautam Buddh Nagar and Bulandshahr in the south in western Uttar Pradesh.
4. *North Central and Eastern India*: comprising the rest of Uttar Pradesh, north and south Bihar, West Bengal and coastal Orissa.
5. *Central India*: comprising Madhya Pradesh, inland Orissa, Chhotanagpur region of Bihar and forested areas of Maharashtra, Gujarat and south-eastern Rajasthan. Agro-climatic conditions in Rajasthan vary from forested hills and valleys in the south to a well-watered plain in the centre to semi-desert and desert in the west.
6. *Not classified*: Assam and the seven hill states of the north-east, with large populations of tribal people; Himachal Pradesh and Jammu and Kashmir.

The rest of this chapter is devoted to description of agricultural[2] and industrial[3] development in the six macro regions, the levels of economic and social development of the people as indicated by per capita income and values of selected indicators of social development. The selected indicators are recognized as indicators of social development by the United Nations and other international organizations and are widely used for cross-country comparisons. For detailed analysis of economic development in each region, state has been used as unit for which data are readily available.

Southern India

Tamil Nadu, Andhra Pradesh, Karnataka, Kerala and Pondicherry.

These states have higher levels than the national averages of

(i) Higher proportion of urban/total population (Table 4.1),
(ii) Higher proportion of workers in factories/proportion of population (Table 4.4),
(iii) Higher yields of principal crops—rice, sugarcane and cotton—in the principal producing areas,

(iv) Higher average and female literacy rates than the national averages (Table 4.2),
(v) Lower and falling rates of population growth than the national averages (Table 4.1),
(vi) Higher proportion of electrified villages than the national averages (Table 4.8), and
(vii) Lower proportion of population below the poverty line than the national average (Table 4.6).

Yields of the principal food crop—rice have increased significantly since the early 1970s as a result of extensive use of dwarf, very high yielding varieties of rice, produced under conditions of assured and adequate water supply along with judicious use of organic manure, chemical fertilizers, pesticides and improved implements. The irrigated areas have increased progressively partly due to more efficient use of water from canals from the principal rivers and partly due to extensive use of electric or diesel driven pumps on wells.

Yields of sugarcane and cotton, the other important crops of the three states (excluding Kerala), have also been increasing progressively due to extension of irrigation, use of improved varieties of seed and better farm management. Increase in yields of plantation crops in Kerala has been less noteworthy.

A number of large cities, Chennai and Coimbatore in Tamil Nadu, Hyderabad and Visakhapatnam in Andhra Pradesh, Bangalore and Mangalore in Karnataka and Kochi in Kerala have emerged as major industrial centres. Employment in factories has increased progressively as new factories have been located in the environs of these centres. The industries range from production of processed foods, textiles (in Coimbatore and Mysore), garments, a variety of consumer goods, consumer-durables (refrigerators, air conditioners, TV receivers, electrically-operated kitchen gadgets and motor vehicles) to building materials. The latest addition in all the three states except Kerala is information technology industries. Bangalore is the principal centre of these industries, the turnover of which is in billions of dollars and is increasing rapidly. Chennai and Hyderabad are also emerging as centres of the I.T. industries.

Tamil Nadu

The environs of Chennai have been favoured since the 1960s for location

Table 4.1: Population and Growth Rates 1971-81 and 1981-1991

Sl.No.	*State and Region*	*Population (millions)*	*Growth Rate 1971-81*	*Growth Rate 1981-91*	*Proportion of Urban Population in 1991 (Per cent)*
			Percent per decade		
(1)	(2)	(3)	(4)	(5)	(6)
I.	**Southern Region**				
	Andhra Pradesh	66.3	23.1	23.8	26.9
	Karnataka	44.8	26.8	20.7	30.9
	Kerala	29.0	19.2	14.0	26.4
	Tamil Nadu	55.9	17.5	15.0	22.0
III.	**Western Region**				
	Goa	1.17	26.7	16.0	41.0
	Gujarat	41.2	27.7	20.8	34.5
	Maharashtra	78.3	24.5	25.4	38.7
III.	**North Western Region**				
	Punjab	20.2	23.9	20.3	29.5
	Haryana	16.3	28.8	26.3	24.6
	Delhi	9.4	55.5	51.6	89.9
IV.	**North Central and Eastern Region**				
	Bihar	86.4	24.0	22.4	13.1
	Orissa	31.7	20.1	20.2	13.4
	Uttar Pradesh	139.0	25.5	25.2	19.8
	West Bengal	68.0	23.2	24.6	28.5
V.	**Hilly Forested and Desert**				
	Madhya Pradesh	66.1	25.3	26.8	23.2
	Rajasthan	43.7	33.0	28.0	22.9
VI.	**Not Classified**				
	Assam	22.3	23.6	23.6	11.1
	Himachal Pradesh	5.1	23.7	19.4	8.7
	Jammu and Kashmir	7.7	29.6	23.5	23.8
	All India	**84.3**	**24.7**	**23.5**	**25.7**

Sources: (Cols. 3 to 5) Census of India 1991: Paper No. 1, Provisional Population Totals. Census Commissioner and Registrar General of India, New Delhi. Col. 6—Tata Consultancy Services: Statistical Outline of India 1998-99, Mumbai, Table 93, p. 51.

Table 4.2: Average and Female Literacy Rates in 1991

Sl.No.	*State and Region*	*Average Literacy Rate (%)*	*Female Literacy Rate (%)*
I.	**Southern Region**		
	Andhra Pradesh	45.1	33.7
	Karnataka	56.0	44.3
	Kerala	90.6	87.0
	Tamil Nadu	63.7	52.3
II.	**Western Region**		
	Goa	77.0	68.2
	Gujarat	60.9	48.5
	Maharashtra	63.0	50.5
III.	**North Western Region**		
	Punjab	57.1	49.7
	Haryana	55.3	40.9
	Delhi	76.1	68.0
IV.	**North Central and Eastern Region**		
	Bihar	38.5	23.1
	Orissa	48.6	34.4
	Uttar Pradesh	41.7	26.0
	West Bengal	57.7	47.2
V.	**Hilly Forested and Desert**		
	Madhya Pradesh	43.5	28.19
	Rajasthan	38.8	20.8
VI.	**Not Classified**		
	Assam	53.4	43.7
	Himachal Pradesh	63.5	52.5
	Jammu and Kashmir	na	na
	All India	**52.1**	**39.4**

Source: Census of India 1991. Paper No. 1. Provisional Population Totals, Registrar General and Census Commissioner, India, 1991: p. 62.

of factories manufacturing motor vehicles—trucks, buses, passenger cars, motor bicycles and scooters. Two factories, one for the manufacture of buses and trucks and the other for two-wheelers were established in the late 1950s. Their capacity has increased steadily. A Korean company has been established in the 1990s, for manufacture of passenger cars in a suburb of Chennai.

Coimbatore is the centre of the cotton textile industry which developed there following production of high quality cotton in the area irrigated by a canal from the Pykara River. It is now a multi-industry centre with manufacture of textiles, garments and textile machinery as the principal industries.

Chennai benefited greatly from the flight of capital due to militancy of trade unions from Kolkata in the late 1960s. Its principal advantage is a disciplined labour force, willing and able to learn industrial skills quickly and free from militant trade unionism. Furthermore, because of location closest to Singapore and Hong Kong, it is likely to be favoured as an industrial centre for establishment of industries by Singapore and Hong Kong based Indian industrialists.

Just over half of the cropped area in Tamil Nadu is unirrigated and subsistence farmers produce sorghum or millets as the food crops and oil seeds, preferably groundnut as the cash crop. But there are pockets of prosperity in the lands, irrigated by the Kaveri river and in the areas irrigated by wells fitted with electric or diesel driven pumps in which high yield rice is the principal crop. Sugarcane is a second crop in and around Coimbatore.

Although Chennai and Coimbatore are the principal industrial centres in the state, there are smaller centres such as Madurai, Tiruchirapally and Salem. The principal cottage industry is weaving of cotton and silk textiles by handloom and power looms. The State Government has taken effective measures since the 1950s for protection of these industries on which millions of poor handloom weavers depend for their livelihood. As a result, cotton and silk sarees made in Tamil Nadu have a ready market all over India. Certain kinds of handloom cloth have an export market also.

The values of most of the indicators of social development are higher than the national averages and have been rising steadily. The growth rate of population and infant mortality rate are lower than the national level and have been falling. Adult and female literacy rates are higher than the national averages. However, per capita income and proportion of population below the poverty line are close to national averages. A part of the reason for industrial development in the state is that the State Government has since the 1960s taken effective measures to promote it.

Educated Tamil Brahmins deprived of opportunities for white collar jobs in their home state have since the late 1920s been migrating to work in these jobs in Delhi, Mumbai, Kolkata and other large cities. They are also among the top ranking professionals—lawyers (jurists), physicians, teachers and scientists. In recent years, large numbers have joined as executives in the Indian public sector and private companies as well as Indian branches of multinational companies. The best among them have risen to the highest positions in all these fields. The latest trend among (Tamil and Bangalore based) software specialists is to migrate to the Silicon Valley in California, the largest centre of information technology industries in the U.S.A., in which salaries for software specialists are much higher than in India.

Table 4.3: Infant Mortality Rates, 1996

Sl.No.	*State and Region*	*Infant Mortality Rate (per 1000 children)*
I.	**Southern Region**	
	Andhra Pradesh	66
	Karnataka	53
	Kerala	13
	Tamil Nadu	54
II.	**Western Region**	
	Goa	na
	Gujarat	62
	Maharashtra	48
III.	**North Western Region**	
	Punjab	57
	Haryana	68
IV.	**North Central and Eastern Region**	
	Bihar	72
	Orissa	95
	Uttar Pradesh	85
	West Bengal	55
V.	**Hilly Forested and Desert**	
	Madhya Pradesh	97
	Rajasthan	86
VI.	**Not Classified**	
	Assam	75
	Himachal Pradesh	62
	All India	**72**

Source: Tata Consultancy Services: Statistical Outline of India, Mumbai, 1998-99, p. 15.

Karnataka

Bangalore, the capital of Karnataka is today one of the fastest growing industrial centres in India. The industries located in and around it include:

(i) Hindustan Aircraft, established during second World War for servicing and repair of aircrafts which has diversified into manufacture of small trainer aircraft;

(ii) Manufacture of telephone receivers and other telecommunication equipment;

(iii) Manufacture of a variety of consumer goods and consumer durables—from textiles and garments to air conditioners;

(iv) Manufacture of precision machine tools and watches;
(v) Computer software and other information technology industries;
(vi) Manufacture (or assembling initially from imported kits but progressively from domestically manufactured components) of passenger cars and heavy trucks for the regional and national market.

The initial advantages of the city were a salubrious climate and well developed infrastructures (it was once a city of gardens) and a disciplined labour force. These have largely disappeared and it is now a busy, highly polluted city with serious deficiencies of infrastructure (such as adequate water supply, well maintained roads and an international class airport). The presence of two institutes of science and of a large number of men and women trained in the sciences has led to the development of computer software and other information technology industries from the 1970s. The turnover of these industries is in hundreds of millions of dollars and is increasing by the year (Table 4.4a).

The strip of about 175 km. between Bangalore and Mysore city is well irrigated by a canal from the river Kaveri. It produces large crops of rice and high yield sugarcane and has a number of rice and sugar mills. Climatic conditions are most suitable for rearing silk worms on mulberry leaves. This has led to silkworm rearing and weaving of silk cloth as remunerative cottage industries. Mysore city has a large mill manufacturing silk textiles. Thus, there is a sizeable class of people of middle income groups—professionals and white collar workers, well paid skilled industrial workers and well-to-do farmers among which there is a large market for manufactured consumer goods and consumer durables—from processed foods through refrigerators and air conditioners to two-wheeler scooters and passenger cars.

Another emerging industrial centre in Karnataka is Mangalore, situated along the south west coast. It is a port and has a petroleum refinery. The uplands between Karnataka and Kerala have plantations of coffee and tea. While the planters are rich, the workers in the estates are poor.

The rest of Karnataka is poor and backward. Rainfall is low and variable. Millets, cotton and oilseeds are the principal crops but yields vary with the vagaries of the monsoon. There are very few industries. The values of most of the indicators of social development are not very high.

Per capita income, growth rate of population, the proportion of workers in factory industries/proportion of national population, adult and female literacy rates, infant mortality rate and proportions of villages having access to electricity and safe and adequate drinking water are somewhat higher or at par with national averages.

Kerala

Kochi with a deep-water harbour, a shipyard and a naval base, a petroleum refinery and an international airport is the largest industrial centre in Kerala. There is a high propensity to migrate to the Gulf countries in Kerala, south-west Karnataka and Goa. These areas receive several thousand million dollars every year in remittances from migrants. The remittances have helped the families of migrants to raise their level of living and improve, enlarge or rebuild the family house and/or farm. Migrants use a variety of imported consumer durables. But the demand for them has not led to development of industries manufacturing them. There is large migration of residents of Kerala, south west Karnataka and Goa to work as white collar workers in Mumbai, Delhi and various cities in South India. Nurses from Kerala work in hospitals in India and abroad. Thousands of educated women work as teachers in schools run by churches throughout India. However, remittances home of these workers have also not sparked significant industrial development in the state. Industries in Kerala remain confined to handloom weaving, processing of coir, cashewnut (locally grown or imported) and shell fish for export and domestic consumption and manufacture of metalware. The reasons for lack of industrial development in the state need to be investigated.

Production of rice and plantation crops—coconuts, rubber, coffee and spices have been increasing steadily but not spectacularly. Kerala has also a large potential for development of winter tourism. Its sunny, storm-free beaches, good rail and air connections with the rest of India and two airports are its main attractions. Its handicrafts could have a large market among domestic and foreign tourists.

The values of indicators of social development—adult and female literacy rate, growth rate of population, infant mortality rate, proportion of villages having electricity and located within two km of motorable road are very high in Kerala and only marginally lower in Goa and Mangalore. Indeed Kerala has been held up as a model state by the UNDP in having achieved high values of social development despite not having very high per capita income.

Andhra Pradesh

There are a large number of rice and sugar mills in coastal Andhra Pradesh. The region receives dependable irrigation from canals from the Godavari and Krishna rivers. Some areas in coastal Andhra Pradesh are the principal producers in the country of flue cured tobacco which is used in the manufacture of cigarettes. Large quantities are exported and the rest is used in manufacture of cigarettes within India. Hyderabad has a large factory manufacturing cigarettes. Other factories are located in various other cities in different regions of India.

Hyderabad, the capital of Andhra Pradesh, is the principal industrial centre in the state. It has in its environs, a number of defence related industries, and a factory of Bharat Heavy Electricals, a Government of India undertaking which manufactures machinery for generation, transmission and distribution of electricity; machine tools, refrigerators and other consumer durables. Visakhapatnam in the extreme north east, on the border with Orissa is the other industrial centre in Andhra Pradesh. It has a shipyard and a large steel mill. However, it is too far from the rest of Andhra Pradesh to have much impact on its economy.

Values of most of the indicators of economic or social development—growth rate of population, literacy rate, female literacy rate, infant mortality rate, per capita income, and proportion of population below the poverty line, percentage of villages electrified or within 2 km of motorable roads are not high. One reason for this is that Telengana, which constitutes more than half of Andhra Pradesh, is a backward region.

Western India

Maharashtra, Gujarat and Goa and Union Territories of Daman, Diu and Dadra-Nagar Haveli

Maharashtra and Gujarat are the most industrialized states in India. They have 14 per cent of the population but 36 per cent of the employment in factory industries (Table 4.4). Both states benefited from the flight of capital from the Calcutta Metropolitan District (including both Calcutta and Howrah) in the late 1960s due to militancy of trade unions in the CMD. In this period, many non-Bengali owners and managers of factories had to go through a period when they were harassed and felt unsafe. Many Gujarati entrepreneurs closed their factories in the CMD to reopen them in coastal Gujarat or in the environs of Mumbai.

Table 4.4: Distribution of Total Population, Proportion of Workers in Factory Industry among Total Workers and of Workers in Value Added Industry among Workers in Factory Industry by States (Per cent)

Sl.No.	*Regions and States*	*Proportion of Workers in Factory Industries of Total Workers in each State (per cent) 1995-96*	*Workers in Value Added Industries as Proportion of Total Workers in Factory Industry in each State*	*Population in Each State as Proportion of Total Population*
(1)	(2)	(3)	(4)	(5)
I.	**Southern Region**			
	Andhra Pradesh	11.8	7.0	8.0
	Karnataka	5.1	4.8	5.3
	Tamil Nadu	12.3	10.2	6.6
II.	**Western Region**			
	Gujarat	9.5	12.6	4.9
	Maharashtra	15.1	23.7	9.3
III.	**North Western Region**			
	Punjab	4.7	2.9	2.4
	Haryana	na	na	2.0
IV.	**North Central and Eastern Region**			
	Bihar	3.3		10.2
	Uttar Pradesh	8.9		16.3
	West Bengal	8.2		8.0

Source: Tata Consultancy Services: Statistical Outline of India 1998-99, Mumbai 1998, p.88. Percentages calculated from absolute figures.

Table 4.4 (a): Electronics Production Profile

(Rs. in crores)

	1993-94	*1997-98*
Electronic Hardware	14.0	22.0
Increase (per cent per year)		14.5
Computer Software	15.8	32.0
Increase (per cent per year)		25.5

Source: Tata Consultancy Services: Statistical Outline of India, 1998-99. Table 80, p. 79.

Coastal Gujarat has been called an industrial workshop. The factories located in it include manufacture of textiles, garments, and a large variety of machine tools, various consumer goods, consumer durables and pharmaceuticals. The discovery of crude oil off its coast has led to the establishment of petroleum refineries and factories manufacturing petro-chemicals, synthetic yarn and various plastic goods. The area benefited from the return of Gujarati traders from the East African countries—Uganda, Tanzania and Kenya—in the 1960s and the 1970s. They started manufacturing a variety of machine tools and other goods. The development of dairying to supply milk to Mumbai and the manufacture of dairy products (butter, cheese and baby food) has led to the emergence of a sizeable class of well to do farmers among which there is a sizeable market for consumer durables.

The other parts of Gujarat, Saurashtra and Kutch are relatively poor and backward. Most of the cropland is unirrigated and production of the principal crops—sorghum and millets for food and groundnuts and cotton as cash crops varies greatly with the adequacy and timeliness of rain from the summer monsoon. However, completion of the Sardar Sarovar Dam on the Narmada River in Madhya Pradesh will lead to a major increase in the irrigated area and in agricultural output in Saurashtra. The recent completion of India's largest petroleum refinery and petrochemical plant located at Jamnagar on the coast of Saurashtra could lead to growth of industries processing petrochemicals and plastic goods including textiles and garments. Industrial development in the duty-free export zone located at port Kandla on the coast of Saurashtra would also receive a major stimulus with the completion of the refinery.

Maharashtra

Maharashtra is the most industrialized state in India. Most of the industries in it are located in the environs of Mumbai (including New Mumbai and Thane), in Pune and in towns located along the rail-*cum*-road strip of 175 km between the two cities and Nasik. Textile mills established since the 1970s are still important. A number of them are closed; others have diversified to manufacture cloth using mixtures of cotton or wool with polyester fibre. The proprietors of several mills which have closed have established powerloom clusters in New Mumbai and Thane. Cost of production in them is much lower than in integrated spinning and weaving mills because of lower costs of land and labour.

Western Maharashtra is a major producer of sugarcane with high sucrose content and high yield per hectare of land. Production is

Table 4.5: Per Capita Net State Domestic Product at Factor Cost Current Prices in 1996-97

Sl.No.	*State and Region*	*Rs. (00)*
I.	**Southern Region**	
	Andhra Pradesh	99
	Karnataka	103
	Kerala	91
	Tamil Nadu	112
II.	**Western Region**	
	Goa	197
	Gujarat	139
	Maharashtra	173
III.	**North Western Region**	
	Punjab	182
	Haryana	162
	Delhi	198
IV.	**North Central and Eastern Region**	
	Bihar	38
	Orissa	64
	Uttar Pradesh	67
	West Bengal	94
V.	**Hilly Forested and Desert**	
	Madhya Pradesh	74
	Rajasthan	85
VI.	**Not Classified**	
	Assam	66
	Himachal Pradesh	99
	Jammu and Kashmir	74
	All India	**109**

Source: *Economic and Political Weekly,* Research Foundation: National Accounts Statistics of India 1950-51 to 1996-97 Mumbai, 1998, p. 84.

concentrated in the valleys of several small streams that flow from the Western Ghats to the sea. The establishment of sugar mills in the towns in these valleys has led to the establishment of enterprises for manufacture or repair of sugar mill machinery.

The industries located in Mumbai and its environs include besides textiles, machine tools, garments, cosmetics, consumer durables including passenger cars, light commercial vehicles and trucks and office and hospital furniture. The factory for manufacturing passenger cars was established in the late 1950s; that for manufacturing light commercial vehicles and trucks was established in the 1960s. Mumbai is the largest

Table 4.6: Proportion of Population Below Poverty Line 1993-94

Sl.No.	*State and Region*	*Population below Poverty Line %*
I.	**Southern Region**	
	Andhra Pradesh	22.2
	Karnataka	33.2
	Kerala	25.4
	Tamil Nadu	35.0
II.	**Western Region**	
	Goa	14.9
	Gujarat	24.2
	Maharashtra	36.9
III.	**North Western Region**	
	Punjab	11.8
	Haryana	25.1
	Delhi	14.7
IV.	**North Central and Eastern Region**	
	Bihar	55.0
	Orissa	48.6
	Uttar Pradesh	40.9
	West Bengal	35.7
V.	**Hilly Forested and Desert**	
	Madhya Pradesh	42.5
	Rajasthan	27.4
VI.	**Not Classified**	
	Assam	40.9
	Himachal Pradesh	28.4
	Jammu and Kashmir	n.a
	All India	**36.0**

Source: Tata Consultancy Services: Statistical Outline of India 1998-99, Mumbai 1998, p. 213.

producer of films and television serials in India. Although employment and value added in the industry is difficult to estimate, there is little doubt about the large size of both.

Pune is the second largest city and industrial centre in Maharashtra. The industries located in it include manufacture of machine tools, motor vehicles, defence related industries and manufacture by the Kirloskars of pumps, compressors for air conditioners and refrigerators and passenger cars and trucks. A large number of Mumbai-based industrialists have established their factories in New Mumbai, Thane and in towns located along the 170 km. rail-*cum*-road strip between Mumbai and Pune to avail of lower costs of land and labour than in either of the two cities.

Development of horticulture—grapes, citrus fruit, onions and other vegetables in several districts of western Maharashtra has added a sizeable class of prosperous farmers who produce sugarcane or fruit and vegetables. The latter are sent all over India and also to the Gulf countries. Thus, western Maharashtra which was once a poverty stricken, famine prone area in which relief works had to be undertaken from time-to-time until the 1960s has been transformed during the last three decades into a prosperous agro-industrial region.

The other parts of Maharashtra—Vidarbha and Marathwada have little industrial development. Cotton, millets and oil seeds are the principal crops. There is little development of irrigation so that most of the farmers are poor subsistence farmers. The stated policy of the State Government is to decentralize location of industries away from the Mumbai-Pune region to Vidarbha and Marathwada. However, the policy has not been implemented effectively so that these regions remain industrially under-developed.

The region around Nagpur is the principal centre for growing loose jacket oranges (tangerines) which are sent all over India. Fruit processing is a well-established industry in the city. It could become a centre for producing a variety of consumer goods and consumer durables for the regional market. It has suffered in recent years by poor rail or air connectivity with the other large cities and neglect of industrial development by the state government.

The values of indicators of social development are not so high in Gujarat and Maharashtra but are rising. Most of the villages are electrified. Adult and female literacy rates are rising. Rates of population growth are high and there is no indication of their decline. Further, the proportion of cropland irrigated is low.

Goa

Values of indicators of social development are high in Goa. Overall literacy and female literacy rates are the second highest among Indian states. The rate of population growth is only marginally higher than in Kerala. Almost all villages are within two km of a motorable road, are electrified and have access to safe and adequate water supply. Goa has also a large tourism industry. Both Indian and foreign tourists flock to its sunny beaches in the winter. The music and dances of its population, influenced greatly by the Portuguese, are a major attraction for foreign and domestic tourists.

Table 4.7: Net Irrigated Area as Per Cent of Net Cultivated Area

State and Region	*Net Irrigated Area/Net Cultivated Area (per cent)*	
	1993-94	1996-97
I. Southern Region		
Andhra Pradesh	37.5	40.6
Karnataka	21.6	21.9
Kerala	14.5	15.7
Tamil Nadu	47.4	52.7
II. Western Region		
Gujarat	27.0	n.a.
Maharashtra	14.9	14.4
III. North Western Region		
Punjab	93.2	93.0
Haryana	75.8	n.a.
IV. North Central and Eastern Region		
Bihar	47.5	49.4
Orissa	33.2	35.0
Uttar Pradesh	65.6	68.7
West Bengal	35.0	35.0
V. Hilly Forested and Desert		
Madhya Pradesh	27.1	32.3
Rajasthan	28.3	33.3
VI. Not Classified		
Assam	21.1	20.9
Himachal Pradesh	17.5	18.8
Jammu and Kashmir	42.4	42.7
All India	**36.0**	**38.6**

Source: Tata Consultancy Services: Statistical of India, Mumbai 1998-99, p. 15 and 2000-2001, p. 132.

Goa is not an industrial centre at present. But with development of the port of Marmagoa and construction of the Konkan railway which provides access to the Konkan, western Maharashtra and eastern Karnataka, it has the potential for industrial development in the foreseeable future.

There is a high propensity to immigrate to the Gulf countries in Goa, and to Britain, the U.S.A. and Canada among the people of Gujarat. Mumbai is expected to remain the biggest financial centre in India. It has the best and busiest port in India. The building of another harbour at *Uran* on the mainland and improvement of the port of

Marmagoa in Goa have added to the freight handling capacity along the west coast.

North Western India

The region includes the states of Punjab and Haryana, the National Capital Territory of Delhi and a tract 100-150 km in breadth extending from Dehra Dun in the north to Bulandshahr in the south in western Uttar Pradesh.

The region has high levels of agricultural production because of extensive development of irrigation from canals, tubewells and shallow wells fitted with electric or diesel pumps. Wheat, rice and fodder crops in Punjab and Haryana and in addition to these sugarcane and oil seeds in western Uttar Pradesh are the principal crops. Completion of the Bhakra-Nangal irrigation-*cum*-power project greatly increased the irrigated area in Haryana and to a lesser extent in Punjab.

Agricultural output in the entire region has increased rapidly from the late 1960s due to use of very high yielding varieties of dwarf seed of wheat and rice along with chemical fertilizers, pesticides, improved ploughs and power driven implements including mechanical threshers and tractors. The region has the best milch animals in India which are fed on nutritious fodder crops grown in the summer. It is a large producer of milk and dairy products which are consumed however within the region itself.

Industrial development received a big boost in the Punjab in the late 1950s when large supplies of electricity began to be available with the completion of (the Nangal part of) the Bhakra-Nangal project. The government of the state actively assisted local entrepreneurs and those who were returning home with capital accumulated through stay in Thailand and Malaysia to establish small, medium and large sized industrial units in different cities of the state. Ludhiana, which has an enormous number of factories manufacturing or repairing farm implements, machine tools and consumer durables—electric fans, sewing machines, bicycles, motor bicycles etc.—is the largest industrial city in the state. Production in its woollen hosiery industry, established since the 1920s has increased rapidly to meet increasing domestic and foreign demand. Exports from the late 1950s to the late 1980s were mainly to the Soviet Union.

Amritsar, which has a large mill manufacturing carpets and woollen textiles, is another large industrial centre. Kapurthala has a factory manufacturing coaches for the railways. A factory manufacturing precision machine tools and watches has been established in the environs of Chandigarh, the capital of both Punjab and Haryana.

A large proportion of the industrial units in Haryana are located in two satellite cities of Delhi—Gurgaon and Faridabad. Elsewhere in the state the industrial units are concerned primarily with processing of agricultural produce, wheat and rice mills and cotton gins. Production of the traditional handicrafts—manufacture of brass utensils in some cities and furnishings on power looms at Panipat has also increased steadily to meet both domestic and export demands.

Punjab and Haryana have the highest levels of per capita income. All the villages are electrified and except in parts of Haryana are within two km of a motorable road and have access to adequate and safe drinking water.

However, the values of other indicators of social development—adult literacy rate, female literacy rate, infant mortality rate and rate of growth of population although rising slowly are not high. They are low particularly in Haryana.

In the strip of 100-150 km in western U.P. that extends from Dehra Dun to Bulandshahr, wheat, sugarcane and oilseeds are the principal crops. Most of the cropland is irrigated by canals and tubewells owned by the state or shallow wells fitted with electric motors or diesel driven pumps owned by the farmers. As in Punjab and Haryana, production of wheat increased spectacularly in this area with introduction from the late 1960s of dwarf, high yielding varieties of wheat. Yields of sugarcane and oil seeds have also been increasing steadily but not spectacularly, with improved farm management by the hard working farmers.

As in Punjab and Haryana, production of fodder crops to feed milch animals is an important part of the crop rotation system so that the area has high quality milch animals and is a large producer of milk, all of which is consumed locally.

There are a large number of sugar and a few cooking oil mills in the area. Sale of wheat and of sugarcane and oilseed to the mills is the principal source of cash for the farmers.

The area includes the multi-industry complex at Modi Nagar. Besides, a large number of medium sized and large industrial units are located in the two satellite cities of Delhi—Ghaziabad and Gautam Buddh Nagar. Meerut, with a population of almost 1 million also has a number of industrial units. Per capita income and level of living of the farmers and residents of urban areas are not as high as those in Punjab and Haryana. However, they are far higher than those in other parts of Uttar Pradesh.

Furthermore, although most villages have adequate water from wells, they are not kept clean so that water borne diseases of the respiratory tract are endemic. No significant effort has been made by the government to promote industrial development.

Domestic and foreign tourism is a source of income for the population of several cities in the region. Agra, one of the largest cities in the region, is visited by millions of foreign and domestic tourists every year because of the Taj Mahal. Millions of domestic tourists visit the region which is also the birthplace of Lord Krishna and has several other places of pilgrimage along the Ganga at the foothills of the western Himalayas. There is however an acute shortage of tourist infrastructure—hotels for tourists of high or middle-income groups, bus services, taxis and tourist guides.

It is not possible to comment on the values of indicators of social development because the region forms part of Uttar Pradesh and separate data are not available for it.

North Central and Eastern India

The region includes West Bengal, north and south Bihar, coastal Orissa and Uttar Pradesh, except the strip mentioned above.

The region is densely populated, and despite the fact that it is endowed with well watered plains the great majority of the farmers are poor subsistence or below subsistence farmers. The Kolkata Metropolitan District (CMD) which includes the cities of Kolkata and Howrah and a number of jute mill towns located along the river Hooghly and the Durgapur-Asansol multi-industry complex are the principal industrial areas in West Bengal. In Bihar, the principal industrial centres—Jamshedpur and Bokaro both of which have large integrated steel plants and several industries processing steel and chemicals and Ranchi which has a factory manufacturing heavy machines are all located in the Chhotanagpur region. There are few industrial units in north or south Bihar.

There was a large flight of capital from the CMD in the late 1960s on account of militancy of trade unions and insecurity of life for managers and owners of many industrial units. A large number of non-Bengali industrial entrepreneurs closed their works in the CMD to re-open them in Chennai, Mumbai, and Pune or in coastal Gujarat. A number of industrial units fabricating large steel structures such as bridges, owned by the Government of India were closed on account of militancy of trade unions. There has been significant reversal of these conditions, thanks to the efforts of the present Communist Party government which has been in office for more than 30 years. The government has eliminated shortages of water and power which had been endemic in the 1970s and the 1980s and greatly reduced militancy of trade unions. The jute mills and tea packaging units have experienced expansion on account of increase in output of both crops, and many of the steel fabricating units have reopened.

There are literally thousands of industrial units in the CMD manufacturing or repairing machinery for mines or making spare parts or components for such machines, for repair of ships and manufacturing a variety of consumer goods—garments, hosiery, pharmaceutical drugs and toiletries. A new harbour with a petro-chemical complex has come up at Haldia about 60 km south of Calcutta. There is a large factory manufacturing passenger cars in the environs of CMD.

Land reforms and extension of irrigation through installation of large number of electric pumps on irrigation wells has increased agricultural production and has created a class of well-to-do farmers in West Bengal. The frequency and intensity of floods has also been reduced to an extent by flood control works on the Damodar and Teesta rivers. There is good potential for development of information technology industries. Due to location of the Institute of Technology at Kharagpur, the Institute of Management and the Indian Statistical Institute at Barrackpur in the CMD and two reputed universities—Kolkata and Jadavpur—in the city itself, there is a large number of graduates in the sciences who could provide the manpower for establishment of the industries for which the state government should create the infrastructures. The industries can cater initially to the demand of banks and other financial institutions, business houses and manufacturing units in the CMD but could develop progressively an export market.

Irrigated area has increased also in parts of Orissa as a result of the Hirakud Dam on the Mahanadi River at Sambalpur. There is a large integrated steel mill at Rourkela, with its associated metallurgical and chemical industries. However, there has been little development of industries or improvement in agriculture in the rest of the state.

On the other hand, due to insecurity of life and property in large parts of Bihar, and parts of U.P. where dacoity, kidnapping and murder of wealthy merchants and entrepreneurs are not uncommon, there has been little industrial investment.

The poor, below subsistence farmers of eastern U.P. and Bihar have a high propensity to migrate to large metropolitan cities, particularly Kolkata, Mumbai and Delhi to work there as unskilled industrial workers or doing a variety of odd jobs such as of rickshaw-pullers, doormen in banks and other commercial establishments. They have also been migrating in large numbers since the 1970s to Punjab and Haryana to work as casual agricultural labourers in the busy agricultural season when there is a shortage of local labour.

During the last century, they migrated in large numbers to work on tea plantations in Assam or as indentured labour to work on sugar plantations in various British possessions from Trinidad and Tobago in the Caribbean to Natal in South Africa to Fiji in the South Pacific. They have settled there and in some countries such as Mauritius and Fiji their leaders are heads of governments. However, migration to metropolitan cities in India has only kept hunger at bay and has not led to significant improvement in the level of living of the migrant families.

The values of indicators of economic and social development—growth rate of population, overall and female literacy rates, infant mortality rate, per capita income, proportion of population below the poverty line, proportion of villages electrified are close to the national averages in West Bengal. However, they are very low in the other three states. In Bihar, per capita income is one-third of the national average and the proportion of population below the poverty line is 50 per cent higher than the national average. The indicators in the other two states are significantly higher than in Bihar, but are still quite low.

A part of the backwardness of the region is due to the legacy of the *zamindari* system of land tenure. Although the system was abolished in the 1950s, its psychological impact in terms of lack of initiative among farmers to improve productivity of their small land holdings through more intensive cultivation still persists. A second factor is the class struggle in Bihar between the high castes who were the former non-cultivating owners of land but now have to cultivate the land left to them with the use of hired labour and the low castes who have now become peasant proprietors. A third and more important reason is that U.P. with a population of 138 million and Bihar with 86 million in 1991 are so large that it is extremely difficult to govern them effectively. Division of the states into smaller states, proposed from time to time, is difficult in the present political environment but cannot be postponed indefinitely.

Flood control in north Bihar, where large areas of fertile lands get covered every year with coarse sand and gravel brought down by the

Table 4.8: Proportion of Villages Electrified

Sl. No.	*State and Region*	*As on 31-3-1996*
I.	**Southern Region**	
	Andhra Pradesh	100.0
	Karnataka	98.0
	Kerala	100.0
	Tamil Nadu	100.0
II.	**Western Region**	
	Goa	na
	Gujarat	98.8
	Maharashtra	99.4
III.	**North Western Region**	
	Punjab	100.0
	Haryana	100.0
	Delhi	100.0
IV.	**North Central and Eastern Region**	
	Bihar	70.8
	Orissa	73.6
	Uttar Pradesh	77.0
	West Bengal	76.9
V.	**Hilly Forested and Desert**	
	Madhya Pradesh	95.1
	Rajasthan	88.0
VI.	**Not Classified**	
	Assam	99.5
	Himachal Pradesh	100.0
	Jammu and Kashmir	96.9
	All India	**86.8**

Source: Tata Consultancy Services: Statistical Outline of India, Mumbai, 1998, p. 76.

floods of the Kosi, Gandak and other rivers and parts of northern U.P.; and curing alkalinity of soil by suitable reclamation measures would contribute greatly to increase in agricultural production. However, a beginning in regional development has to be made with a massive effort to improve indicators of social development.

The State Governments have shown little inclination to promote industrial development. There could be significant industrial development through improvement of quality and expansion of output to meet domestic and export demands of the traditional handicrafts of U.P. such as manufacture of decorative brassware in Moradabad, weaving of carpets in and around Mirzapur and of silk sarees in a suburb of Varanasi.

Table 4.9: Proportion of Children in Primary Schools

Sl.No.	*State and Region*	*Proportion of Children in Primary Schools*	
		1996-97	1997-98
I.	**Southern Region**		
	Andhra Pradesh	82	90
	Karnataka	106	105
	Kerala	91	90
	Tamil Nadu	106	109
II.	**Western Region**		
	Gujarat	115	na
	Maharashtra	111	113
III.	**North Western Region**		
	Punjab	81	82
	Haryana	80	na
IV.	**North Central and Eastern Region**		
	Bihar	71	76
	Orissa	89	99
	Uttar Pradesh	73	62
	West Bengal	104	92
V.	**Hilly Forested and Desert**		
	Madhya Pradesh	97	102
	Rajasthan	94	97
VI.	**Not Classified**		
	Assam	109	109
	Himachal Pradesh	95	90
	Jammu and Kashmir	68	67
	All India	**91.0**	**90**

There is a potential for development of the information technology industries in U.P. also. There is an Institute of Technology at Kanpur and three universities in the state. Allahabad, Varanasi and Lucknow were considered to be centres of excellence until the 1950s. Standards of teaching and research in them could be improved to provide the basis for training of graduates in the sciences who would provide the manpower for establishment of the industries. As in West Bengal, they will cater initially to the domestic banks and financial institutions and manufacturing units.

Bihar and U.P. could develop religious tourism by promoting the needed infrastructures in the places of birth, enlightenment and preaching of the first sermon by Lord Buddha which are located in Bihar, or the border of Nepal and Bihar and near Varanasi in U.P. and which are visited by millions of Buddhist pilgrims from south east and east Asia, from Thailand to Japan. The Japanese have indicated their willingness to provide financial and technical assistance for development of tourism infrastructure. However, the State Governments have shown no inclination to accept the offer and provide the infrastructures for development of tourism—from well maintained, deluxe and lower priced hotels, well maintained roads, improvement and expansion of the airports at Varanasi and Patna to bring them to international standards.

Varanasi and Allahabad in U.P. and Gaya in Bihar are visited by millions of Indian pilgrims. However, infrastructure (such as small, clean, low priced inns for their stay in comfort) is woefully lacking. Development of tourism besides providing employment to large numbers of people could generate the capital and foster growth of entrepreneurs for promoting industrial development and improving agriculture.

Hilly Forested and Desert India

The region includes Madhya Pradesh, inland Orissa, Chhotanagpur region of Bihar, forested areas of Maharashtra and Gujarat and Rajasthan. The region has a large population of scheduled tribes who subsist on cultivation of their small plots and judicious use of forests to obtain fuelwood and thatch for building or repair of their huts, for food during some seasons of the year and for medicinal herbs. The region is rich in mineral resources and has a large potential for development of both thermal and hydro-power. There are four large integrated steel mills, a heavy machinery plant at Ranchi in Bihar, plants for making trucks, machines for generation, transmission and distribution of electricity, several cement mills, plants for manufacture of rolling stock (wagons) for the railways and a number of hydro-electric or thermal power based electricity generating stations that supply power to cities in northern India—from Kolkata to Delhi and to cities/towns and villages in the region itself.

However, exploitation of the rich mineral and power resources by these units and/or of forests to obtain timber and plywood for construction of houses, commercial and office buildings in the cities in northern and western India have not benefited the tribals. On the contrary, they have been badly exploited by the mining and forest contractors. The tribals work as unskilled labour in mines and industrial units at subsistence wages. The location of the industrial units and power plants etc. has displaced large numbers of them from their traditional village homes. Schemes for their resettlement in villages chosen by the State Governments have been most unsatisfactory. They have not been provided with large enough plots of cultivable land and are also virtually denied access to neighbouring forestlands. Even adequate and safe drinking water is not available in many resettlement villages.

During the last two decades a number of socially concerned citizens and organizations have protested so vehemently against exploitation of the tribal that the concerned State Governments are being forced to pay attention to their grievances. Their protests have induced a change in the attitude of some State Governments and it is hoped that greater attention will be paid in future to their welfare including rehabilitation in sites in which their traditional life style is not disturbed.

There is acute scarcity of food in parts of the region whenever the monsoon fails and starvation deaths are not uncommon in the most backward districts of Orissa. In the desert region of western Rajasthan, large numbers of livestock perish in years of acute drought which is common. Famine relief works have to be undertaken and fodder has to be imported to save the livestock which are the principal wealth of the people.

Values of indicators of both economic and social development are low in both Madhya Pradesh and Rajasthan. Per capita income is lower than the national averages in both states. Rates of population growth are high, average and female literacy rates are low. The female literacy rate in Rajasthan is barely half the national average. Almost all the villages in Madhya Pradesh have electricity but the proportion is less than 90 per cent in Rajasthan.

Not Classified

Assam and the Seven Small Hill States of the North East

These states have poor communications with the rest of India. Assam, which comprises most of the Brahmaputra valley, has fertile plains which are subject however to floods during the monsoon season. Rice in the plains and tea on the hill slopes are the main crops. There is hardly any industry except for a small refinery which processes crude oil; the products are transported by a pipeline to Barauni in Bihar. The tea gardens, owned before independence by Scots are now owned mainly by non-Assamese businessmen. The tea is sent to Kolkata for packaging for consumption within India and abroad. Although production has increased progressively to meet rapidly rising demand within India and to maintain a sizeable export, the benefit does not accrue to the Assamese because the labourers and the tea plantation owners are all non-Assamese. One large multinational Anglo-Dutch company has a commanding position in packaging and sale of tea for both the domestic and foreign markets.

The hill states, small in size have subsistence agriculture, with rice as the main crop, as the principal means of livelihood. Levels of social development are high in states such as Mizoram and Nagaland in which most of the population has been converted to Christianity. Nagaland was in the grip of insurgency for a long period, which has been contained through action by the Indian Army. In occasional periods of scarcity when the rice crop fails, food has to be dropped by air and road in order to avert starvation because of lack of rail and poor road communications with the rest of India.

Himachal Pradesh

Himachal Pradesh was formed in 1948 through the merger of a large number of tiny hill states in the north of Punjab and Haryana and two districts of Punjab. Simla, the capital, which was the summer capital of British India for more than a century and was a beautiful hill station, is now an overgrown medium sized city which suffers from serious problems of air pollution and shortage of water during the summer which is also the busy tourist season. Besides subsistence agriculture, catering to tourists and growing apples for consumption in the plains are the principal means of livelihood in some parts of the state. Industrial development is limited to packaging of fruit, processing it to make fruit juice, jams, honey etc. and making woollen shawls on handlooms. Parts of the state remain snowbound for four to five months in the year. Since it is located on the border with Tibet, there is a large presence of the army. Repair of border roads and catering to the needs of the army provide employment to thousands of men.

Jammu and Kashmir

The state has three distinct regions:

(i) *Jammu*: An area of plains and hills which borders Punjab and has a mixed Hindu and Muslim population.

(ii) *The Kashmir valley*: A densely populated extremely fertile valley with a predominance of Muslim population which lies between the lesser and greater Himalayas. Rice is the main food crop.

There are large orchards of temperate fruits in the hills—apples, pears, peaches, apricots and cherries. Growing the fruits and packaging them for sale in the plains is the major source of income for large numbers of the people.

Production of rice is not sufficient to meet the needs of the population and large quantities have to be imported. All other foods—sugar, tea and cooking oil have also to be imported.

Before the insurgency which gripped the state during a part of the 1990s, catering to the needs of hundreds of thousands of tourists and export of its superb handicrafts—delicately embroidered fine woollen shawls, woollen and silk carpets, silk cloth, wood work, papier mache, etc., were and continue to be a major sources of income for the population. These activities have now resumed with control over insurgency.

There is a very large presence of the armed forces because of the strategic location of the state on the border with Pakistan and Tibet. Catering to the needs of the army provides employment to large numbers of people.

The available data on values of indicators of social development indicate that they are close to the national average.

(iii) *Ladakh*: a thinly populated dry mountainous area located on the border between India and China. The capital, Leh is at an altitude of about 13,000 feet. The population is mixed—Buddhist and Muslim.

Conclusion

This broad ranging survey of levels of economic and/or social development among different states and within different regions of some large states indicates that there are large inter-state and intra-state differences in these levels. These differences will increase unless determined efforts are made by the National and State Governments to reduce them.

To give two examples, first the Green Revolution, as a result of which large increases in output and yields per hectare of the two main cereal crops—wheat and rice—have occurred is confined to certain limited areas in which certain favourable conditions were met. Similarly, high yields of cotton and sugarcane-important cash crops—are obtained in areas with adequate and assured moisture provided by assured rainfall and/or irrigation. However, there has not been a similar increase in yields of these cereals or of sorghum and millets, which are the principal food crops, cotton or oil seeds which are the principal cash crops of farmers in the nearly 70 per cent of the cropland which is totally dependent on rainfall. Similarly while cotton and sugarcane give very high yields in certain limited areas, the yields of these are low in the rest of the areas in which they are grown. The crops are grown because they happen to be the only available cash crops. As a result, large differences have appeared in income and levels of consumption among the farmers and the rural population in different states and regions.

Second, factory industries are concentrated in the environs of some large metropolitan cities or in some regions of some states. Thus, there are differences in levels of industrial development between these states and regions and the rest of the country. These have led in turn to large differences in income, consumption and levels of social development of the people of these states and regions and of those in the rest of the country. While some regions such as the dry areas of Rajasthan and certain hilly areas may remain backward because of agro-climatic or physiographic reasons, there is no reason why large areas in regions which are well endowed with these to be highly productive and have high levels of economic or social development should remain economically or socially depressed. This despite the efforts of the governments to decentralize industrial development.

Differences in levels of social development as indicated by the values of social indicators are also sharp and will increase unless vigorous steps are taken to reduce them by the State Governments where they are low. As examples of several developed countries in the U.S.A. and many countries in Europe indicate it is extremely difficult to reduce intra-national differences in level of economic and social development despite the efforts of the governments of the various countries.

In India, while some regions such as the desert and semi-desert areas of Rajasthan and the hilly or mountainous regions of some states, might remain backward because of agro-climatic or physiographic reasons, there is no reason why large areas in well watered plains, which are well endowed to be highly productive should remain economically and/or socially depressed. If differences in levels of development between these backward and advanced states are allowed to persist or be accentuated they will generate social and political tensions which could be reduced only through continuous action over a long period.

The determined efforts of the present government of West Bengal have raised the productivity of farmlands and incomes of farmers as also halted and to an extent reversed the industrial decline in the Kolkata

Metropolitan District. Governments of other backward states—Uttar Pradesh, Bihar, Madhya Pradesh and Orissa should make similar efforts to raise levels of social and economic development of their people. A beginning should be made with raising levels of social development because a literate and healthy population will itself make a determined effort to raise income and consumption levels. In Uttar Pradesh and Bihar it is necessary also to improve the law and order situation so that there is security of life and property for the citizens and entrepreneurs can invest in industrial development. In Madhya Pradesh and Orissa, exploitation of the large tribal populations by mining and forest contractors should be minimized and schemes for rehabilitation of the displaced as a result of construction of dams, power stations or large industrial units are so designed that they can resume their traditional economic activities and social life.

Notes

1. V. Nath, "Regional Disparities in Economic and Social Development in India", *National Geographical Journal of India*, Banaras Hindu University, Varanasi, Vol. 44 Parts 1-4, March-December 1998, pp. 27-48.
2. A detailed regional analysis of agricultural growth/development forms part of a chapter, *The Growth of Indian Agriculture: A Regional Analysis* in the book by the author; *Regional Development and Planning in India*. Concept Publishing Co., 2008. Also published in *Economic and Political Weekly*, Vol. 7 No. 12 December 1970.
3. See *Ibid*: (i) *Industrial Location and Employment in India*. (ii)'*Trends in Industrial Location*. (iii) *Entrepreneurship in India: Distribution by Caste and Levels of Economic Development*.

5

Planning in India: The Experience, 1950-2000

Introduction

Economic development is a tumultuous, stressful process in which although the GDP increases at a faster rate than earlier, some economic or social groups gain at the expense or *vis-à-vis* the others. This is borne out by India's experience with economic and social development during the over 50 years since it became independent in 1947.

Historical Background

During the closing years of Second World War, there was much interest in India in comprehensive economic and social planning as a means to promote its economic and social development. A group of industrialists and big businessmen based in Mumbai produced in 1945, a Twenty Year Plan, 1945-65, for economic development of the country known as the Bombay Plan. The plan emphasized the need for modernization and expansion of existing industries for selling their products at home and in the developing countries of South Asia and East Africa and establishing new industries. It emphasized also the need for providing basic infrastructures such as approach roads, safe and adequate water supplies to villages and cities, opening of schools in villages and primary health centres within easy reach and increasing agricultural output by modernization of techniques to meet the food needs of the people and fibre needs of industries. Veterinary hospitals and dispensaries were to be built in order to provide facilities to farmers for their livestock.

The British Government joined the movement by producing a Ten Year Plan for reconstruction of the economy after the war. Emphasis in this plan was on construction of roads to break the isolation of villages so that a large proportion of them could be reached by motorable roads and improving national and state highways to match the existing network of railways.

Earlier in the 1930s the National Planning Committee established by the Indian National Congress had published a series of studies on various sectors of the economy. The members of the Committee included besides political leaders, economists, sociologists, engineers and scientists. The committee had as its chairman, Pandit Jawaharlal Nehru.

The Planning Commission

The Commission was established in January 1950, almost immediately after the Government of India had got over the daunting tasks of providing relief to and ensuring rehabilitation of millions of displaced persons who had migrated from Pakistan to India. The Prime Minister, Pandit Jawaharlal Nehru was its chairman. He had become an ardent believer in planning after he had seen the very rapid progress that the Soviet Union had made under its first and second five year plans during his visit to the country in the 1930s. The five other members included a Congressman who had a distinguished record of resolving labour disputes, two distinguished civil servants, a retired chairman of a large shipping company and an expert in agriculture and rural development. They were chosen for their expertise and not because they were Congressmen.

Goals and Policies for Development at National and State Levels have been:

(1) Increase growth of Gross Domestic Product (GDP) through expansion of output in agriculture and industries (including small industries and handicrafts) and services.

(2) Alleviation/eradication of poverty through undertaking food for work programmes for landless labourers and marginal farmers mainly in unirrigated areas to supplement their income and provide employment when they would otherwise be unemployed. The programmes would expand and improve rural infrastructures; increase in number of wells for drinking water and for irrigation; soil conservation and land reclamation works: construction of check dams for both irrigation and soil conservation in the hilly areas.

(3) Eradicate illiteracy and greatly increase attendance in primary schools for boys and girls of school going ages. Undertake

programmes for adult literacy and campaigns to increase enrolment of children in schools in states with low enrolment rates.

(4) Provide preventive and curative health care to all from health centres within easy reach of the villagers and in cities. Providing facilities for pre- and post-natal health care and family planning for women in the reproductive age group and for lactating mothers.

(5) Improvement and Expansion of Urban Infrastructures: Electricity and water supply, facilities for disposal of solid and liquid wastes in cities; expansion and improvement of intra-city roads.

(6) Assistance for self-help housing for people of low and middle income groups in villages and cities. Relocation and improvement of slums in large cities.

(7) Vocational education to train primary and secondary school teachers, nurses and dispensers, Doctors would be trained at state level colleges and teaching hospitals); repairmen of electric and electronic appliances and motor vehicles. The candidates should be selected primarily from boys and girls from low and middle-income families so that the trainees can then get jobs and raise the incomes of their families.

(8) Training for work in traditional handicrafts of the cities and for work in sun-rise industries, e.g. manufacture of garments; work in the information technology industries. Training as draftsmen, clerks of lawyers, income and other tax advisers; training for work as tourist guides, customs inspectors, passport officers at airports. The departments concerned would organize training.

There is a hiatus in the existing training facilities: those for training of professionals are adequate or in excess of requirements (especially of lawyers). However, those for sub-professionals or nurses and dispensers, lawyer's clerks and tax consultants, and repairmen of electric or electronic gadgets or motor vehicles are either woefully inadequate or non-existent. The reasons for the hiatus need to be investigated and training facilities organized.

(9) Development of large and small scale industries, khadi and village industries and protection of handloom weavers. Tariff protection for Indian industries against dumping of imports of

foodgrains (wheat, rice, and course cereals), sugarcane, cotton and groundnut to protect income of farmers. Fixing prices for chemical fertilizers. Fixing prices of cereals, sugar, cooking oil and kerosene distributed through the public distribution system in order to alleviate hardship to the poor and fixing prices of petroleum products keeping in view international prices of crude oil.

(10) Privatization of public enterprise.

(11) Improving efficiency in operation of nationalized banks, LIC and GIC to increase their profits and to make them competitive with foreign institutions. Voluntary retirement schemes to reduce number of surplus employees. Nationalized banks and other public financial institutions to be actively involved in development of large and small scale industries. Banks to provide medium term loans to farmers for buying tractors, installing tube wells, etc.

(12) Reduce corruption in government at national, state and local levels.

Five Year Plans

First Five Year Plan

The Commission produced the First Five Year Plan 1951-56 in December 1951, two years after its establishment. Emphasis in the Plan was on agriculture and rural development. The investment envisaged under it was modest and could be financed easily from domestic funds without any foreign aid.

Priorities in the Plan were dictated by the problems that the Government of India had faced in the three to five years following Independence. With the partition of India all the areas which produced surplus wheat for domestic consumption and medium staple cotton for making fine cloth in the canal irrigated areas of West Punjab and Sindh had gone to Pakistan. Import of medium staple cotton required scarce foreign exchange. Import of food, mainly cereals, also involved foreign exchange. Besides the Government has had considerable difficulty in importing food. It could be imported only from the U.S.A. and Canada, which had in addition to supply wheat to Western Europe and the Soviet Union, the fields of which had suffered extensive damage during Second World War.

The Plan was widely hailed by the media as being realistic because of its priorities and because the modest investment envisaged in it did not require any foreign aid or investment. The Plan was successful. Output of cereals and medium staple cotton increased enough to eliminate the need for their imports. Two favourable monsoons in 1954-55 and 1955-56 together with extension of irrigation by canals, tube wells and surface wells helped in achieving of these targets. The Community Development Programme launched by the Government of India in October 1952 provided funds from the State Governments to villages to construct thousands of kilometres of approach roads, improvement of water supplies for drinking and for irrigation, opening of tens of thousands of primary schools in villages and thousands of secondary schools in large villages to increase the number of children going to schools. Primary health care centres established under the programme provided facilities for preventive and curative health care. Similar facilities were created at the community development block/*taluka* levels to advise farmers on prevention of diseases among livestock.

The Second and Third Five Year Plans: 1956-61 and 1961-66

Buoyed by this experience, the Planning Commission prepared these two plans. The emphasis now was on industrialization. Large integrated steel mills, mills for processing bauxite to make alum and aluminium metal, factories for making heavy machine tools, machines for generation, transmission and distribution of electricity, light machine tools, telephone receivers and other telecommunication equipments were established. Factories for manufacturing rails, wagons and coaches for the railways were established also during this period. A factory for making electric and diesel locomotives for the railways had already been established during the First Five Year Plan.

After the discovery of oil off the coast of Mumbai and offshore and on-shore Gujarat, large investments were made in exploration and development of the oil fields, establishing refineries for processing crude oil to produce petrol and diesel oil for motor vehicles; kerosene and cooking gas for cooking or lighting in villages in some parts of the country. Some of the refineries were established in collaboration with companies based in oil producing countries of the Gulf. Large investments were made also for constructing pipelines for carrying petroleum products from the oil fields to the consuming centres.

Technical and financial assistance for establishing these factories was provided by the Soviet Union, Germany and Britain and to a much smaller extent by Canada. Technical assistance was given on a commercial basis by Switzerland and the U.S.A.

The light machine tools and telecommunication equipment factories were profit-generating and so were petroleum refining and construction of pipelines and distribution of petroleum products. The factories manufacturing machines for generation, transmission and distribution of electricity became profit making after a period of losses. But the steel and aluminium processing mills and several other factories incurred large losses due to difficulties of management and infrastructures.

It is significant that during this period dominated by public investment in heavy industries, private companies like the Tatas were allowed to expand capacity and modernize their steel mill at Jamshedpur with loans guaranteed by the Government of India and were assisted also to expand capacity of their hydroelectric and water supply capacity units in order to meet the increasing demands of electricity and water of rapidly growing Mumbai. The two foreign oil companies that had been distributing petroleum products in India for decades were also allowed to establish oil refineries in a suburb of Mumbai and were allowed to expand their networks of dealers throughout India.

No new large industrial investments have been made in subsequent plans. However, diversion of such large investment to industrial projects which were slow in yielding returns had resulted in neglect of agricultural development. As a result, there was a food crisis in mid-1960s when famine was averted only by large imports of cereals (Wheat and Milo) from the U.S.A. under its PL 480 programme.

Cessation of the exports of foodgrains by order of President Johnson, coincided with rapid use first of high yielding dwarf varieties of wheat and then of rice developed in Mexico and the Philippines respectively and adapted to Indian conditions by Indian researchers. Extensive use of these varieties increased production of wheat and rice so rapidly that the country did not need to import any cereals by 1970-71.

Production of both cereals has been increasing rapidly with increasing areas brought under conditions of assured and adequate supplies of water provided by dependable rainfall or rainfall-*cum*-irrigation. By the mid-1990s production of cereals had increased to nearly 200 million tonnes—three and half times the production in the mid-1950s. Production has been adequate to meet the increasing needs of the population, which at 840 million in 1991 was two and half times the population in 1951. Production of sugar and medium staple cotton has also been increasing steadily so that there has been no need for imports. Production of tea and jute has increased rapidly enough to meet increasing export demand despite increase in domestic consumption. The only food for which there is a shortage met by imports is cooking oil.

The fever of nationalization continued during the 1960s despite the losses of the industrial projects. Twenty largest banks were nationalized in 1969; life and general insurance companies had already been nationalized. Air India, the profit making international airline, established by the Tatas was nationalized at the same time and Indian Airlines was established to cater to the needs of the increasing volume of air travel between metropolitan cities and a small airline was established for operation in Assam and the north eastern states. The rail and road link with Assam and road communication with the north eastern states could be easily disrupted during the monsoons. The Government of India established also a chain of hotels in Delhi and some other cities and places of tourist interest. Private hotel operators were also encouraged to establish hotels in these places, some in metropolitan cities were established by or through collaboration between domestic and foreign operators.

State Governments also made investments in establishing industrial units. But most of their investment has been in agricultural and rural development and constructing and improving infrastructures such as roads.

During the next 20 years, 1970-90 the efforts of the Government of India and of State Governments were concentrated on minimizing the losses of public enterprises in order to provide funds for expansion of the infrastructure particularly roads and water supplies and facilities for secondary, university and technical education and running the existing institutes of science and technology and management.

In the 1990s planning has been reduced to outlining policies and programmes by adopting which Government ensures that balance of payments remains positive and India does not land in a situation similar to the one in 1991 when foreign exchange reserves were exhausted and India had to abolish most of the export and import controls, under the dictates of the IMF and the World Bank in order to get a loan from the IMF and aid for projects financed by the Bank.

The Tenth Plan 2000-2005 has fixed targets to be achieved of various sectors of the economy. However, the targets will be continually modified keeping in view the progress in different sectors of the economy.

To conclude the country still persists in making Five Year Plans and fixing targets of achievement in different sectors. The Plans serve also as an envelope for coordinating the development plans of different states and Union territories; but the Plans have to be modified continually keeping in view the fiscal and balance of payments situation in the country and the international situation, particularly prices for India's imports and prospects for exports. The fiscal deficit must be within acceptable limits and the foreign exchange resources must be on the increase so that the country can finance the investments envisaged in the plans. Emphasis henceforth would be on making monetary and fiscal policies every year, providing funds for implementation of the Plans for expansion of infrastructures—improvement in inter-state highways, ports, power supplies for cities and rural areas, drinking water and irrigation etc. Development of industries and provision of modern services is left to the leaders of business and industry the plans should only facilitate their investments. Following India's lead, most of the developing countries of South and South East Asia and Africa, prepared five year plans. Many of them still persist with five year plans. But there too plans have met a similar fate as in India.

Although the life and general insurance companies remained profitable, the losses of nationalized banks mounted because they were forced to open branches in villages and lend to non-credit-worthy borrowers, under the slogan of *Gharibi Hatao* (Remove Poverty).

By 1991, when the country was faced with a balance of payments crisis all these policies were reversed in order to get bridging loans from the IMF and the World Bank.

The policy now is to abolish most of the controls on imports and exports in order to enable private industrialists to improve the quality of their products to make them internationally competitive. Increased exports of products such as garments, leather goods, consumer durables ranging from furnishing for home and office to chasses for buses and trucks and a variety of other goods and finally, rapidly expanding exports of computer software have enabled India to have a positive balance of payments.

Fiscal, monetary and developmental policies are now made by the Ministry of Finance in consultation with the Chambers of Commerce and Industry and planning is reduced to incorporating the results in various plans. The Plans still serve as instruments of fixing targets for increasing production of products ranging from food grains to consumer durables and coordinating the plan of the Centre and State Governments. But planning has lost the glamour that it had earlier. It is felt now that in the rapidly changing economic and political situation in the world, five years is too long a period to be useful for projecting trends of investment or its allocation between different sectors of the economy.

In India, there is now a consensus that most of the industries and infrastructures such as distribution and transmission of power and water supply; telecommunications are better managed by companies than by the government. Denationalization of the banks that have started making profits is also being considered actively; certain areas of insurance have been thrown open to foreign insurance companies in order to provide competition to the domestic insurance corporations.

Institutions for Planning

India soon after Independence decided to have a plan for development for which an apex body called the Planning Commission was set up. Besides other institutions were set up and some existing ones were strengthened. These were:

The Planning Commission; the National Development Council which included Chief Ministers, Advisers, Ministers of Finance, Commerce, Rural and Urban Development, Health, Education, Industry, Tourism and Surface Transport; the Prime Minister's Council of Economic Advisers; Estimates Committee of Parliament;

Federation of Chambers of Commerce and Industries; Associated Chambers of Commerce and Industries; Confederation of Indian Industries;

Labour Unions; State Level Planning Boards and all state level ministries; and similar institutions as at the central level; District Collector; the *Zilla Parishad* President; the Panchayat Samiti Chairman;

Village or multi-village level Panchayat Chairman; Municipal Committees/Corporations.

6

Rural Development

In 2001, more than forty years after Independence nearly 72 per cent of the population lived in villages; in 1950-51 the proportion was more than 80 per cent (both estimates are according to the censuses conducted during the two years). Development with welfare would have no meaning if the level of income and welfare of the rural people did not increase. Since most of the rural people are farmers or agricultural labourers their levels of income depend principally on increase in agricultural output. Their welfare depends also on their access to basic service facilities—approach roads; clean and adequate water supplies; facilities for adult, primary, secondary or technical education for all; easy access to facilities for preventive and curative medical care within a short distance from their villages.

The Community Development Programme

These were precisely the objects of the Community Development Programme, which was launched in October 1952; initially in about 2000 villages in all the states and extended in a diluted version allover the country during the next ten years. The principal objects of the Programme were two:

(i) To make major investments in rural infrastructure, i.e. to provide approach roads, safe clean and adequate water supplies; primary and secondary schools and primary health centres; preventive and curative health care.

(ii) To assist the villagers to use improved methods of farming to increase agricultural output. The diseases of livestock would be controlled by providing veterinary facilities within easy reach and also improved methods of animal husbandry.

The villagers were expected to pay half the cost of expansion of some of the infrastructure facilities through their labour or materials. Thus for construction of roads and schools, the villages would provide land and labour; the government would metal and maintain the roads and provide school teachers and equipment for running the schools.

To increase agricultural output, the State Governments would provide extension workers to teach improved methods of cultivation and farm management. Financial assistance was provided to improve tanks for irrigation and construct new wells. Later when electric supplies became available as a result of completion of the various irrigation and power projects started in the First Five Year Plan (1951-56) the farmers were assisted to install pump sets on their wells. Augmented supplies of irrigation water also increased greatly the areas with assured supplies of water for farming.

The extension workers provided by the community development programme, supplemented by specialists in use of chemical fertilizers and pesticides assisted the farmers to plant dwarf varieties of wheat and rice in areas with assured water supply which gave two to three times the yield of the older varieties. By the end of the 1990s the country was producing almost 200 million tonnes, which provide the bulk of calories for India's population,

Per capita consumption of cereals has increased by about 10 per cent during the period 1970-71 to 1996-97. At the same time, there is an imbalance between the farmers of the 70 per cent cropped area that is not irrigated because yield of the cereals 'sorghum' and 'millets' grown in these areas has not recorded increases in the areas growing wheat and rice.

Production of sugarcane has also increased so rapidly that per capita consumption of sugar is also much higher than in the 1950s and even as late as the 1970s. However, the increase is concentrated in areas which get adequate and assured moisture. Similarly, per capita consumption of milk, vegetables, poultry products (eggs and chicken) and fish has also increased. Excepting fish, which is produced and consumed mainly in coastal areas, milk and chicken and vegetables are produced also in areas which have facilities of assured water supply provided mainly by irrigation. After meeting the local consumption needs of milk, poultry and vegetables the remainder is sold through cooperatives or by individual farmers for sale in the cities.

Thus, regional imbalance is a dominant characteristic of the agricultural revolution that India has witnessed since the late 1960s and there does not seem to be any prospect of its reduction in the next decade.

Panchayati Raj Institutions

An establishment of these institutions was first recommended in 1954 by a committee appointed by the Ministry of Community Development to evaluate progress of community development and national extension service. It recommended establishment of three institutions (Ministry of Community Development and Cooperation, 1957): *panchayats*, *panchayat samitis* and *zilla parishads* at the levels of the village, the community development block and the district. Beginning with Rajasthan in October 1959, the governments of all the states established these institutions in the early or mid-1960s. This was hailed by the political leaders in the central and state governments as a major step forward in the direction of "direct democracy".

The three institutions, their mode of establishment and their powers and functions are as follows:

The Panchayats: A body constituted for every village with a population of 1000-5000 (up to 10,000 in Kerala) or a group of villages with similar population.

The Panchayat Samiti: A body constituted for every community development block, an area with rural population between 60,000 (less in mountainous areas) and 150,000 or more in some southern states. The country had been divided into about 5,000 blocks for implementation of the community development programme. The *panchayat samiti* was a body consisting of *sarpanches* (chairmen) of all the *panchayats* in its area. It was a rather large body of up to 50 *sarpanch* members.

The Zilla Parishad: A body constituted at the district level, in order to oversee community development and other rural development programmes within its jurisdiction. It would distribute the grants given by the state government for implementation of the programmes. Since the country had nearly 500 districts in 1951 and about 5,000 blocks and every *zilla parishad* had an average of 10 blocks within its jurisdiction. Every MLA was an *ex-officio* non-voting member of one or two *panchayat samitis* within his constituency. Similarly, every M.P. was an *ex-officio* non-voting member of all the *panchayat samitis* and *zilla parishads* within his constituency.

The *panchayat* was to be a directly elected body. All adults (men and women) in the village or villages within its jurisdiction were entitled to vote for election of its chairman (*sarpanch*) and other members. The *panchayat samiti* and the *zilla parishad* were both constituted through indirect election. The *samiti* consisted of the *sarpanches* of all *panchayats* within its jurisdiction as its members. The *zilla parishad* had as members all the chairmen (*pradhans*) of all the *samitis* within its jurisdiction.

In Maharashtra and some southern states, an older administrative unit *taluk* and the community development block were coterminous.

There was at the level of the *panchayat samiti*, a team of one or more extension officers for raising agricultural output, a veterinarian who treated diseases of farm animals and advised villagers on improving livestock and a veterinary dispensary, a 6-bed hospital with a doctor, a dispenser and one or more nurses. It had also a lady health visitor who advised the rural women on basics of hygiene, nutrition and childcare. There were also one or more dispensaries in every community development block. This organization provided villagers with curative and preventive health care. There was also an inspector of education, who supervised the working of all the primary and secondary schools within the *panchayat samiti* under his supervision. The area of every *panchayat* had to have a primary school. A number of secondary schools in large villages or small towns were to provide secondary school education to students within its jurisdiction. Every primary school had one or more teachers. Every secondary school had a number of teachers. A *samiti* had also an inspector of cooperative societies and a secretary of a cooperative society in every large village. Their duty was to provide the villagers with loans for buying improved seeds and fertilizers at low rates of interest and to ensure that they were repaid in time.

According to the Committee, the Collector was supposed to be the friend, philosopher and guide of the Panchayati Raj Institutions. He had a senior officer of the state administrative service to assist him in his duties relating to rural development programmes. This officer, designated as District Development Officer was also the Secretary of the *zilla parishad*.

The Collector was supposed to attend all meetings of the *zilla parishad* which had its own chairman called *pramukh*. He could attend the meeting of any *panchayat samiti* that he considered necessary. His duties were to keep the state government informed about the functioning of the Panchayati Raj Institution. Thus, he could report to the government any major deficiencies in the functioning of any *panchayat samiti* or even the *zilla parishad*. On receiving his report, the state government would direct him to conduct an enquiry and submit his report for necessary action. He would enquire also about corruption or unacceptable behaviour of any *sarpanch*.

The district and division level officers of the development departments were expected to attend all meetings of the *zilla parishad* and if requested by the Collector also attend meeting of any *panchayat samitis*. Their attendance would acquaint them with the views of these representatives of the people about the functioning of their departments. They were supposed to rectify immediately complaints about malfunctioning of their departments.

The governments of several states abolished the *zilla parishad* and *panchayat samitis* in the late 1960s or early 1970s—barely 10 years after their formation because their functioning was not considered satisfactory by the governments. They began to be revived with greatly increased powers and grants and loans given by the State Governments in the 1980s and 1990s. Establishing them has been made mandatory by the 73rd Amendment to the Constitution, which was enacted in 1995. However, some State Governments have still not revived them.

The Committee, which had recommended establishment of these institutions in 1957, had expected that these institutions would be non-political. This was an unrealistic expectation in the social situation in the villages with great inequalities in income and social status of influential members of the high castes and those of the scheduled castes. In reviving the institutions, the governments have realized that the institutions cannot but be political, so much so that loss of control of these institutions in a large number of districts or of municipal bodies of the most important cities is considered by the political party in power in the State Government to be an indicator of decline in its popularity. Consequently, the party in power in the state government tries very hard to remain in power in these institutions.

Rural Development Programmes

Employment Generation by Building or Repair of Public Works in Selected Regions

These programmes have received varying emphases during this 50-year period depending upon the commitment of the various governments to eradication of poverty among the rural poor—landless agricultural labourers belonging mainly to the scheduled castes, in villages in the plains; members of the scheduled tribes in the hilly, tribal areas of peninsular India; both farmers and landless labourers in the western and eastern Himalayan regions where the fields are small and there is heavy soil erosion during the summer monsoons and many fields get washed away; the semi-desert and desert areas of western Rajasthan.

The programmes include:

(i) Building or repair of roads; Construction or repair of drinking water sources; Construction and repair of irrigation sources; Soil conservation-*cum*-irrigation works.
(ii) Construction and repair of roads, check dams and drinking water sources constitute the most widespread work undertaken in all the regions mentioned above.

In the semi-desert and desert areas of western Rajasthan, the programme consists of:

(a) Construction of new wells and repair of old tanks, step wells and wells.
(b) Clearing croplands of silt and coarse sands deposited during the drought.

In areas affected by natural disasters such as cyclones which visit coastal areas of the east and west coasts, and in Assam which gets flooded during the monsoon, clothing and blankets are air dropped to sustain the people until the floods recede. Thereafter money is provided to clear the land of water, to replace livestock that had perished. Money is also provided to help rebuild their huts. The offices of the collectors and sub-divisional offices also distribute building materials such as cement and corrugated iron sheets. These officers are in charge of overseeing the relief work.

The programmes can also be called food for work. The men and women employed in them are provided a part of their wages in balanced food (cereals, sugar and cooking oil) and the rest as money to enable them to buy other needs including kerosene for cooking. An efficient public distribution system, i.e. ration shops in which they can buy basic foods at prices fixed by the government is an integral part of the programme. The programmes are most effective when distribution of balanced food is accompanied by education of pregnant and lactating mothers and those with small children, the basics of nutrition, personal hygiene and care of children.

Finance for these programmes is provided partly by the Central Government and partly by the governments of the states. Such programmes are financed also by the World Food Programme of the Food and Agricultural Organization of the United Nations, several western donors and by the World Bank and the Asian Development Bank as part of their efforts for alleviation of poverty. Finance for the disaster relief programme is provided mainly by the Central Government. The International Red Cross distributes clothes and blankets to people marooned in floods and also sends doctors and para-medical personnel to prevent spread of epidemic diseases in the extremely unsanitary conditions around the marooned people.

Rural development programmes also included campaigns for reducing illiteracy and securing admission of all children in schools; and campaigns for eradicating widespread diseases and improving health of mothers and children; family welfare (including family limitation) for all women in reproductive age groups. These programmes have received increased emphasis during the last decade because of increasing realization that an educated and healthy population is a *sine qua non* of sustained economic growth. The programmes have received emphasis also because of the findings of the Census of 1991 and of various rounds of the National Sample Surveys that India has the largest number of illiterates in the world. The illiteracy rates in several states are larger even than in some of the least developed countries of Africa.

Similarly, despite 50 years or more of providing health care to all, millions of people suffer from easily preventable diseases such as those of the digestive and respiratory tracts and malaria.

In some states, particularly Bihar, large parts of Uttar Pradesh, Madhya Pradesh and Rajasthan, illiteracy rates are very high and incidence of the above-mentioned communicable diseases is also very high.

Among the states mentioned above, Madhya Pradesh has undertaken with considerable success a campaign for increasing literacy. No other state has launched such a campaign.

A nearly insuperable obstacle in reducing illiteracy is that in most of these states, the rural people feel that literacy, particularly of girls is useless. Among the state governments that of Madhya Pradesh has during the last decades organized a programme for increasing literacy with considerable success. No other state government has taken such an initiative so far.

Regional Imbalance in Rural Development

During the last 50 years of rural development there has emerged a large and increasing imbalance between areas with assured and controlled irrigation and others in which crop production depends upon the rains. In the former, the farmers obtain high yields of the principal cereals—wheat and rice with use of very high yielding dwarf varieties along with use of chemical fertilizers and/or organic manure and pesticides. Farmers with large plots use tractors and other machines such as mechanical hullers of wheat and maize. Some of these areas produce sugarcane or cotton; yields per hectare are high because improved high yield varieties of the crops can be grown. Farmers get employment through most of the year because raising two crops from most of the fields is the norm. Agricultural labourers can also find employment for most of the year in agriculture in handling produce in the markets, in the processing industries, in mills for producing rice or wheat flour, in cotton textile mills, sugar mills and those producing cooking oil or *vanaspati*. Production of perishable foods—milk, poultry products and vegetables is also concentrated in these areas.

The level of living of the rural population is high because they have the income to buy mill made clothes, furnishings, soap and toiletries and cooking gas for their homes. Most of the homes are *pucca* and may have electricity. The villages are also located along motorable roads. The landless agricultural labourers can find adequate employment also in the numerous industries in these areas.

In the unirrigated areas on the other hand the principal cereals grown are coarse grains—sorghum and millets and gram. Oilseeds (ground nut) and cotton are the principal cash crops. Yields are generally low and vary greatly depending upon whether rainfall has been adequate or timely. Farmers as well as agricultural labourers cannot get more than 100 days' work and food for work programmes have to be undertaken for them.

This regional imbalance between farmers and agricultural labourers in the irrigated areas on the one hand and the unirrigated areas on the other is a prominent feature of the Indian rural scene of which there seems to be no prospect for reduction in the foreseeable future.

Further work by the author on rural development programmes, the impact of the imbalance growth on concentration of rural poverty and economic and social change in village India—the two case studies in Rajasthan and Punjab form part of another volume—*Rural Development Planning and Change in Village India.*

7

Urban Growth and Planning[1]

Urban studies are important because (a) they describe the experiences with planning during a period of rapid change—demographic, technological, socio-economic, political administrative and in the concepts and practices of urban and regional planning, and (b) for illustrating the problems of plan formulation and plan implementation in India's small and big cities.

In the case of the growth of metropolitan cities some of the authors on urban issues have stated that rapid growth of urban population and of metropolitan cities since 1941 constitutes over-urbanization. But, the percentage of urban population in India, 33.4 per cent of the total in 2001[2] was not high for Low Developing Countries at similar levels of GDP and economic development; the percentage in most other developing countries is much higher. Furthermore, the growth rates experienced in India's large metropolitan cities, although they may appear high have also been exceeded in most of the large cities of the LDCs.[3]

Most of the metropolitan cities in India have experienced rapid increase in population and economic activities during the period 1951-81. The growth of their populations is indicated by the following figures in the cities mentioned below:

(Population in lakhs)

	1951	*1981*	*1991*
Bombay (Mumbai)	29.7	89.0	225.2
Pune	6.1	16.9	24.9
Hyderabad	11.3	25.5	43.4
Delhi	26.6*	62.2	84.2
Calcutta (Kolkata)	–	–	110.2
Madras (Chennai)	–	–	54.2

* Figures for 1961.

There has also been large spatial expansion for location of industries, markets and other service sector activities, for housing and for expansion of physical and social infrastructures. Also, there has been a structural change in the political environment, with progressive concentration of decision-making powers and of financial resources with the Central and State Governments. The concentration has led, in turn, to erosion of the cities and approval of major development projects in them are now taken by the State Governments (Central Government in case of Delhi and other Union territories). Suppression for long periods of municipal bodies, including corporations of large cities, on grounds of bad management (but often because they are controlled by a political party other than that in power in the State Government) and management of municipal affairs by administrators appointed by the State Government is another aspect of the erosion. The Municipal Corporation of Bombay the richest and most powerful in the country, which could not be superseded for more than a century, is now subject to suppression.

The crises of urbanization or rather the problems of urban proliferation of slums, pressures on urban services, pollution etc., are due in our view primarily to grossly inadequate investment in expansion of housing and urban infrastructures to meet the demands of rapid growth. It should be mentioned that investment in housing was regarded as consumption expenditure by the Planning Commission up to the Sixth Five Year Plan 1981-86 and was given low priority. Public investment in housing which formed almost 20 per cent of the total investment in housing during 1950-1980, was limited to providing subsidized housing to employees of the Central and State Governments and public sector enterprises or to selected weaker sections of the community such as scheduled castes and scheduled tribes and industrial workers. Private investment in housing has been inhibited by legal constraints, particularly the rent control and urban land ceiling acts. Investments in urban infrastructures have also been minimal. The only allocation made for them in the Sixth and Seventh Plans was for improvement or expansion or urban water supplies and constituted less than 2 per cent of the total public investment under the plans. The planners have continued to consider investment in urban infrastructure as the responsibility of municipal bodies, quite unmindful of the fact that these bodies are incapable of making the investment, because the great majority of them depend upon grants (or loans) from state governments to meet even their current operational expenditures.

Shortfall in the implementation of urban plans or deviation from them does not constitute a failure of planning. They have undoubtedly contributed greatly to aggravation of urban problems. Congestion in metropolitan cities with consequent lengthening of journey from home to work, intense pressure on the transport system and rapid growth of slums along pavements and on other available vacant spaces, would have been much less if the recommendations made in all the plans for the cities, for dispersal of industries and of commercial, administrative and other services had been accepted and implemented by the concerned governments. The plans have recommended relocation of industries as well as commercial, financial and other service sector activities from the centre of the cities to the suburbs. The Green-Areas would have been better preserved, with considerable benefit to the quality of the urban environment if recommendations of the plans for these cities to preserve these areas had been followed.

But such deviations from the plan implementation due to financial resource constraints or other reasons are not uncommon in the planning process and one does not give up planning because of them. It has to be recognized that, despite deviations and shortfalls, the plans have served as the principal investment for directing the spatial expansion of the cities in their period of rapid growth, 1951-81. Through their land use components, they have provided the basic design for location of new housing, industries and other economic activities, and for expansion of transport, water supply, waste disposal and other services. The projections of the plans relating to growth of population and employment, and of demands for housing and infrastructure facilities needed to meet the demands of growth or for achieving vital economic or social objectives, have provided the framework for investment to meet those demands. The contribution of the plans to growth and spatial expansion of the cities is fully realized only when we imagine a 'no plan' situation.

The plans prepared for the cities in the pre-Independence period were more successful. They were implemented with greater speed and efficiency and there were fewer deviations from them. But in the post-Independence period this pace has not been continued because of a variety of reasons, including financial resource constraints of municipal bodies and development authorities and long delays in decision-making within the State Governments. The State Governments have often taken five years or more in approving the plans. Approval of major projects included in the plans, allocation of funds for projects and establishment of management structures for their implementation have meant further delays. Deviations from plans are also greater than in the pre-Independence period because of the pressures of public opinion and money power.

Metropolitan and regional plans are prepared by development authorities established and controlled by the State or Central Governments. In recognition of rapid growth of the cities far beyond their municipal limits, a metropolitan region, much larger than the municipal area of the city, is generally designated as a planning region. It includes, besides the city, satellite towns, villages, agricultural areas, waste lands etc., as also new residential, industrial or commercial areas that have come up or are coming up. For example, the Bombay metropolitan region, designated in 1977, extends over an area of more than 2000 sq. miles and includes, besides the whole Bombay island—the Thane and Kalyan districts on the mainland. The rapidly urbanizing areas on the mainland are along the principal highways and railways, and on the coastal strip facing Bombay Island in which 'New Bombay' is coming up, primarily as an industrial township housing private and public sector industries and the onshore installation of the Oil and Natural Gas Commission. The planning regions for other metropolitan cities are also large enough to provide for the anticipated spatial expansions of the cities during the periods of the plans.

The growth and spatial expansion in most of the cities have been so rapid that the plans, first prepared in the fifties have had to be continually revised to take account of new developments. Recognizing the rigidity of the 20 year—'Master Plan' which were popular in the late 1950s and 1960s, most of the plans formulated in the seventies and the eighties have been flexible and have been modified continually in the light of changing conditions and needs. The 'Master Plan' approach suffered from many deficiencies. Some master plans appeared to be so ambitious or ahead of their time that they were not accepted for implementation. And even in the case of the plans that were accepted, there were large deviations or contraventions, which increased as time went on. Furthermore, shortfall in plan implementation due to financial constraints or other reasons, and delays in approval and implementation of major projects and programmes, were so great that the plans became increasingly irrelevant.

Although development has to be implemented primarily by the municipal corporations of the principal cities within the planning regions and the agencies which are responsible for providing physical and infrastructure services in them, the development authorities have the essential functions of overseeing implementation of the plans and of ensuring that their basic design and proposed land use patterns as also their recommendations relating to development policies, projects and programmes are accepted by the implementing agencies. Frequent consultations between the development authorities and the implementing agencies during plan formulation, and effective cooperation between them in plan implementation are, therefore, essential.

Consultations with the State Government at all important stages of plan formulation are of the utmost importance because the development authorities are established by them and are answerable to them. Secondly, the plans have to be approved and financial resources for their implementation have to be allocated by the State Governments. The author explains, however, that the needed cooperation between development authorities and the implementing agencies has not always been forthcoming and that conflicts of perception and of policy have been a major problem in the implementation of the plans of all the five cities, which prepared Master Plans—Mumbai, Delhi, Chennai, Kolkata and Bangalore. The State Governments too have not desisted from deviating from the plans or contravening them through their decisions, even after the plans had been approved by them. An outstanding example of this kind relates to the failure of the Maharashtra Government to shift the capital and to take the decisions needed for dispersal of industries and administrative and other services from the central areas of Mumbai, in keeping with recommendations in all plans for the city. These emphasized the need to reduce overcrowding and congestion and the pressures on the overstrained physical and social infrastructures of Mumbai.

Planning of land use that is determination of locations for housing, industries and commercial and other service activities, of transportation routes and of various physical and social infrastructure facilities forms the core of a development plan. Most plans contain also proposals for decongestion of the central areas of the cities through relocation of industries, markets etc. However, proposals have been conspicuously unsuccessful. Large new residential areas, markets, and other essential service areas, industrial estates and large public or private sector enterprises have undoubtedly come up in new locations within the metropolitan regions, especially around the satellite and other towns. But relocation of existing industries and handicrafts from the central areas has not taken place. On the contrary, new industries, particularly small industries and handicrafts, have mushroomed in them. In central Mumbai, for instance, growth of new industries has gone hand in hand with closure of sick textile mills and other old industrial units. Rapid industrial growth in the Mumbai metropolitan region, particularly on the mainland along the Bombay-Pune Road and in New Bombay (Navi Mumbai)has been primarily for location of new industries, including large public sector industrial units. Residential, commercial and other developments within this area have been primarily for meeting the needs for services of new industries, and other economic activities and of the populations dependent upon them. Location on-shore installations of the Oil and Natural Gas Commission south of New Bombay, although contrary to the plan for the city and building of the Nava Shiva port are other influences contributing to the growth of New Bombay.

Notes

1. Several essays on the subject by the author form part of another publication, '*Urbanization, Urban Development and Metropolitans Cities in India*'. Concept Publishing Co., New Delhi, 2007.
2. Data cover only 12 States and one Union Territory—*Source*: Statistical Outline of India 2001-2002; Tata Services Limited.
3. Indeed the proportion of India's population living in the largest city—Calcutta—16 per cent in 1991 is comparatively low and is moreover, no higher than it was in 1901.

8
Agricultural Growth in the 1970s: An Analysis*

In order to achieve the Fourth Five Year Plan target of growth of agricultural output by 5 per cent annually during the plan period (1969-74) and the rest of the 1970s, the rate of increase in productivity of croplands will have to be higher than the rate envisaged in the Plan. This is because the Plan's projection of increase in the gross cropped area appeared to be too high on analysis of both past trends in growth of the area and future possibilities of extension of cultivation and increase in multiple cropping.

For achievement of a high average rate of increase in productivity, significant increase in the rate is essential in the states, mostly in eastern and north-central India, in which it was lower than the all-India average of 1.77 per cent during 1952-53 to 1964-65. These states account for more than half of both total cropped area and value of agricultural output of the country. Low rates of productivity increase in them are not due to physical handicaps, but appear to be related to socio-economic factors: levels of economic development and the modernization of agriculture are lower in most of them than in the states with relatively high rates of increase in productivity. Significant reduction of inter-state differences in agricultural progress does not appear likely, however, from analysis of recent trends in modernization of agriculture, the pattern of public sector outlays under the Fourth Plan on agriculture, irrigation, rural electrification and related programmes or from targets of important plan programmes such as HYVP.

The specific causes of slow agriculture progress should be identified separately for each lagging state and region and appropriate remedial measures should be taken. But there are some common elements which point to the need of similar measures in most states. First since unirregated

* This article was published in *Economic and Political Weekly*, Vol. 5, No. 52, Review of Agriculture, December 26, 1970.

rice is the principal cereal crop in most of the states, intensive research and extension efforts aimed at evolving and spreading rapidly high yielding varieties of unirregated rice are needed. Second, the socio-Institutional handicaps of these states, arising from prevalence of *Zamindari* or other feudalistic land tenure systems over large areas until the early 1950s and/or inclusion of large areas in backward princely States in the pre-Independence period have not been entirely overcome. The remedial measures should include besides needed land reforms, accelerated development of social services and infrastructures and strengthening of development institutions.

The regional aspect of agricultural growth has not receved adequate attention; its analysis and formulation of suitable programmes to accelerate growth in the lagging region is a necessary corollary to the high area selectivity of the agricultural strategy of the Fourth Plan.

We discuss here two aspects of agriculture growth:

(i) The relative contributions of increase in cropped area and increase in productivity of crop lands in achieving the Fourth Five Year Plan target of increase of agricultural output by 5 per cent annually during the plan period and the rest of the 1990s; and

(ii) Regional differences in increase in productivity and their relation with physical conditions, levels of modernizations of agriculture and overall economic development and with Fourth Plan public sector outlays relating to agriculture, irrigation, rural electrification etc., and important programmes of increasing agricultural output.

The New Agricultural Strategy (NAS), adopted since 1966 and being continued under the Fourth Plan, is capital and technology intensive and has high areal selectivity. It aims at achieving a rapid increase in agricultural output through use of capital and technology intensive inputs such as high yielding seeds, chemical fertilizers and pesticides along with thorough preparation of land and efficient water management. Its principal components in case of cereals are the high yielding varieties and short duration varieties programmes. Most of the projected increase in cereal during the Fourth Plan period will come from them. The HYVP alone contributing 2/3rd of the total (Planning Commission, 1970, p.138).[1] The programmes are being taken up in a carefully selected areas in which the rigorous condition of adequate, assured and well regulated water supply can be met and other agro-economic conditions are also favourable for rapid progress. The total area under the two programmes in the final year of the Plan will be 40 mn hectares, or less than 40 per cent of the total area under cereals.[2] But in spite of the emphasis on intensification and area selectivity and recognition of the fact that the scope of extension of cultivation is limited because "there is virtual exhaustion of uncommitted land resources" (*ibid*, p. 121), the Plan envisages a large increase in the gross cropped area by 1980-81, as is shown in Table 8.1.

Table 8.1: Projection of Cropped Area and Irrigated Area (in mn hectares)

	1966-67	*1980-81*	*Increase*	*Average Annual Increase (%)*
Net sown area	137.0	151.0	14.0	0.7
Gross area sown	156.6	188.0	31.4	1.5
Area sown more than once	19.6	37.0	17.4	6.3
As percentage of net sown area	14.3	24.5		
Gross irrigated area	32.8	58.0	25.2	4.2
As percentage of gross cropped area	29.9	30.8		

Source: Planning Commission: Fourth Five Year Plan, 1969-74, p. 35.

Gross cropped area is expected to increase by more than 20 per cent, at an annual average rate of 1.2 per cent. The increase in physical terms will be 31.4 mn hectares of which 14.0 mn hectares will be due to increase in the net sown area and the balance to increase in the multi-cropped area. The growth rate of 1.2 per cent is lower than the rates of increase of gross cropped area under the First and the Second Plan, but it is double the rate observed during the first four years of the Third Plan (Table 8.2). Further, since there has been no increase in the area after 1961-62[3], achievement of the projected growth rate will mean a reversal of the trends since the early 1950s characterised first by slowing down and later cessation of increase in the area. It may be of interest to mention that the growth rate projected in the Fourth Plan is three times the rate of 0.4 per cent annually over the period 1964-86, projected by the US President's Science Advisory Committee Panel on world food supply, which had advocated for India a production strategy very similar to the NAS (Holst, 1967). The Panel's projection of gross cropped area in 1981 was only 169 mn hectares as compared with 188 mn hectares under the projection of the Plan. The two projections are not entirely comparable—the plan projects a somewhat higher rate of growth of agricultural output—but considering the essential similarity of the two production strategies, the difference in the projections is noteworthy.

Table 8.2: Compound Rate of Increase in Agricultural Production, Area and Productivity in Different Periods

		Production	*Area*	*Productivity*
1.	First Plan (1951-52 to 1955-56)	4.1	2.6	1.4
2.	Second Plan (1956-57 to 1960-61)	3.1	1.3	1.8
3.	Third Plan (1961-62 to 1964-65)	3.3	0.6	2.7
4.	1969-70 to 1980-81	5.0	1.2	3.7

Source: Lines 1 to 3: Fourth Five Year Plan, p. 118. Line 4: *ibid*, pp. 35-37.

Trends in Land Utilization, 1950-51 to 1966-67

The data of Table 8.3 bring out that gross cropped area increased by nearly 25 mn hectares during this period. Three-fourth of the increase was due to increase in the net sown area and the balance came from increase in multi-cropping (area sown more than once). Both net sown area and area sown more than once increased most rapidly during the period of the First Plan; a part of the increase was due to extension of reporting to areas which had been non-reporting earlier. But it may be noticed that while the net sown area continued to increase under each of the three Plans; area sown more than once did not increase after 1960-61. The Fourth Plan projection envisages therefore another significant departure from earlier trends: more than half of the increase in gross cropped area is expected to come from increase in the area sown more than once, which had not shown any increase during the 1960s.

Table 8.3: Trends in Land Utilisation (in mn hectares)

	1950-51	*1955-56*	*1960-61*	*1966-67 (provisional)*
1. Total reporting area	284.3	291.9	298.9	306.0
2. Forests	40.5	51.3	55.8	60.5
3. Area not available	47.5	48.4	50.0	50.6
4. Other uncultivated land excluding current fallows	49.4	38.9	37.4	35.2
5. Total fallow lands	28.1	24.1	22.6	22.6
6. Net area sown	118.7	129.2	133.2	137.0
7. Area sown more than once	13.1	18.2	19.6	19.6
8. Grossed cropped area	131.9	147.3	152.7	156.6
9. Gross irrigated area	22.6	25.6	27.9	32.8

Source: Directorate of Economics and Statistics, Government of India, Ministry of Food and Agriculture, Community Development and Cooperation.

Increase in net sown area during the First Plan period was aided by the stimulus to reclamation of waste lands given by the land reforms such as abolition of *zamindari* and *jagirdari* and various productions increase programmes of the Plan; the slow-down in later years was due to limitation of continued increase in the net sown area. The possibilities of extension of cultivation are limited in a densely populated country like India in which practically all the cultivable land is already under cultivation and the proportion of net sown area to total geographical area is the highest among the large or medium-sized countries of the world (Holst, 1967)[4]. Net sown area can increase in future mainly through reduction of areas classified as "fallow lands" and "other uncultivated land excluding current fallows" in the Land Utilization Statistics. The limited possibilities are indicated by the near stability of the areas of both categories since 1955-66, after the effects of extension of reporting and reclassification of lands in the early 1950s had worked themselves out. The Fourth Plan refers to a "survey of wastelands which suggests that an estimated area of 2.2 million hectares is available for reclamation and cultivation during the Fourth Plan. Of this, land reclamation will be carried out over one million hectares" (Planning Commission, 1970, p. 138). No details are given on how the balance increase of 13 mn hectares in net sown area by 1980-81 is to be achieved.

Apart from physical limitation to extension of cultivation, efficiency in mobilization and utilization of resources in increasing agricultural output through it and alternative means has to be considered also. Extension of cultivation is attractive under conditions of peasant agriculture because it involves minimum changes in technology and organization and can be achieved mainly through fuller utilization of committed but underemployed peasant sector resources such as human labour and bullock power. Increasing productivity of croplands involves on the other hand changes in technology and organization to which there is considerable resistance from the peasants in the early stages, and also large non-peasant sector investments such as on irrigation works or for production of improved seed and chemical fertilizers. But the attraction of extension of cultivation diminishes considerably when technological change and increase in productivity get established within peasant agriculture. Resistance to changes in agricultural practices is much less than earlier, and productivity techniques are adopted by the peasants with increasing speed and efficiency. Secondly, the underemployed peasant sector resources are much smaller (or non-existent) because of fuller utilization of these under conditions of steadily increasing productivity. In India, extension of cultivation is less attractive as a means of increasing agricultural output now than it was in the early 1950s. Technological change and steady productivity increase have got established in agriculture over large areas of the country, and in states like Punjab in which the 'Green Revolution' has been successful, the labour surplus in agriculture has nearly disappeared and seasonal shortage have begun to be reported (Billings and Singh, 1970, pp. A-61-71). As other states achieve similar progress, the attraction of extension of cultivation will decrease further. Indeed, it is not unreasonable to expect, with steady increase in productivity of agricultural labour and rise in wage rates, a reduction in the net sown area in some states, through withdrawal of cultivation from marginal, low productivity lands. The reduction may be expected particularly in States like Maharashtra and Mysore in which the areas of low productivity croplands are particularly large and rising productivity in agriculture and expanding non-agricultural employment will combine to push up wage rates of agricultural labour.

Increase in Multi-Cropping

Increase in gross cropped area through increase in multi-cropping is qualitatively different from the increase through extension of cultivation because multi-cropping is a form of intensification: it increases the intensity of cropping in the existing sown area. It involves changes in the cropping pattern and may require changes in use of inputs and management practices. In India, multi-cropping is closely related to irrigation because of the need to irrigate the second crop in most areas. The planners have projected near doubling of the multi-cropped area by 1980-81, at an average annual increase rate of 6.3 per cent (Table 8.1). The increase is expected to be achieved mainly through use of new, short duration varieties and appears to be dependent upon a number of technological advances, some of which are not beyond the experimental stage. This is clear from the following statement in the Fourth Plan:

> "However in the absence of short duration varieties, cropping intensity could not be made a focal point of agriculture strategy. During recent years, this barrier is being overcome and techniques of inter-cropping and relay-cropping are being developed. A series of new multi-cropping cycles have been evolved and tested. These are likely to have a significant bearing on future development" (p. 139).

Multi-cropping with use of short duration varieties will require also a high degree of efficiency in water management because adequate and well regulated water supplies must be available to all the crops grown in succession. Increase in the irrigated area and even more than the increase, improvement of irrigation in the existing irrigated areas are important in this context. The plan includes large programmes for achieving both objectives: the programmes of construction of tube-wells and installation of electric irrigation pumps are aimed primarily at meeting the needs of areas proposed to be brought under the high-yielding varieties and the short duration varieties programmes.

Since achieving of the projected increase in multi-cropping is dependent upon technological break-through, besides successful execution of irrigation and rural electrification programmes, it is difficult to comment on its prospects. But viewed against the background of stagnation of the multi-cropped area in the 1960s, achievement of a growth rate of more than 6 per cent annually during the 1970s appears to be quite unlikely. A shortfall, perhaps a large one, may be expected.

The emphasis on efficient water management under the NAS has led to significant and welcome change in the irrigation programmes—from mere extension of irrigation to extension-*cum*-improvement. As mentioned above, the programmes of construction of tubewells and installation of pumps are aimed primarily at improving the quality of irrigation. Moreover, the Plan gives, for the first time in any plan document, an estimate of the area on which irrigation is to be improved (p. 254). But the Plan's target of increase in the total irrigated area to 58 mn hectares by 1980-81 is quite ambitious: it envisages an average growth rate of 4.2 per cent annually, as against the growth rates of 2.2 per cent during the 1950s and 2.6 per cent between 1960-61 and 1966-67. It will not be easy to achieve such a sharp step-up in the growth rate of the irrigated area, especially as intensification/improvement of irrigation over large areas is sought to be achieved at the same time. It may be mentioned that actual increase in the irrigated area were much below the targets in case of all the earlier Plans.[5]

Increase in Productivity of Croplands

It is clear from this discussion that notwithstanding the emphasis on intensification in the New Agriculture Strategy, the Fourth Plan contains quite ambitious targets of increase in the gross cropped area, through both extension of cultivation and increase in multi-cropping, and in the gross irrigated area. The projected rates of growth are in all cases much higher than the rates achieved under the earlier Plan. To the extent the actual increase in gross cropped areas falls short of target, the rate of increase in productivity of crop-lands will have to be higher than 3.7 per cent annually, envisaged in the Plan (Table 8.2). The figure of table show a progressive rise in the rate of increase in productivity—from 1.4 per cent under the First Plan to 2.7 per cent between 1960-61 and 1964-65. But a more realistic comparison is with the average rate for the period, 1960-61 to 1968-69. This rate works out to be less than 1 per cent, so that achievement of the required rate of about 4 per cent will mean a fourfold increase over the average rate during the eight years immediately preceding the Fourth Plan.

Regional Aspects of Agricultural Growth

In this context, crop-and-region-wise analyses of growth of output assume importance, because slow growth in case of important crops or over large regions will depress the overall growth rate of the agricultural output. The difference in the growth rates of the principal cereal crops since introduction of the NAS—rapid growth in case of wheat and stagnation in case of rice and millets—have attracted considerable attention and the Plan provides for an intensive research effort to achieve technological break-throughs in rice and millets, similar to that for wheat (p.159).[6] But regional differences in agricultural growth, though noted in the Plan (p. 119), do not appear to have received similar attention: the plan does not appear to have included any special effort to accelerate growth in the lagging regions.

State-wise data on rates of growth of agricultural output and increase in productivity during the period, 1952-53 to 1964-65, are given in Table 8.4. Table 8.4 presents data also on a number of variables—proportion of cropped area irrigated, index of availability of moisture, average productivity per hectare of cropped area and selected indicators of modernization of agriculture—which are of interest in analysis of inter-state differences in increase in productivity. The data on irrigation and the indicators of modernization are given for a year in the early 1960s and the latest year for which they are available; comparison of the data for the two years brings out recent trends. The average rate of growth of agricultural output during this period was just above 3 per cent for all-India with inter-State variation from 4.56 per cent in Punjab and Haryana to 1.17 per cent in Assam. Only 5 states—*Punjab, Haryana, Gujarat, Tamil Nadu and Mysore*—had rates higher than the all-India average. In case of

Tables 8.4: Growth of Agricultural Output and Productivity and Data on Variables Affecting Productivity

Sl. No.	State	Compound Rate of Growth during 1952-53 to 1964-65 (Per cent)		Percentage of Gross Cropped Area Irrigated in		Index of Moisture Availability	Index of Average Productivity per Hectare (Average of 1956-57 to 1958-59, India=100.0)	Consumption of Chemical Fertilizers ($N+P_2O_5+K_2O$), kg per Hectare of Gross Cropped Area		Co-operative Credit Loans Advanced by Primary Societies to Members (Rupees per Hectare of Gross Cropped Area)		Use of Mechanical Power (Units per Thousand Hectares of Gross Cropped Area)	
		Productivity of Croplands	Agricultural Production	1962-63	1966-67			1962-63	1968-69	1963-64	1966-67	1961	1966
(1)	(2)	(3)	(4)	(5)	(6)	(7)	(8)	(9)	(10)	(11)	(12)	(13)	(14)
1.	Gujarat	4.09	4.55	7.8	10.5	140.4	64.6	2.3	9.0	33.8	45.5	5.7	11.3
2.	Tamil Nadu	3.04	4.17	45.2	46.1	251.7	176.2	11.0	19.5	56.3	43.0	18.9	41.9
3.	Mysore	2.71	3.53	9.2	11.4	151.9	64.9	3.1	12.9	14.3	21.1	2.3	4.4
4.	Punjab	2.61	4.56	42.2	64.8	157.3	131.7	3.4	29.1	19.2	48.1	3.4	13.9
	Haryana				37.7				10.4		17.4		3.7
5.	Maharashtra	2.45	2.93	6.7	7.3	192.2	65.1	2.3	10.2	30.2	40.2	3.9	8.5
6.	Andhra Pradesh	2.45	2.71	29.5	30.2	194.9	103.7	8.6	11.3	21.3	14.5	4.6	7.9
7.	Bihar	2.25	2.97	19.9	21.8	296.9	118.9	2.4	4.1	4.7	13.5	0.7	1.2
8.	Orissa	1.66	2.48	16.4	15.3	316.4	132.7	1.0	1.6	8.3	11.1	0.3	0.3
9.	West Bengal	1.34	1.94	21.5	22.6	321.5	168.8	3.3	9.7	10.1	14.9	0.7	1.2
10.	Madhya Pradesh	1.21	2.49	5.6	6.1	261.2	80.6	0.9	2.6	13.7	19.9	0.9	1.3
11.	Kerala	0.96	2.27	21.0	20.0	321.0	126.2	9.4	24.8	42.7	52.8	2.8	3.9
12.	Uttar Pradesh	0.94	1.66	26.6	32.4	222.8	128.3	2.2	16.8	22.2	19.4	1.2	3.0

(Contd.)

(1)	(2)	(3)	(4)	(5)	(6)	(7)	(8)	(9)	(10)	(11)	(12)	(13)	(14)
13.	Assam (-----)	0.08	1.17	23.3	21.6	323.3	174.0	0.3	3.1	0.6	5.9	0.4	0.8
14.	Rajasthan (----)	0.11	2.74	12.5	13.7	124.5	51.7	0.5	1.8	3.6	4.5	0.7	1.5
	Co-efficients of correlation with rate of increase of Productivity			0.09		–0.39	–0.18						
	India	**1.77**	**3.01**	**18.9**	**20.9**	**217.5**	**100.0**	**3.1**	**10.7**	**19.5**	**23.3**	**2.6**	**6.9**

Notes: Data are not available for Jammu and Kashmir and Nagaland.

Sources: *Cols 3 and 4*: Planning Commission, Fourth Five Year Plan 1969-74, p. 119. Based on "Growth Rates in Agriculture" published by Economic and Statistical Adviser, Ministry of Food and Agriculture.

Col 5 and 6: Computed from data on gross cropped area and gross irrigated area published by the Directorate, Economics and Statistics, Ministry of Food and Agriculture, CD and Co-operation.

Col 7: Computed from data on distribution of gross cropped area by rainfall regions (Directorate of E and S Ministry of FA, CD and C: "Indian Agriculture in Brief", Tenth Edition, 1970, pp. 22-23 and percentage of gross cropped area irrigated given in Col 5 above).

Col 8: J.G. Anand: "Measurement of Actually Realised Agricultural Productivities Per Acre and Per Worker in the Different Crop Regions of India" in Agricultural Situation of India, Annual Number, 1964.

Cols 9 and 10: Fertiliser Association of India, New Delhi, Fertiliser Statistics (Annual).

Cols 11 and 12: Reserve Bank of India, Bombay: "Review of Co-operative Movement in India".

Cols 13 and 14: Computed from data on numbers of oil engines, electric pumps and tractors in Livestock Censuses of 1961 and 1966.

rate of increase in productivity, the range of inter-state variation was larger and as many as 7 states had rates exceeding the all-India average. Further, while there was a correspondence between the two rates in most states, there was a marked divergence in some states, such as Rajasthan. The state experienced very rapid increase in the cropped area, of 2.85 per cent annually, and the decline in productivity indicates that a part of the increase was on land of low productivity (Ministry of Food and Agriculture, 1966, p. 40). It will be noticed also that the states with rates of productivity increase lower than the all-india average are concentrated in the eastern and north-central regions. Five out of the 6 states in these regions all except Bihar, had lower rates than the national average. [7] In contrast, most of the southern and western States had higher rates than the national average.

Increase in productivity is the result of two factors: (i) increase in yield of the crops grown, and (ii) substitution by more remunerative crops of less remunerative ones. A comprehensive analysis of increase in productivity has not been made in "Growth Rates in Agriculture". The source book of the data on agricultural growth rates. But from data on growth rates of area and production of different crops given in it, it appears that substitution made an important contribution to increase the productivity in some States. The most notable example is of Gujarat, where there was a phenomenal increase in the area under groundnut (10.08 per cent annually) at the expense of the less remunerative jowar and bajra, areas under which declined by 1.68 per cent and 5.14 per cent annually, respectively (Ministry of Food and Agriculture, 1966, Appendix 5.38).

Influence of Irrigation and Availability of Moisture

Table 8.4 shows that while in some states with high rates of increase in productivity, such as Punjab-Haryana and Tamil Nadu, the proportions of irrigated cropped area are high; in others such as Gujarat, Maharashtra and Mysore, the portions are quite low. The coefficient of correlation between the proportion of the cropped area irrigated and the rate of increase in productivity is only 0.1 indicating lack of significant relationship between the two. There is no significant relationship also between rate of productivity increase and index of availability of moisture based on proportion of cropped area failing in different rainfall zones and provided with irrigation.[8] The indices are quite high in most of the eastern and north-central states with low rates of increase in productivity and are low in several states with low rates. The co-efficient of correlation is negative –0.39, and is not significant. Indeed superimposition of the map showing states' rates of increase in productivity on maps of annual rainfall, soils and topography in the National Atlas of India showed that in three states—Gujarat, Maharashtra and Mysore—high rates had been achieved in spite of considerable physical disadvantages of low rainfall, plateau or hill topography and thin, low fertility soils over large areas while in states like Assam, West Bengal and Uttar Pradesh, the physical advantages of abundant or adequate rainfall, extensive plains and fertile alluvial soils had not been adequately exploited and rates of productivity increase had remained low. It is interesting to note that the indices of average productivity per hectare of cropped area (col. 8) were considerably higher in most eastern and north-central states with low rates of productivity increase than in most southern and western states with high rates. The co-efficient of correlation (–0.18) is negative, but not significant, in this case also.

Increase in Productivity and Modernization of Agriculture

Data are presented in Table 8.4 on 3 indicators of modernization of agriculture—consumption of chemical fertilizers, use of mechanical power and loans advanced by primary cooperative societies to their members. The quantum of cooperative credit has been taken as an indicator of modernization because it shows capacity of farmers to work successfully with a modern, democratic institution of self-help and to avail themselves of a modern aid to development. Data on consumption of chemical fertilizers and on cooperative credits were readily available; the index of use of mechanical power was constructed from data on number of tractors, oil engines and electric irrigation pumps, available in the livestock censuses. Each tractor was given a weight of 2 and the other machines weights of 1 each.

Two major facts emerge from the data:

(i) large inter-state differences in the values of all the three indicators, and

(ii) high values in most states with high rates of productivity increases and low value in most of the states with low rates.

The range of inter-state differences in consumption of chemical fer[illegible]izers (1962-63) was from 11.0 kg per hectare of cropped area in Tar[illegible]l Nadu to 0.3 kg in Assam. In case of cooperative credit (1963-64), the [illegible]nge was much larger, from Rs. 56.3 per hectare of cropped area to Rs. [illegible]6; but Tamil Nadu and Assam were again the states with the highest and [illegible]he lowest value. The range in case of the index of use of mechanical power in agriculture was also large. The inter-state differences are due to an extent to differences in need or potential for use of particular inputs in particular states. The potential for use of chemical fertilizers is under present techno-economic conditions much greater in Punjab and Kerala where moisture conditions are favourable than Rajasthan, Gujarat or Maharashtra, where the conditions are much less favourable. But in the main, the differences reflect differential progress in modernization of agriculture. One indication of this is provided by the sharp increases in the values of the indicators between the two years, for which data are given in the Table, under the influence of intensive agricultural development programmes. In case of both consumptions of chemical fertilizers and use of mechanical power the increases were more than three fold for the country as a whole. Among states increases in fertilizer consumption were most noteworthy in case of Punjab, Haryana, and Uttar Pradesh, where they were related to the success of the high-yielding varieties of wheat, and in the southern State of Kerala. Increases in use of mechanical power were most rapid in Tamil Nadu, Gujarat, Punjab and Haryana where the use of irrigation pumps and tractors was already well established. On the other hand, in states like Orissa and Assam where use of these machines was almost non-existent in 1961, progress during the next five years was also slow. Increase in cooperative credit was comparatively small, less than 20 per cent between 1963-64 and 1966-67 for the country as a whole. But increase in Bihar and Assam deserve notice because they give evidence of strengthening of the cooperative movement in states in which it had very low levels of performance earlier.

A rough idea of the relationship between the rate of increase in productivity and indicators of modernization can be obtained by counting the number of ranks among the first seven for each indicator, obtained by the States having the first seven ranks in rate of increase in productivity. The results of the count given in Table 8.5, indicate a fair degree of association, because five or more of the first seven ranks of the indicators are taken by the states with higher rates of productivity increase. The counts are similar for the earlier and the latter years for which data are given in Table 8.4. A better measurement of the relationship between the rate of productivity increase and the modernization indicators is given by spearman co-efficients of rank correlation. The co-efficients appearing at line 10 to 12 of Table 8.5 are more than 0.5 in case of all three indicators, but only that for the index of use of the mechanical power is significant at 5 per cent level.

The data of Table 8.4 show also that Bihar and Kerala are the two states in which the ranks according to the rates of productivity increase and those for the modernization indicators differ most. Bihar has a high productivity increase rank but low ranks on all the three modernization indicators; in Kerala the position is the reverse. It has been mentioned above that the figure of the rate of productivity increase for Bihar is in doubt. The figure for Kerala also need further investigation because an exceptionally large proportion of the agricultural output of the state consists of plantation and tree crops, in which depressed conditions may have prevailed during the period to which the productivity increase rate relates. Modifying the productivity increase rate rank somewhat, Kerala was placed above Bihar and was included among the group of seven states with relatively high rates of productivity increase (the High states of Table 8.6). With the modification, both the results of the counts and the spearman co-efficient changed towards stronger association between the rate of productivity increase and the indicators, as shown in Part II and IV of Table 8.5.

Table 8.5: Distribution of First Seven Ranks of Modernization Indicators Among States with High (H) and Low (L) Rates of Productivity Increases

			H States	*L States*
I.	**Use of:**			
1.	Chemical fertilizers	1962-63	5	2
2.	Chemical fertilizers	1968-69	5	2
3.	Co-operative credit	1962-63	5	2
4.	Co-operative credit	1966-67	5	2
5.	Mechanical power	1961	6	1
6.	Mechanical power	1966	6	1
II.	**Distribution in latest year after placing Kerala above Bihar Use of:**			
7.	Chemical fertilizer	1962-63	6	1
8.	Co-operative credit	1966-67	6	1
9.	Mechanical power	1966	7	
III.	**Spearman co-efficients of rank correlation Rate of productivity increase and use of:**			
10.	Chemical fertilizer	1962-63	0.56	
11.	Co-operative credit	1963-64	0.54	
12.	Mechanical power	1961	0.74	
IV.	**Rate of productivity increase, modified as at II above and Use of:**			
13.	Chemical fertilizer	1962-63	0.68	
14.	Chemical fertilizer	1968-69	0.53	
15.	Co-operative credit	1963-64	0.71	
16.	Co-operative credit	1966-67	0.75	
17.	Mechanical power	1961	0.79	
18.	Mechanical power	1966	0.79	

Table 8.6:

Sl. No.	State	Rank According to Index of Economic Development	Fourth Plan Public Sector Outlay on AIRE Programmes: Total (million rupees)	Fourth Plan Public Sector Outlay on AIRE Programmes: As Percentage of Value of Agricultural Output of 1964-65	Percentage of Total AIRE Outlay Allocated to: Agriculture and Allied Programmes	Percentage of Total AIRE Outlay Allocated to: Major and Medium Irrigation	Percentage of Total AIRE Outlay Allocated to: Flood Control	Rural Electrification	High-Yielding Varieties Programme: Percentages of Area to Area under Cereals in 1966-67: 1968-69	High-Yielding Varieties Programme: Percentages of Area to Area under Cereals in 1966-67: 1973-74	Percentages of Area under the Crop which was Irrigated in 1966-67: Rice	Percentages of Area under the Crop which was Irrigated in 1966-67: Wheat	Number of Electric Irrigation Pumps (thousands): 1966	Number of Electric Irrigation Pumps (thousands): 1969	Number of Electric Irrigation Pumps (thousands): 1974*	Percentage of Villages Electrified on 31-3-1969	Length of Surface Roads per 100 sq km on 31-3-1967
(1)	(2)	(3)	(4)	(5)	(6)	(7)	(8)	(9)	(10)	(11)	(12)	(13)	(14)	(15)	(16)	(17)	(18)
	High																
1.	Gujarat	3	1962.3	36.1	40.8	52.5	3.6	3.1	9.2	33.3	17.9	–	7.0	42.0	57.0	15.5	8
2.	Tamil Nadu	2	1925.0	28.8	58.8	18.4	1.2	21.4	15.6	45.5	92.5	--	256.6	410.1	562.3	62.0	31
3.	Mysore	7	1866.5	32.6	50.3	40.2	1.0	8.5	4.7	15.0	60.7	–	16.9	91.9	130.6	23.2	13
4.	Punjab }	6	933.6	24.0	51.5	17.0	12.8	9.6	34.2	70.0	85.6	72.1	25.3	59.1	81.6	37.0	12
	Haryana }		880.0		44.4	34.0	10.2	11.4	13.3	49.4	71.9	68.9	3.5	45.4	7.4	22.0	13
5.	Maharashtra	1	3751.0	44.0	55.0	38.0	0.6	6.4	8.9	30.5	18.5	–	7.2	125.0	225.0	22.4	10
6.	Andhra Pradesh	8	1726.5	19.6	41.4	44.0	5.7	8.8	3.6	30.8	92.1	–	57.2	122.3	172.3	20.3	10
7.	Kerala	5	958.2	31.6	60.4	28.0	7.0	4.6	17.4	60.0	53.0	–	2.7	13.9	25.2	72.1	50
	Low																
8.	Bihar	13	2699.0	35.0	41.8	41.1	4.0	13.8	7.4	18.3	29.5	45.4	3.2	49.4	138.4	8.8	8
9.	Orissa	14	835.5	25.0	60.4	30.0	2.4	7.2	3.4	15.7	20.8	–	–	0.5	2.0	1.8	6
10.	West Bengal	4	1111.1	18.2	68.6	17.1	5.3	9.0	7.0	30.2	28.2	–	0.4	1.2	3.6	6.3	18

(Contd.)

(1) (2)	(3)	(4)	(5)	(6)	(7)	(8)	(9)	(10)	(11)	(12)	(13)	(14)	(15)	(16)	(17)	(18)
11. Madhya Pradesh	10	2058.1	25.0	49.7	40.3	–	10.0	2.0	6.0	13.0	–	1.8	24.6	74.6	3.9	6
12. Uttar Pradesh	11	3803.5	20.0	58.2	23.7	2.0	16.0	19.3	23.4	17.9	59.1	17.6	75.5	225.5	11.4	9
13. Assam	9	1089.2	43.7	55.0	7.0	28.0	10.0	3.1	8.3	33.6	–	–	–	3.2	1.5	4
14. Rajasthan	12	1380.2	33.5	23.5	54.3	2.1	10.1	3.6	12.0	24.1	66.2	6.9	18.8	53.8	6.3	5
India								**9.3**	**24.5**	**37.9**	**48.1**	**512.9**	**1087.5**	**2337.5****		

Note: Outlays on Central and Centrally Sponsored Schemes, for which state-wise breakdowns are not available, are not included. Data are not available for Jammu and Kashmir and Nagaland.

* Projected.

** Includes 500,000 pumps to be energized under REC financing programme for which state-wise breakdown is not given in the Plan document.

Source: *Col 3*: Nath V.: "Levels of Economic Development and Rates of Economic Growth in India—A Regional Analysis", *National Geographical Journal*, Varanasi, India (Forthcoming).

Cols 4, 6, 7, 8 and 9: Fourth Five-year Plan, 1969-74, pp. 261, 265 and 281, and unpublished data furnished by the Programme Administration Division, Planning Commission.

Col 5: Estimates of Value of Agricultural Output, prepared by the State Statistical Bureaus, and made available by the Central Statistical Organisation.

Cols 10 and 11: Data on areas under HYVP are from "Fertilizer Statistics 1968-69" (Fertilizer Association of India, New Delhi, 1970) pp. 514 and 521, *Source*: Ministry of Food, Agriculture, CD and Co-operation.

Cols 12 and 13: Directorate of Economics and Statistics, Ministry of Food, Agriculture, CD and Co-operation: "Indian Agriculture in Brief", Tenth Edition 1970, Table 2.13.

Cols 14, 15 and 16: Forth Five-year Plan, pp. 280-81

Cols 17 and 18: Ministry of Finance, Government of India: "Pocket Book of Economic Information, 1969", New Delhi, 1970, p. 39.

Increase in Productivity Level, of Economic Development and Agricultural Development Programmes

The relationship between the rate of productivity increase, the level of economic development and the agricultural development programmes were examined next. The modified productivity ranks of states as obtained above were used (column 2 of Table 8.6). The ranks of the states of column 3 of the Table are according to a composite index of economic development developed by the author and based on per capita income, proportion of urban population to total population, proportion of workers engaged in manufacturing industries to all workers, literacy rate for the population 5 years old and over, and the proportions of population living in districts at two higher levels of economic development, as given in the 1961 Census publication, 'Levels of Regional Development' (Registrar General of India, 1964, p. 19). Columns 4 to 11 and 15 to 17 of the Table present data on proposed public sector outlays under the Fourth Plan on agriculture, irrigation, rural electrification (AIRE) and related programmes and on physical magnitudes of two programmes—high-yielding varieties and rural electrification. Data on total investment in agriculture are needed to assess the prospect of agricultural growth in different states and to determine whether the observed inter-state differences are likely to be accentuated or reduced in future. But since total investments data were not available, data on public sector outlays which constitute an important component of total investment were used. They give an indication of the effect of public investment on agricultural growth. The total outlay figures are given in column 4 of the Table and their relation to total value of agricultural output of each state is indicated in column 5. The percentage distribution of total outlays among the principal programmes is shown in columns 6 to 9. These figures give an identification of the relative emphasis on different programmes in different States, and of the effort to meet particular problems in some states. Thus allocation of a high proportion of the total outlay to flood control programmes in Assam indicates emphasis on them in a state in which floods constitute a serious problem.

The positive association between the rate of productivity increase and the level of economic development is shown both by the counts of rank positions and the Spearman co-efficients of rank correlation. Six out of the 7 higher ranks according to the index of economic development were taken by states with relatively high rates of productivity increase (the High state of column 2), and the Spearman co-efficient was 0.66. Total AIRE outlays vary from Rs. 3803.5 million in Uttar Pradesh to Rs. 880.0 million in Haryana. The percentages, total AIRE outlay/value of agricultural output, vary from 44.0 in Maharashtra to 18.2 in West Bengal. A positive association between the percentages and the rates of growth of agricultural output or of increase in productivity would indicate that the outlays will have the effect of accentuating inter-state differences in the rates; a negative association would indicate the reverse. No significant association was observed, however, the Spearman co-efficients between the percentage and the two rates were very low, 0.11 and 0.13 respectively. Data on distribution of total outlays among the main components indicate that the proportion allocated to major and medium irrigation are high in several states in which the proportion of cropped area irrigated are low at present. Gujarat, Rajasthan, Mysore and Madhya Pradesh are examples of such states. The proportions allocated to rural electrification are relatively high in Tamil Nadu, Uttar Pradesh and Bihar. Tamil Nadu had led in this programme for more than a decade. It has by far the largest number of electric irrigation pumps than any state and had, in 1969, the second highest proportion (after Kerala) of electrified villages. The emphasis of the programme in U.P. and Bihar indicates beginning of attention to it in states in which it had been neglected earlier.

Rural electrification, especially installation of electric irrigation pumps, and the high yielding varieties programme are perhaps the most important programmes for increasing agricultural output under the Fourth Plan. The total number of electric pumps in the country doubled between 1966 and 1969 and is projected to more than double again by 1974. Among the states the increases have been notable in Tamil Nadu and Punjab where the numbers were large even earlier, and also in several other states such as U.P., Bihar, Haryana and Madhya Pradesh where they were quite small. The HYVP has its principal concentration at present in U.P., Punjab and Haryana, where wheat is grown under irrigation, because the high-yielding varieties have been most successful in case of irrigated wheat. Nearly half of the total area under the programme in 1968-69 was in the three states. But the distribution is expected to change during the Fourth Plan period on account of rapid expansion of areas under the programme in other states, following expected research breakthrough in rice and other cereals. By the end of the Plan less than 30 per cent of the total area under the programme will be in the 3 states. But inter-state differences in the proportions of the cereal area brought under the programme will continue to be large (column 11 of Table 8.6). Moreover the proportion will remain very low in several states such as Assam, Madhya Pradesh, Rajasthan, Bihar and Orissa. Rice is the principal cereal crop in all of them except Rajasthan, and as the data of the column 12 indicate, most of it is grown without irrigation. In U.P. where also rice is the principal cereal crop in the Eastern region and is grown mostly without irrigation, the proportion of cereal area under HYVP will increase only marginally during the Fourth Plan period indicating that after a high proportion of the area under irrigated wheat, grown in the western region of the state, has been covered by the programme, further progress will be slow. Accordingly, the HYVP will have only limited coverage, even at the end of the Fourth Plan, in the large areas growing rice without irrigation in the eastern and north central states, and little influence in breaking the agricultural stagnation in them.

High and Low States—A Summary

The position of High and Low States of Table 8.6, in respect of total cropped area, total value of agricultural output, indicators of modernization of agriculture and the two Fourth Plan programmes discussed above is summarized in Table 8.7. It will be seen that the Low States had more than half of both the total cropped area of the country and the total value of agricultural output. But they accounted for less than one-third of the totals of the country for both consumption of chemical fertilizers and quantum of cooperative credit, and a bare 12.5 per cent of the total units of mechanical power used in agriculture. Average levels for all the three indicators were much lower in them than in the High states. Nearly 60 per cent of the total area under HYVP in the country was in the Low States in 1968-69 (mainly because of the large area in U.P.), but the percentage will go down to 38 by 1973-74. The share of the Low states in the total number of irrigation pumps will increase during the Plan period, but the change will not be large enough to affect the dominance of the High states.

Conclusion

From this summary and the earlier more detailed presentation it is clear that half of the states of India, having more than half of the total cropped area and the total value of agriculture output, are not participating adequately in agricultural progress. The Fourth Plan, while it contains

Table 8.7: High and Low States—Summary Position

	States		*Total*
	High	*Low*	
1. Gross cropped area, 1966-67			
Total ('000 hectares)	17,900	82,122	156,638
Per cent of all India total	46.0	52.4	100.0
2. Value of agricultural output, 1964-65			
Per cent of all-India total	46.6	52.3	100.0
3. Consumption of chemical fertilizers			
($N+P_2O_5+K_2O$), 1968-69	13.5	6.9	1.07
Average per hectare of gross cropped area	57.7	32.2	100.0
(kg) Per cent of all-India total			
4. Co-operative credit, 1966-67			
Average per hectare (Rupees)	33.6	14.4	23.3
Per cent of all-India total	66.2	32.6	100.0
5. Use of mechanical power in agriculture, 1966			
Average per hectares (Units)	11.7	1.7	6.9
Per cent of all-India total	76.1	12.5	100.0
6. Area under the high-yielding varieties programme			
Per cent of all-India total, 1968-69	43.9	59.2	100.0
Per cent of all-India total, 1973-74	58.0	38.4	100.0
7. Number of electric irrigation pumps			
Per cent of all-India total, 1969	83.7	15.5	100.0
Per cent of all-India total, 1974	71.6	27.8	100.0

programmes for achieving rapid increase in some directions in some Low States, such as rural electrification in U.P. and Bihar, or for meeting particular problems, such as of floods in Assam will not reduce significantly inter-state differentials in rates of growth of agricultural output or of increase in productivity in croplands. What is more important it does not have an adequate content, such as by way of the HYVP, for greatly accelerating agricultural growth in the Low states. But persistence of a low growth rate over a large part of the country will make achievement of a high overall rate of growth of agricultural output very difficult. Moreover, persistent regional disparities in agricultural growth will lead to a regional dichotomy in economic development and growth, which will complicate enormously the task of economic development. The causes of slow agricultural progress in the Low state should be identified and suitable remedial measures should be taken. This should be done separately for each state and for each region within the larger states because of the diversity of physical and economic conditions among and within the Low states. But there are some common elements which indicate the need for similar programmes in most areas. First, since unirrigated rice is the principal cereal crop over large areas, developing high yielding varieties of the crop and propagating the new varieties rapidly are important techno-administrative tasks. The second need is for socio-institutional changes, particularly land reforms. Most of the areas of the Low states were under *Zamindari* or other feudalistic land tenures until the early 1950s; large parts of Rajasthan, Orissa and Madhya Pradesh had formed part of small backward princely states. The handicaps of these areas arising from institutional and cultural factors, have apparently not been overcome adequately through progress under the Plans. One reason for this may be the abolition of the older land tenure system had not been followed by structural changes which could set in motion a change reaction of rapid change and growth. This is brought out by several studies, including those of the Planning Commission 1966 and Thorner 1962 Part I Land and Labour. The process of reform and change must be carried further through suitable land reform measures and complimentary measures of social change and institutional development. Reference has been made above to the weakness of the cooperatives in most of the Low states; the institutional development measures must extend also to Panchayati Raj Institutions, particularly in states like Bihar and Madhya Pradesh in which the block and district level institutions have not yet been established (p. 228). Finally, special attention will need to be given to expansion of infrastructures such as communication and rural electrification which have particular relevance for development of agriculture and in which the data of Table 8.6 indicate that the Low states are much behind the High states.

The areal selectivity embodied in the NAS and the Fourth Five Year Plan is a short term optimization strategy. It will need to be complemented by measures aimed at overcoming structural obstacles to agricultural growth over large parts of the country and preparing them for rapid growth over a long period. Without such measures the short term strategy will soon reach its limits and achievement of the ambitious targets of agricultural growth during the 1970s will be jeopardized.

Appendix Table: Growth Rates in Agriculture and Related Data for India and Fourteen States

	India	*Punjab*	*Gujarat*	*Madras*	*Mysore*	*Bihar*	*Maharashtra*	*Rajasthan*	*Andhra Pradesh*	*Madhya Pradesh*	*Orissa*	*Kerala*	*West Bengal*	*Uttar Pradesh*	*Assam*
(1)	(2)	(3)	(4)	(5)	(6)	(7)	(8)	(9)	(10)	(11)	(12)	(13)	(14)	(15)	(16)
Linear Growth Rates 1952-53 to 1964-65 (% per year)															
All crops															
1. Output	3.42	5.56	5.12	4.91	4.06	3.21	3.19	3.08	3.06	2.79	2.72	2.52	2.07	1.82	1.25
2. Area	1.28	2.06	0.46	1.13	0.83	0.71	0.44	3.23	0.27	1.35	0.84	1.38	0.60	0.74	1.32
3. Productivity	1.91	2.86	4.52	3.46	3.03	2.39	2.62	–0.08	2.72	1.30	1.78	1.00	1.41	1.01	–0.07
Food grains															
4. Output	2.75	4.30	2.09	4.89	3.71	3.28	2.29	2.68	3.65	2.58	2.60	4.37	1.16	0.91	0.80
5. Area	1.02	1.63	–2.19	0.75	0.91	0.64	0.33	3.03	0.84	1.28	0.79	0.51	0.26	0.40	1.36
6. Productivity	1.60	2.26	5.34	3.92	2.64	2.55	1.94	–0.23	2.63	1.16	1.75	3.74	0.90	0.49	–0.48
Non-food grain crops															
7. Output	4.79	9.46	8.03	4.96	4.91	2.61	5.15	4.89	1.83	4.50	3.40	1.83	4.23	4.28	1.62
8. Area	2.56	4.90	5.93	2.45	0.59	1.84	0.83	5.13	–1.59	1.67	1.65	2.06	4.29	2.19	1.21
9. Productivity	1.79	3.08	1.64	2.05	4.03	0.78	3.65	–0.09	3.93	2.44	1.54	–0.20	–0.09	1.72	0.35
10. Growth rate of population, 1951-1961 (%)	21.50	25.84	26.88	11.85	21.57	19.78	23.60	26.20	15.65	24.17	19.82	24.76	32.79	16.60	34.45
11. Growth rate of male agricultural workers, 1951-1961 (%)	26.38	12.00	28.56	41.34	42.11	19.89	28.56	29.04	31.90	20.68	31.86	–5.70	36.76	15.57	35.33

(Contd.)

(1)	(2)	(3)	(4)	(5)	(6)	(7)	(8)	(9)	(10)	(11)	(12)	(13)	(14)	(15)	(16)
Relative Growth Rates (% per year)															
12. Of agricultural production relative to population	1.05	2.36	1.92	3.33	1.57	1.03	0.67	0.36	1.29	0.30	0.61	0.03	–0.91	0.14	–1.63
13. Of food grain production relative to population	0.49	1.36	–0.47	3.31	1.28	1.09	–0.06	0.05	1.80	0.13	0.52	1.52	–1.60	–0.64	–1.97
14. Of agricultural production relative to number of male agricultural workers	0.62	3.89	1.76	0.55	0.99	1.02	0.25	0.14	–0.10	0.60	–0.35	3.28	–1.18	0.23	–1.69
Linear Growth Rates 1952-53 to 1964-65 (% per year)															
Food grain crops:															
Rice															
15. Output	3.64	12.31	5.98	6.04	5.96	3.63	3.38	5.56	5.15	2.34	2.88	4.42	1.42	5.08	0.78
16. Area	1.57	9.21	1.13	3.19	1.97	0.23	1.75	6.48	3.19	1.28	1.14	0.53	0.13	1.97	1.32
17. Productivity	1.80	1.80	4.61	2.19	3.33	3.36	1.41	–0.50	1.56	0.93	1.60	3.70	1.29	2.61	–0.47
(Per cent)	(100.0)	(1.5)		(11.0)	(4.1)	(12.8)	(3.8)		(11.5)	(8.5)	(11.5)	(3.1)	(14.4)	(9.0)	(4.9)
Wheat															
18. Output	3.80	6.79	3.59		4.88	2.35	4.17	2.24		3.61				1.65	
19. Area	2.57	3.92	0.15		0.98	0.98	2.10	3.36		4.50				0.78	
20. Productivity	1.00	2.09	3.22		3.46	1.18	1.85	–0.85		–0.53				0.80	
(Per cent)	(100.0)	(27.2)	(3.3)		(0.9)	(4.1)	(3.7)	(9.3)		(18.5)				(30.2)	
Jowar															
21. Output	1.99	0.66	1.28	4.61	2.71		2.95	–0.59	1.62	2.81				–1.31	
22. Area	0.40	0.42	–1.59	0.10	1.78		0.87	0.59	0.18	–0.24				–0.78	
23. Productivity	1.57	0.15	3.21	4.46	0.91		1.91	–1.10	1.26	3.22				–0.58	
(Per cent)	(100.0)	(0.5)	(4.5)	(6.2)	(14.6)		(34.4)	(3.8)	(13.9)	(16.0)				(5.9)	
Bajra															
24. Output	1.34	–2.32	–0.37	3.60			1.48	4.13	0.74					–1.12	
25. Area	–0.20	–2.59	–4.04	–2.24			–1.12	3.73	–0.89					–0.94	

(Contd.)

(1)	(2)	(3)	(4)	(5)	(6)	(7)	(8)	(9)	(10)	(11)	(12)	(13)	(14)	(15)	(16)
26. Productivity	1.62	0.55	5.96	7.63			3.10	0.51	1.88					–0.27	
(Per cent)	(100.0)	(8.0)	(16.1)	(7.7)			(12.3)	(25.2)	(8.0)					(15.2)	
Gram															
27. Output	0.85	1.35				–0.29		5.19		1.91				–0.04	
28. Area	1.16	2.01				–0.80		6.12		0.91				–0.08	
29. Productivity	–0.24	–0.66				0.57		–0.50		0.95				0.05	
(Per cent)	(100.0)	(27.4)				(4.8)		(12.9)		(16.4)				(31.2)	
Non-food grain crops:															
Cotton															
30. Output	3.81	9.35	6.48	5.56	2.06		2.45	5.85	0.74	–0.98					
31. Area	1.27	5.78	2.65	1.11	0.66		0.63	2.70	–0.48	–0.87					
32. Productivity	2.25	2.89	3.08	3.87	1.23		1.70	2.74	1.29	–0.17					
(Per cent)	(100.0)	(19.7)	(26.6)	(7.6)	(7.2)		(24.3)	(3.2)	(2.9)	(7.0)					
Groundnuts															
33. Output	5.64		11.04	5.49	0.72		6.06		–2.00	11.12					
34. Area	4.40		15.04	3.69	0.87		1.28		–3.16	8.15					
35. Productivity	0.84		–1.11	1.24	–0.10		4.18		1.58	1.84					
(Per cent)	(100.0)		(24.0)	(20.0)	(10.9)		(14.1)		(14.3)	(5.4)					
Sugarcane															
36. Output	7.83	9.28	17.86	10.50	14.58	0.65	9.83	6.34	13.21	7.96			6.73	4.13	3.18
37. Area	4.93	5.71	16.83	10.56	7.60	2.20	7.97	7.76	8.56	9.91			7.32	3.72	1.23
38. Productivity	1.93	2.26	0.53	0.04	4.02	–1.21	1.02	–0.53	2.52	–1.03			–0.31	0.28	1.76
(Per cent)	(100.0)	(8.9)	(1.4)	(6.1)	(5.7)	(5.2)	(10.4)	(0.6)	(9.5)	(1.4)			(1.5)	(46.0)	(0.9)
Jute															
39. Output	5.20					–1.83					4.05		7.21	12.13	0.10
40. Area	4.01					2.29					3.50		6.00	6.18	1.20
41. Productivity	0.85					–2.82					0.50		0.92	3.29	–1.00
(Per cent)	(100.0)					(17.7)					(6.8)		(56.9)	(2.7)	(14.7)
Gross Cropped Area Distribution of Annual Rainfall (%)															
42. Abundant (more than 75")	4.32	2.58	–	–	4.05	–	3.14	–	–	2.77	–	100.00	12.78	0.19	67.95

(Contd.)

(1)	(2)	(3)	(4)	(5)	(6)	(7)	(8)	(9)	(10)	(11)	(12)	(13)	(14)	(15)	(16)
43. Assured (45"-75")	26.80	3.19	–	24.85	9.30	81.43	9.73	–	–	68.23	100.00	–	87.22	16.70	32.05
44. Medium (30"-45")	33.49	25.73	32.63	54.25	18.55	18.57	39.56	4.50	73.43	28.24	–	–	–	69.34	–
45. Low (less than 30")	35.40	68.50	67.37	20.90	68.10	–	47.57	95.50	26.57	2.31	–	–	–	13.77	–
46. Gross irrigated area/gross cropped area (%)	18.88	42.22	7.79	45.21	9.24	19.89	6.74	12.53	29.48	5.63	16.42	20.96	21.53	26.62	23.33
47. Index of moisture availability	214.62	179.25	140.32	249.16	154.49	301.33	172.04	117.03	202.91	277.12	316.42	320.96	321.53	229.74	323.33
Index of Productivity (based on averages of years 1956-1957 to 1958-1959; India = 100.00)															
48. Per hectare	100.00	131.71	64.58	176.21	64.91	119.53	65.08	51.65	118.85	80.55	132.72	126.17	168.75	128.25	174.04
49. Per agricultural worker	100.00	215.99	105.90	111.24	88.71	62.83	88.94	88.24	103.68	94.35	132.72	110.06	144.15	101.11	111.49
Use of Modern Inputs															
50. Consumption of chemical fertilizers ($N + P_2O_5 + K_2O$), 1965-1966 (kg per hectare of gross cropped area)	5.30	5.22	4.70	14.49	4.63	3.31	4.60	0.82	9.74	1.64	2.99	14.49	7.61	4.52	3.02
51. Cooperative credit: loans advanced by agricultural cooperatives to members in 1963-1964 (rupees per hectare of gross cropped area)	19.52	19.22	33.78	56.31	14.34	4.73	30.24	3.56	21.25	13.73	8.31	42.74	10.06	22.17	0.62

(Contd.)

	(2)	(3)	(4)	(5)	(6)	(7)	(8)	(9)	(10)	(11)	(12)	(13)	(14)	(15)	(16)
52. Use of mechanical power in agriculture in 1960-1961 (units per thousand hectares of gross cropped area)	2.58	3.36	5.65	18.86	2.31	0.73	3.88	0.66	4.61	0.88	0.28	2.76	0.72	1.18	0.40
53. Composite index of use of modern inputs in agriculture (India = 100.00)	100.00	109.06	160.24	430.96	83.45	38.32	130.69	19.89	157.13	45.13	36.61	199.81	74.34	81.53	25.22
Development of Services															
54. Rural literacy rate (%)	19.0	18.4	24.1	24.7	20.0	16.1	21.5	10.9	16.8	12.7	20.1	45.4	21.6	14.3	24.9
55. Number of doctors per million of population	227	382	230	192	209	157	316	133	196	134	127	215	481	127	257
56. Length of surfaced roads (in kilometers) per thousand square kilometres	76.91	93.62	70.22	259.4	194.4	64.04	83.38	44.89	99.17	54.91	52.44	207.2	155.0	75.03	31.20
Number of towns per million rural population	7.49	11.65	11.82	13.73	12.61	3.60	9.37	8.59	7.50	7.89	3.77	6.41	6.77	4.15	5.47
58. Composite index of development of services (India = 100.00)	100.00	135.60	119.32	183.80	154.61	71.29	121.47	72.26	100.96	75.65	69.94	172.16	155.04	71.05	89.47
59. Composite index of agricultural development (India = 100.00)	100.00	162.54	138.62	228.55	96.96	65.00	104.29	66.06	116.79	73.69	82.95	127.85	93.00	78.62	57.72

Note: Numbers in parentheses show percentages of all-India output produced in the state in the triennium ending 1964-65.

Sources: Lines 1-9 and 15-41: "Growth Rates in Agriculture" [see text footnote 3];
Lines 10, 11, 54, and 57: Census of India 1961, Paper No. 1 of 1962, Final Population Totals (Delhi, 1962);
Lines 42-46: *Indian Agricultural Statistics 1962-63* [see text footnote 5];
Lines 48 and 49: J.G. Anand: Measurement of the Actually Realized Agricultural Productivities per Acre and per Worker in the Different Crop Regions of India, *in Agricultural Situation in India: Annual Number 1964*, Directorate of Economics and Statistics, New Delhi, 1964, pp. 401-411;
Line 50: *Fertilizer Statistics 1965-66,* Fertilizer Association of India, New Delhi, 1967, p. 101;
Line 51: "Statistical Statements Relating to the Cooperative Movement in India 1963-64" (Reserve Bank of India);
Line 52: "Livestock Census of India, 1961" (Directorate of Economics and Statistics, New Delhi);
Line 55: "Stock of Health and Medical Manpower," *Institute of Applied Manpower Research Working Paper No. 6*, New Delhi, 1965 (mimeographed), pp. 17-18;
Line 56: *Statistical Abstract of the Indian Union 1965*, Central Statistical Organization, Delhi, 1966, pp. 314-315.

Notes

1. Unless stated otherwise, quotations are from and page numbers relate to Fourth Five Year Plan, 1969-74 (Planning Commission, New Delhi, 1970).
2. The target of areas under the high-yielding varieties and short duration varieties programmes by 1973-74 are 25 mn hectares and 15 mn hectares, respectively. The total area under cereals which was 99 mn hectares in 1968-69 would total about 105 mn hectares by 1973-74 if it increases at the rate of 1.2 per cent projected for the gross cropped area.
3. The total cropped area fluctuated between 155 mn and 158 mn hectares between 1961-62 and 1968-69.
4. W. Holst, 1967, p. 704. Table below gives:

Total Land Area and Percentages of Arable Land to Total Land Area in Some Selected Countries

Country	*Total Land Area (mn hectares)*	*Percentage of Arable Land to Total Land Area*
World	13395	11.3
USSR	2240	10.8
USA	1090	16.2
China	956	11.5
India	327	49.7
Pakistan	95	30.0
France	55	37.0
Japan	37	15.5

Source: Production Year Book, FAO, 1968, Vol. 22.

5. The targets and achievements of irrigation programmes under the first three Plans are shown below:

	Major and Medium		*Minor Target*	*Irrigation Achievement*
	Target	*Irrigation Achievemen*		
First Plan	3.4	1.3	4.5	3.8
Second Plan	4.2	2.2	3.6	3.6
Third Plan	5.2	2.2	5.2	5.3

Source: Directorate of Economics and Statistics, Ministry of Food and Agriculture, Community Development and Cooperation, "*Indian Agriculture in Brief*", Tenth Edition, 1970, pp. 150-51.

6. The output indices for wheat, rice and jawar were as follows:

	1964-65	1967-68	1968-69
Wheat	182.1	244.9	258.7
Rice	155.1	149.4	157.2
Jowar	141.0	144.5	141.0

Source: Indian Agriculture in Brief 1970, p. 96.

7. The figures for Bihar are of doubtful accuracy because the following note appears in *Growth Rates in Agriculture* under the Table relating to index number of area, production and production of different crops for the state (Appendix Nos. 2.25 to 2.27): "Due to defects in the statistics of the area and of production of different crops for which no adjustment could be made in the absence of the detailed data at lower levels the index numbers for the period prior to 1956-57 suffer from a number of limitation."
8. Data on proportion of gross cropped area of states falling in different rainfall zones were obtained from *Indian Agriculture in Brief*, Table 2.6, pp. 22-23, and the following weights were given in construction of the index:

Annual rainfall 1150 mm and above	3
Annual rain fall 750 mm to 1150 mm	2
Annual rainfall 750 mm	1
An additional weight of 1 was given for irrigation in all zones	

References

Billings, Martin H. and Singh, Arjan, Mechanization and Rural Employment, *Economic and Political Weekly*, Vol. No. 26, June 27, 1970

Holst, W., 'Evaluation of Population and Food Problems of India,' in the *World Food Problem, Report* of the panel on The World Food Supply of the President's Science Advisory Committee, Washington DC, 1967.

Ministry of Food and Agriculture Economic and Statistical Adviser, *Growth Rates in Agriculture* (Mimeographed), March 1966.

Planning Commission: *Report on Implementation of Land Reforms*, New Delhi. 1966

Registrar General of India: Census of India 1961. Vol. I India Part I (A-1) Text *Levels of Regional Development*, New Delhi, 1964.

Thorner, Daniel and Alice: *Land and Labour in India* Asia, Bombay, 1962, Part I *Land and Labour*.

9

Industrial Development

Industrial Location and Employment in India

The Indian economy has been transformed during 1950-51 to 1997-98 from a primarily agricultural economy in which agriculture contributed more than half of the gross domestic product (GDP) to a diversified economy in which industry and service sectors contribute three-fourths of the GDP while agriculture contributes less than one-fourth.

The transformation has been the result partly of policies and investments by the Government of India and the governments of various states and partly to investments by private companies and initiatives of entrepreneurs.

Economic geographers have long debated the relative importance of different factors—the advantage of an early start, proximity to mineral and non-mineral raw materials, availability of low cost unskilled and skilled labour, initiative of entrepreneurs, policies of governments and finally, proximity to markets in explaining location of factory industries. Analysis of the relevant data, however, shows that the proximity to raw materials in some ways is the least important and proximity to markets the most important factor in location of industries.

Further, there is no likelihood of a major change in the regional location of factory industries during the next decade. On the other hand states and regions which are industrially advanced could increase their lead over those that are industrially backward.

The three decades 1970s–1990s have seen rapid growth of knowledge based industries such as computer software and other information technology industries. Employment and value added in them has gone up exponentially during the past two decades and is expected to increase rapidly in the foreseeable future. Finally, the industries instead of being concentrated in one city—Bangalore as at present, will spread to several other metropolitan cities, as a result partly of efforts of some state governments which are creating the infrastructure for their development.

This chapter presents, in brief[1], the principal facts about distribution, by states, of employment and value added in factory industries in the mid-1990s and to relate them to the distribution of mineral and non-mineral resources, the level of economic development in different states and policies relating to industrial development followed by the State Governments. The present structure of the industrial sector and locational pattern of factories are discussed against the background of the transformation of the Indian economy from a primarily agricultural economy at the beginning of the 1950s to a diversified economy in which industry and service sectors contributed three-fourths of the gross domestic product by the mid-1990s.

Changing Industrial Scenario: 1950s to 1990s

In 1950-51, India was an economy in which agriculture contributed 56 per cent of the gross domestic product while the small industrial sector contributed only 15 per cent (Table 9.1). The sector comprised besides cottage industries and handicrafts, factories processing tea and jute for export and making a narrow range of consumer goods—cotton, wool and rayon, textiles, sugar, wheat and rice flour, cooking oil, shoes and other leather goods and cement and corrugated iron sheets, etc. for construction.

Table 9.1: Distribution of GDP by Major Sectors 1950-51 and 1997-98

Contribution to GDP by Sectors	*1950-51*	*1997-98*
Agriculture	55.8	25.3
Industry	15.2	30.1
Services	29.0	44.6

Source: Government of India, Survey of Industries, New Delhi, p. 1.

The traditional handicrafts—weaving of handloom cloth of cotton, silk or rayon and brassware, etc., were also oriented towards meeting the needs for consumer goods. The basic industries—steel mills, plants manufacturing machinery for mining, generation, transmission and distribution of electricity, manufacture of locomotives, coaches and other equipment for the railways, light and heavy machine tools, vehicles for public, commercial and private transport (trucks, buses, passenger cars, motor bicycles, scooters etc.) were virtually non-existent. By the mid-1990s, however, these industries together with petroleum refining, manufacture of petrochemicals, other chemicals, pharmaceuticals and a wide range of consumer durables contributed the bulk of employment and value added in the factory sector. Furthermore knowledge-based industries such as computer software and other information technology based industries were well established and were experiencing very rapid growth. The contribution of the industrial sector to GDP is estimated to have increased to 30 per cent and of agriculture to have fallen to 25 per cent by 1997-98 (Table 9.1).

Factories and Small Industries: Employment and Values Added

The industrial sector consists of two components:

(i) *Factories*: Industrial units employing 10 or more workers and using power or employing 20 or more workers if not using power, and

(ii) Small industries including cottage industries and handicrafts. During 1995-96 the employment and value added figures for the two segments of the sector were the following:

Table 9.1: Factories and Small Industries: Employment and Value Added, 1995-96

	Employment (millions)	*Per cent*	*Value added (Rs.'000 crores)*	*Gross Output (Rs. '000 crores)*	*Per cent*
Factories	10.05	40	139.4	670.5	66
Small Industries	15.30	60	n.a.	356.4	34
Total	**25.35**	**100**	**-**	**1026.9**	**100**

Source: Government of India, Survey of Industries, New Delhi, pp. 89 and 91.

Thus factories provided employment to about 40 per cent of the workers engaged in industries but contributed almost two-thirds of the gross output, while small industries provided employment to 60 per cent of the workers but contributed only one-third of the output.

Industrial Growth and Location of Industries

Rapid transformation of the economy began in the late 1950s and continued through the 1970s. Heavy investments were made during this period of about 20 years by the Government of India in establishing five large integrated steel mills, a factory for manufacturing heavy machinery, factories for manufacturing a variety of machine tools and equipment for power generation, transmission and distribution, a factory for making telephone receivers and other telecommunication equipment and factories for manufacture of locomotives and coaches for the railways. Economic and/or technical assistance for establishing the factories was provided principally by the Russians, the British or by other European countries.

After the discovery of large deposits of crude oil off the coast of Mumbai and Gujarat in the late 1950s, large investments were made in exploration and exploitation of petroleum deposits, establishing petroleum refineries and a network of dealers for distribution of motor spirit, diesel, kerosene and other petroleum products. Private companies including the multinational corporations that had been distributing petroleum products for decades were also allowed to establish petroleum refineries. Some of these have involved foreign investment. Indian private investors have made large investments in plants manufacturing a large variety of petrochemicals.

Private entrepreneurs made complementary investments also in steel rolling mills, manufacture of wagons for the railways, steel rods and corrugated iron sheets for construction and establishing pig iron plants for manufacture of castings. Their other major investments were in manufacture of telephone receivers and other telecommunication equipment, food processing and manufacture of drugs.

Manufacture of vehicles for public, commercial and private transport was also started by private entrepreneurs in the late 1950s or early 1960s with technical assistance provided by reputed foreign manufacturers. Production of all these as well as of a variety of consumer durables—refrigerators, air conditioners, radio and television receivers, office and hospital furniture, furnishing for home and office—has increased rapidly during the five decades, 1950s to 1990s in response to rapid increase in domestic demand.

The computer software for export industry which began in Bangalore in the 1970s, has experienced very rapid growth during the subsequent two decades so that by the late 1990s, the turnover of the industry is in billions of dollars and the shares of some of the leading software export companies are considered important enough to be listed on the New York

Stock Exchange. According to one estimate, software exports amounted to $ 2.65 billion in 1998-99, 56 per cent higher than $ 1.75 billion in 1997-98 and are expected to reach $ 10 billion within five years (*Times of India*, July 1999).

The value of output of consumer, industrial and other electronic goods more than doubled during the four years 1993-94 to 1997-98 (Table 9.2). Such growth is a portent of trends of the foreseeable future; information technology based industries are poised for very rapid growth during the next decade because of development of the Internet. Furthermore computerization in Indian industries, banking, finance, public administration and other services is just beginning.

Table 9.2: Electronics Production Profile Value of Output

	Rs. Crore	
	1993-94	*1997-98*
Consumer electronics	4150	7600
Industrial electronics	1170	3150
Computers	1820	2900
Communication and broadcasting equipment	3150	3250
Strategic electronics	500	500
Components	2680	4400
Total	**14070**	**21800**
Computer Software for Export	1020	6500
Domestic Software	695	3470
Grand Total	**15785**	**31770**

Another noteworthy development which will affect industrial growth in the next decade is entry during the last few years of Korean, American or other multinationals who have established factories manufacturing or assembling from imported kits passenger cars or trucks and a wide range of consumer durables. Their factories are located in the environs of Chennai, Delhi and Bangalore.

It may be mentioned that the environs of the large metropolitan cities especially Mumbai, Delhi, Bangalore, Hyderabad, Pune and Chennai have been the favoured locations for establishment of a number of such public and private sector industrial units. Excepting the steel mills and the heavy machinery plant, most of the other public sector industrial units are in the vicinity of large cities. The three petroleum refineries established by the foreign companies in the 1950s were located in the environs of Mumbai. Many refineries established later have also been located near cities along the west or the east coast. The problem of pollution of air and water that their location creates for the residents of the cities were however completely ignored.

The agricultural equipment industry is also located in cities closest to the areas affected by the Green Revolution. Thus the Punjab-Haryana-Western U.P. region in which production of cereals has been increasing rapidly from the late 1960s is served by a factory manufacturing tractors in a satellite town of Delhi, while Ludhiana, an industrial city in Punjab manufactures a wide range of power driven agricultural implements. Hyderabad, Chennai, Pune and Coimbatore are some of the other important cities manufacturing power driven implements for use in agricultural regions within their hinterlands in which agricultural output has been increasing rapidly. However, chemical fertilizer factories are in Gujarat and near the petroleum refineries in various parts of the country.

Two other developments in the 1960s which affected location of industries profoundly were:

(i) Flight of capital from the Calcutta Metropolitan District (including both Calcutta and Howrah) due to militancy of trade unions. As a result, some large steel fabricating units which manufactured bridges and other large steel structures for the railways, mining machinery etc., and which were owned by the Government of India were closed. A number of private entrepreneurs also closed their factories to re-open them in southern India especially Tamil Nadu or in the western Indian states of Maharashtra and Gujarat.

(ii) Industrial growth in these three states has been encouraged also by the influence that the industrialists based in them have had with the Ministers and officers in the Central Government responsible for grant of licences for establishing industrial units and providing them various incentives such as concessional credit from financial institutions, tax exemption for the first few years of operation and various facilities for export of products.

There has been no significant returning capital to the Calcutta Metropolitan District despite the fact that the present Communist Party led government of West Bengal, which has been in power for almost 30 years, has kept militancy of trade unions in check. There is no shortage also of electricity or water in the Calcutta Metropolitan District. This shows that while flight of capital from a region can be triggered off by one or more causes, its return is difficult. A further reason for decline of West Bengal as an industrial state is that the elite in the state have always preferred becoming professionals—lawyers, physicians, teachers, scientists, senior executives in large companies owned formerly by the Scots but by Indians after Independence to becoming industrial entrepreneurs.

Distribution of Employment and Value Added by Factories by States

Data on distribution of employment and value added in factories in 1995-96 in selected states are given in Table 9.3. It may be noted that 25 per cent of the employment but as much as 36 per cent of the value added in factories was accounted for by factories in the two states of Maharashtra and Gujarat. Maharashtra alone contributed 15 per cent of the employment and 24 per cent of the value added in factories. Tamil Nadu and Andhra Pradesh ranked next to Maharashtra and Gujarat as important industrial states. Together these four states accounted for almost half of both employment and value added in factories. On the other hand, Bihar and West Bengal, which have large deposits of coal, iron ore and other minerals and in which there are three integrated steel mills, the heavy machinery plant at Ranchi, the old multi-industry complex of Jamshedpur, the post-1960s complex of Durgapur Asansol besides the industries in Calcutta and Howrah contributed only 11.5 per cent of the employment and 8.5 per cent of the value added in factories.

Table 9.3: Shares of Selected States in Population and Employment and Value Added in Factories

States	*Population (Millions)*	*Per cent of all India*	*Employment (000's)*	*Per cent of all India*	*Value added (Rs. Crores)*	*Per cent of all India*
Andhra Pradesh	68.5	8.1	1180	11.8	987	7.0
Bihar	86.4	10.2	336	3.3	5296	3.8
Gujarat	41.3	4.9	967	9.5	17621	12.6
Karnataka	45.0	5.3	512	5.1	6750	4.8
Madhya Pradesh	58.8	8.0	525	5.2	9522	6.8
Maharashtra	79.0	9.3	1518	15.1	32975	23.7
Punjab	20.3	2.4	473	4.7	4008	3.9
Rajasthan	44.0	5.2	–	–	–	–
Tamil Nadu	55.6	6.6	1237	12.3	14261	10.2
Uttar Pradesh	138.1	16.3	797	7.9	11675	8.4
West Bengal	68.0	8.0	825	8.2	6493	4.7
Others	–	–	1675	16.7	20979	15.0
Total	**846.3**	**100.0**	**10,045**	**100.0**	**139397**	**100.0**

Source: Government of India, Survey of Industries, New Delhi, p. 88.

These figures bring out the fact that the old mineral resource based industries—steel mills, heavy machine building units, plants making machinery for mines, locomotive rails, passenger coaches and rolling stock (wagons for transport of goods) for the railways, cement mills etc. contribute relatively small shares of both employment and value added in industries and that much larger shares are contributed by industries manufacturing machines for generation and distribution of electricity, transport equipment, consumer goods and consumer durables.

The data of Table 9.4 give some indication of this. Food processing, beverage and textile industries contributed 40 per cent of the total employment but only 17 per cent of the value added in factories. On the other hand, machinery other than transport and transport equipment accounted for about 15 per cent of employment but more than 20 per cent of value added in factories. The importance in value added of chemicals is due primarily to the high value of pharmaceutical drugs. The basic metals group consists largely of steel mills. The heavy investment in them may be noted.

Table 9.4: Share of Major Industry Groups in Factory Sector, 1995-96 Per cent Share

Group	*Employment*	*Invested Capital*	*Value Added*
Food products	13.3	7.3	6.6
Beverages	6.5	1.0	1.9
Cotton Textiles	9.8	4.0	3.1
Wool and Silk Textiles	3.8	3.5	2.7
Jute Textiles	3.2	0.4	0.7
Textile Products	3.7	1.3	2.3
Paper	3.4	2.5	3.3
Rubber, Petroleum and Coal Products	3.2	5.3	6.6
Basic Chemicals and Products	6.7	14.5	17.0
Non-metallic Minerals	5.0	4.2	4.1
Basic Metals	7.3	16.1	10.0
Metal Products	2.7	1.7	2.3
Machinery other than Transport	8.5	8.4	12.6
Transport Equipment	6.0	4.3	7.7
Electricity	9.8	23.3	14.7
Repair Services	0.6	0.2	0.3
Others	4.3	1.3	3.2
Total	**100.0**	**100.0**	**100.0**

Industrial Centres[2]

In brief the industries are concentrated in Maharashtra in or around

Mumbai (including New Mumbai and Thane) or Pune. In coastal Gujarat which has often been called an industrial workshop while Saurashtra and Kutch are industrially underdeveloped. In Karnataka, a number of large public sector industrial units are located in the environs of its capital, Bangalore. Hindustan Aircraft about 30 km from the city was established during Second World War for servicing and repair of aircraft; it has diversified into manufacture of small trainer aircraft. Hindustan Machine Tools, which manufactures a variety of precision tools and watches and Indian Telephone Industries which manufacture telephone receivers and other telecommunication equipment were established in the 1960s. There are also number of private companies. A rapidly growing export oriented computer software industry was established in Bangalore in the 1970s which has been followed by the Government of Andhra Pradesh on the outskirts of Hyderabad and in Gurgaon about 30 km from Delhi. The next few years should see the emergence of a number of information technology parks near Pune, Mumbai, Ahmedabad, Chennai, Kolkata, Lucknow, Thiruvananthapuram and Chandigarh. The principal factor inhibiting revival of industrial growth in West Bengal where industries were concentrated in the Calcutta Metropolitan District is a crisis of confidence. In Tamil Nadu, Chennai and Coimbatore are likely to remain the principal industrial centres. In coastal Andhra Pradesh sugarcane and tobacco are the principal crops and the area has a number of rice and sugar mills. In Punjab, manufacture and/or repair of machine driven agricultural implements, consumer durables, and the woollen/hosiery industry will continue to grow.

Prospects for the Next Decade 2010

Several indications of the prospects for industrial growth are given below:

(1) There must be sustained growth in basic industries such as manufacture of steel, cement, heavy, light and precision machine tools; equipment for generation, transmission and distribution of electricity; transport equipment for both railways and roads; petroleum refining and manufacture of petrochemicals. These industries provide the infrastructure of industrial growth. But most of the employment and value added in industries will continue, as at present, to be in food processing, manufacture of textiles and apparel and other consumer goods and consumer durables.

(2) Maharashtra, Gujarat, Tamil Nadu and Andhra Pradesh are likely to continue to be the states with larger shares of both employment and value added in factories than their shares of the population of the country. The states have besides the advantage of an early start, large and rapidly growing urban and rural middle classes.

(3) Karnataka should continue to have similar shares of both employment and value added in industries as its share of the total population of the country. The information technology industry and the industries manufacturing machine tools and telecommunication equipment in and around Bangalore should continue to experience rapid growth in the next decade. Use of computers in industries, trade and public services has scarcely begun in India and will increase rapidly in the foreseeable future. Growth of the computer hardware industry, viz. manufacture of small and medium sized computers initially by assembly of imported components in the environs of Bangalore is the prospect. Manufacture or assembly of heavy trucks and passenger cars which started in the 1990s is also expected to increase rapidly for two reasons. First, there is a large and expanding market for the vehicles in southern India. Second, the companies manufacturing the vehicles are reputed multinationals with access to the latest technology.

(4) The principal advantages of Punjab are an innovative class of skilled workers and a large market for consumer goods, consumer durables and modern farm implements to meet the needs of its progressive and well-to-do farmers and middle income residents of the urban areas who have got accustomed to using manufactured consumer goods and consumer durables. Highly developed infrastructures—rail and road transport and near universal rural electrification—creates a large market for trucks, buses, passenger cars, motor bicycles, scooters, etc. Its share of employment and value added in factory industries should continue to be larger than its share of the population of the country.

(5) Steady growth of factory industries will continue to be experienced in the satellite cities of Delhi-Gurgaon and Faridabad in Haryana and Ghaziabad and Gautam Buddha Nagar (NOIDA) in U.P. A variety of consumer goods—processed foods, clothes for domestic consumption and export,

consumer durables such as passenger cars, refrigerators, air conditioners, office furniture, furnishings for home and office, tractors and other farm equipment are already being manufactured in these cities.

(6) There should be a relatively rapid growth of industries in Rajasthan because of the policies adopted by the government. The government has built in various parts of the state a number of townships in which developed land with adequate and dependable supplies of electricity and water and good telecommunication facilities as well as good rail or road connections (for import of raw materials and export of products) are provided to the industries established in them. Furthermore, entrepreneurs are given tax exemption of profits for the first few years. They are assisted also in getting concessional loans from financial institutions. One such township, Bhiwadi, about 100 km south of Delhi is fully occupied by factories owned by entrepreneurs based in Delhi or Jaipur. Another factor assisting industrial growth in the state will be the growth of tourism. The traditional handicrafts of the state—jewellery, tie and die cloth and decorated leather work should have a large market among foreign tourists.

(7) Bihar, Orissa, Madhya Pradesh, U.P., and Assam will continue to have much smaller shares in both employment and value added in factories in comparison with their shares of the population.

(8) Relatively small shares of U.P. and Bihar, which have 37 per cent of the population of the country but only 11 per cent of the workers in factories and contribute only 12 per cent of the value added in factories need to be explained. One reason is that except for a few districts of western U.P. both states are poor and backward. Furthermore, the governments of the states have not made any noteworthy attempts to promote industrial development. An additional factor impeding industrial growth in Bihar at present is lack of security of life and property. There is literally a class war in parts of Bihar between former non-cultivating owners of land and their labourers most of whom have become peasant proprietors.

(9) Madhya Pradesh and Orissa remain industrially backward despite the fact that they have large mineral resources and established industrial centres in the steel mill cities that are

located in them. Rourkela in Orissa and Bhilai in Madhya Pradesh. Madhya Pradesh has also the industrial city of Indore in which there could be considerable expansion of industries due to availability of an experienced industrial labour force.

(10) Apart from packaging of tea and a small petroleum refinery located near Guwahati and its traditional handicrafts, there are very few industries in Assam. One reason is the relative isolation of the state from the rest of India. However, a determined effort has to be made, initially by the Government of India to establish industries such as a petrochemical plant in the state. With improvements in quality, the products of the distinctive handicrafts of the state should also have a sizeable market in India and abroad.

(11) Industrial growth could pick up in U.P. if it is actively promoted by the government. The productivity of the large area irrigated by canals, tubewells and wells fitted with electric or diesel pumps in western U.P. could also be increased through vigorous agriculture extension efforts. There is a potential also for large increase in output and employment through modernization and improvement in techniques of some of the handicrafts of U.P., such as weaving of carpets around Mirzapur, silk saris in a suburb of Varanasi and of decorative brassware in Moradabad which have large domestic and export markets. The expansion could be more rapid especially for export, if some exploitative practices such as use of child labour in carpet weaving and payment of bare subsistence wages to weavers are ended. Industrial promotion efforts should concentrate on modernization of design and introduction of improved equipment—larger looms in sari weaving and use of power in larger manufacturing units.

There is a prospect also for growth of the computer software industry (principally to meet local demand) in Kanpur which has an Institute of Technology and is an old industrial centre. Lucknow, Allahabad and Varanasi which have universities which had high standards of teaching until recently could be other centres for growth of this industry.

(12) Industrial growth should accelerate in Kerala. Kochi with its naval base, a shipyard and a petroleum refinery is already a large industrial city. There is a prospect for the establishment of consumer durable industries for the local market. Kerala receives remittances of thousands of million dollars every year

from its residents working in the Gulf countries. Thus there is a sizeable market for consumer durables among the large class of well-to-do residents of the rural and urban areas of the state. Thiruvananthpuram could become the centre of an information technology industry based on an adequate supply of educated manpower and the facility of export of products through its airport. Kerala is also well equipped for winter tourism because of its excellent beaches and a warm, largely storm-free winter. The distinctive handicrafts of the state—decorative bell metal ware and products of coir—should also find an expanding market both within India and abroad.

Conclusion

There are likely to be only marginal changes in the spatial distribution of factory industries during the next decade. Inter-state and intra-state disparities in industrial development are likely to increase instead of decreasing during this period.

Economic geographers have often discussed the relative importance of different factors—an early start, proximity to raw materials, access to a disciplined or skilled labour force, capital, entrepreneurs with vision and ability to take risks, professionals with innovative skills and proximity to large markets in explaining location of industries. It appears, however, that among these factors proximity to raw materials, mineral or non-mineral, is the least important. Industries processing raw materials—steel, heavy machinery, cement, paper, sugar, jute, wheat and oil mills, and petroleum refineries, factories producing chemical fertilizers and other petrochemicals, although they involve heavy investment contribute relatively small shares of both employment and value added in factory industries. Much larger shares of both employment and value added in industries are contributed by factories which make a variety of machine tools, equipment for generation, transmission and distribution of electricity, transport equipment including motor vehicles and a large variety of consumer goods and consumer durables. These industries are located typically in the metropolitan areas of large cities which are close to the principal markets for them.

The militancy of trade unions, induced in the late 1960s shift of industries from the Calcutta Metropolitan District to the South and West Indian states of Tamil Nadu, Maharashtra and Gujarat. Return of capital to CMD has not been significant despite the efforts of the present Government of West Bengal.

The phenomenal growth of the computer software and other information technology based industries in and around Bangalore shows the influence of skilled professionals in the beginning and rapid growth of an industry. The next decade should witness establishment and progressive growth of this industry primarily to meet domestic demand in a number of other centres.

The successful efforts of the Punjab Government to promote industrial development in the state in the late 1950s and early 1960s aided by an abundance of skilled workers and venturesome entrepreneurs has led to the establishment of a variety of industries ranging from manufacture of carpets and woollen textiles to agricultural machinery in different cities of the state.

On the other hand the indifference of the Governments of U.P., Bihar, Orissa and Madhya Pradesh towards promoting industrial development in their states is partly responsible for the industrial backwardness of these states. Their shares in both employment and value added in factories are much smaller than their shares of the population of the country. However, government policies also have their limitations. The effort of the Government of Maharashtra to promote industrial development in the backward regions of the state has had little success so far.

The environs of metropolitan cities including their satellite cities are the most favoured locations for factories. Even resource based industries such as petroleum refineries and factories making machine tools and motor vehicles, besides those making a variety of consumer goods and consumer durables locate in them. The developments of the last decade indicate that such spatial distribution is unlikely to change in the next decade. A detailed analysis of the reasons for such location in one metropolitan area would be a fascinating study.

Notes

1. A detailed regional analysis of '*Industrial Location and Employment in India*' is given in the book by the author on *Regional Development and Planning in India*, V. Nath, New Delhi, Concept, 2008. The article was also published in *The Journal of Association of Population Geographers of India*, Vol. 19, Numbers 1 and 2, June—December 1997.
2. A detailed state-wise analysis of concentration and expansion of some industries in some regions but not in others are discussed in details in the publication mentioned above (Nath V., 2008).

10

Sustainable Economic Development 1950-2000: The Experience

Introduction

Self-sustaining development according to W.W. Rostow in 'Economics of Take Off' is that economic and social development should reach a stage when the economy and society propel themselves to further progress. India has reached that stage in some areas of social development but not yet in economic or political development. This is explained in the following:

I. Social Development

(a) The Scheduled Castes

The position of the scheduled castes has changed due to several factors: (i) After abolition of *Jagirdari* in the princely states and of *zamindari* in British ruled provinces, millions of members of the scheduled castes have become peasant proprietors by getting allotted cultivable land which was held by the *jagirdars* and *zamindars* as pastures or woodland. With this change, they have ceased to do lowly work such as flaying hides and skins of dead animals and making shoes and other leather goods used on the farms. They have stopped doing also their traditional duties during life cycle events such as births and marriages in the homes of the *jagirdars* and *zamindars*. The latter have taken the change in their stride regarding this as the inescapable result of the abolition of *jagirdari* and *zamindari*. (ii) With increasing numbers of young men in white-collar jobs, including those in the offices of the Government of India and the State Governments, it is no longer possible for the high castes to discriminate against them or exploit them as they used to. (iii) Since their support is essential for votes for the high castes, the candidates must do all that is possible to win them. Since one-fourth of the seats in Parliament and legislatures of most states are reserved for the scheduled castes and the scheduled tribes, the support of their representatives is essential for the governments in power or for enactment of important legislation. (iv) Even in *Panchayati Raj* Institutions, there is adequate representation for these groups so that discrimination against them is difficult to maintain in these institutions also.

(b) Position of Women

The position of women has also improved greatly. Illiteracy and ignorance about prevention and cure of common diseases of children and women is appreciably less than in the 1950s, thanks to the work of school teachers and physicians (including women doctors), nurses and family planning advisers posted at the community development block/*taluka* level health centres and of private practitioners and health centres run by the municipalities in urban areas. Although the birth rate and the rate of population growth continue to be high in several states, they are falling in an increasing number. The two or three child norm has been adopted by low income group women such as domestic servants in Delhi and other metropolitan cities. In Kerala and Goa where female literacy and acceptance of family planning are both high, rates of population growth are only marginally higher than replacement levels.

There has emerged in the metropolitan cities an expanding class of educated and trained women who combine home making with work outside the home. All the telephone operators and receptionists are women and in most of the corporate offices and in many Central and State Government offices women are accepted as secretaries as a matter of course. Educated women are in the forefront of the movement for preventing violence and crime against women. An increasing number of those guilty of such offences are prosecuted. Under pressure from the women's movement leaders many new laws and changes in the old laws have been undertaken to bring about gender equality and to provide physical security to women in homes and in work places.

The Growth and Role of Middle Class

The middle class has an enormous influence on economic policies for several reasons. First, most of the ministers, legislators, government employees as well as executives and employees of Panchayati Raj Institutions belong to this class. They run the electronic and print media and mould public opinion. They constitute the largest group of voters and consumers. No government can stay in power without their support.

The rise in size and influence of the middle class is in line with development during the last century or 150 years in the countries that are now developed. The numbers of the middle class and its power and influence are bound to increase as a result of successful implementation of anti-poverty programmes.

II. Economic Development

The rate of economic growth has increased progressively from 3-4 per cent per annum during the period 1960-80, just about 1-2 per cent above the rate of increase of population, to 5-6 per cent per annum and 3-4 per cent above the rate of population growth during the 1990s (growth rate of GDP was more than 9 per cent during 2007 and is projected to stay above 8 per cent from 2008 onwards[1]. As a result, per capita income of an average Indian is significantly higher today than it was during 1960-80. It is not certain if it will be possible to maintain this growth given the large oil pool deficit and the government's difficulty in reducing its fiscal deficit. However, since rate of inflation is also high, the impact of increase in per capita income on levels of living gets eroded somewhat; there is need to have a rigorous policy for control in inflation (cost of living).

The economy has not yet reached the stage at which maintenance of average growth rate of GDP attained during the last decade would be automatic. It is very much dependent upon a favourable external environment and the government not making any serious mistakes in formulation or implementation of macro-economic or fiscal policies. The growth rate of the 1990s was achieved because prices of crude oil, import of which forms a significant proportion of the country's foreign exchange expenditure were stable at a rather low level. Furthermore, exports increased rapidly because the rupee was undervalued, keeping in view its domestic purchasing power. Keeping bureaucratic red tape in check also encouraged exporters and other entrepreneurs. These favourable factors may not operate for ever. Steep rise in prices of crude oil is making a large demand on foreign exchange earnings of the country. Furthermore, India's exports are facing increasing competition from China and western developed market economies. Although foreign direct investment is increasing, it remains much lower than projected. It is concentrated in production of goods and rendering services such as banking in which large profits can be made quickly. There has been some increase in investment in infrastructures such as construction of high-speed four or six lane expressways, improvement or reconstruction of ports. However, appreciation in exchange rate of the rupee has made Indian exports expensive.

The increase in rate of economic growth has been due also to increasing efficiency of information technology industries which has made it competitive in foreign markets. It is not clear whether the benefits of economic growth have trickled down to the poor. The percentage of population below the poverty line is estimated to have declined steadily from about 55 per cent in 1973-74 to a projected 18.00 per cent during 2001-02. There has been a sharp decline in the 1990s; the rate was 36.0 per cent in 1993-94 and is estimated at 26 per cent in 1999-2000. The decline is being attributed to the trickle down effect of the rapid growth of gross domestic product achieved during the 1990s. There are, however, large inter-state and intra-state sub-regional variations in rural poverty due to environmental and/or man-made reasons (V. Nath, 2005).

A second change has been in the agents of accelerating economic growth. During the late 1950s to the 1980s the Government of India and of the states made large investments aimed at increasing agricultural production, in establishing industries and expansion of infrastructure. Private entrepreneurs with some notable exceptions concentrated on production of consumer goods and consumer durables where large profits were made in satisfying domestic demand. In the 1990s, large investments in some basic industries such as petroleum refining and manufacture of petro-chemicals and expansion of power supplies is being made by private entrepreneurs. Furthermore, some of the largest private companies are offering to take over loss making public enterprises such as airlines, tourist hotels, banks and state electricity boards. The IT industries that have grown exponentially during the last three decades are the product entirely of private entrepreneurs.

Consistent with this change, there has been a major shift in the groups that influence economic policies of the government. Earlier, the most powerful pressure group was that of labour unions of public enterprises—railways, post and telecommunications, nationalized banks and life and general insurance corporations and public sector industrial enterprises. They insisted on preservation of their employment, pay and other perquisites in spite of losses in public sector units. Their influence remains strong. However, the chambers of commerce and industry have acquired an influence on economic policies that they did not have before. Foreign investors including non-resident Indians have also emerged as an important pressure group influencing economic policies of the government.

In the 1950s and 1960s, the government established institutes of technology and management. Now, the products of these institutions who have become multi-millionaires abroad as software professionals and information service providers are offering to take over the responsibility for management, expansion and modernization of these institutes. The most affluent alumni of the best universities are offering to take over expansion and modernization of some departments of their *alma maters*. Earlier, the government established some world-class hospitals in Delhi, Chandigarh and some other cities. Now physicians/surgeons trained abroad have established hospitals that are both efficient and profitable in several metropolitan cities and are planning to open them in others. Benefits of newly established hospitals are not reaching the poor, accessibility of the poor to these institutions should be ensured.

The unions of employees of public sector enterprises still have enormous power. But they are acquiescing with the fact that they have to accept voluntary retirement packages. Furthermore, they have accepted the fact that the employees retained after privatization of the enterprises must improve their productivity in order to remain in employment. With increasing privatization unemployment is growing and living and working conditions of the workers are deteriorating. Policy makers should make an attempt to avert this situation.

III. Foreign Aid to India

Some aid for Development Planning was given by the Soviet Union, Britain and Germany and to a much smaller extent by Canada, and the U.S.A. Aid from the first three countries was utilized principally in building large steel mills, mills for processing bauxite into aluminium and metallic aluminium, factory for making heavy machine tools, factories for making locomotives, wagons and coaches for railways. Technical assistance for establishing them was given on a commercial basis by companies in Germany, Japan and Italy.

For exploitation of large deposits of crude oil off the coasts of Mumbai and offshore and on-shore Gujarat, also in exploration and development of the oil fields, establishing refineries and a country-wide network of vendors for distribution of products—motor spirit and diesel as fuel for motor vehicles and kerosene and natural gas for cooking, assistance was given by the Soviet Union and on a commercial basis by other countries.

American assistance for development of agriculture and rural development began with start of the community development programme in 1952. However, it was terminated soon because the Administrator of the programme and the Development Commissioners who implemented the programme in the states found that they knew more about agriculture and rural development in India than did the foreign experts and the equipment that they brought was not too useful. Later, in the mid-1960s U.S. assistance was given mainly as surplus cereals (wheat and milo) under its PL 480 programme when there was a severe shortage of grains in the country.

In later years, there has been little assistance from America, Britain or Germany. The principal role of these countries has been to support assistance from the World Bank for some poverty eradication programmes and from the IMF for balance of payments support.

The acceleration of economic growth from 3-4 per cent per annum during 1960-90 to 5-7 per cent of GDP per capita in the 1990 has been due entirely to India's own developmental effort. Foreign direct investment has come in running tourist hotels and banks in which large profits are assured and can be recaptured. There has been little assistance in construction of essential infrastructures such as four to six lane highways or for construction or modernization of ports.

Foreign aid amounts to about six billion dollars per year. Some of it is for the poverty eradication programmes from the World Bank the rest is to finance equipment for industrial or infrastructure projects assisted by the aid giving countries.

In 2000-01 with all the facilities extended to foreign investors, foreign direct investment was estimated at less than two million dollars, scarcely more than 4-5 per cent of the GDP. India's economic development would be the result of India's own economic development effort.

Reference

V. Nath, 'Regional Dimensions of Rural Poverty in India' in *Reinventing Regional Development* (eds.) Surya Kant *et al.*, Rawat Publications, New Delhi. 2005,

Note

1. As per Human Development Report 2001, average per capita income in 1999 was $2248 in purchasing power parity terms between India and the U.S. (p. 20).

11

Growth Poles in the Economy: 1950-2000

Introduction

The concept of growth pole was first advanced and elaborated by the French economist, Francois Perroux soon after Second World War. He defined a growth pole as an innovation or industry or discovery of a natural resource, exploitation of which propels a region and the nation to a higher growth path or aids development of a backward region. Perroux advanced the concept to justify the efforts of the French Government to develop industries in the backward south based on the use of natural gas which had been discovered in the region in the 1950s. The effort failed because the power stations and industries using natural gas remained isolated developments and did not lead to regional development. Winter and summer tourism, rather than industries processing natural gas, remain the dominant providers of employment and source of foreign exchange since the last quarter of the nineteenth century and especially after First World War. However, the concept became popular among regional planners and economists seeking to reduce metropolitan concentration and stimulate economic growth in lagging, backward or depressed regions with the location, specifically of a town (Perroux, 1955).

To be able to fulfil its regional growth-inducing role, the town should have that complex of economic and social infrastructure facilities needed by modern industries, and the 'growth pole strategy' of regional development has come to be identified with the creation of such infrastructures in a few well located towns in lagging regions and attracting industries to them through fiscal and other incentives (Boudeville, Chapter 7).

The strategy has considerable appeal for planners in developing countries, who wish to secure dispersed economic development, both in the interest of regional balance, and as a solution to the economic and social problems caused by too rapid growth of the national capital or other large cities in which all modern enterprises tend to concentrate. In the situation of scarcity of capital, and low levels of infrastructural development, characteristic of these countries, the strategy offers a feasible way to affect dispersed development and achieve regional balance. Writing about India, John Lewis advocated building up of medium-sized towns with populations of 20,000 to 300,000 as focal points of disbursed economic development (Lewis, 1962, pp. 179-185). To these arguments for reducing metropolitan concentration and securing regional balance, he added that of serving the needs of rural modernization; the towns would have a host of service facilities, ranging from markets and seed, fertilizer depots to schools and hospitals, needed for modernization of the surrounding rural regions and various processing, consumer goods and other industries with local or micro-regional orientation would be located in them (Lewis, 1962, pp. 195-200). However, several other factors and developments can be identified as growth poles in the process of economic development due to planning for them or as a result of several technological developments.

It is possible to identify eight growth poles in India's economic development during the fifty years, 1950 to 2000.

(i) Community Development Programme

With the start of the first community development programme of integrated rural development in October 1952, this was extended to the whole country in the next ten years. Under the programme hundreds of thousands of kilometres of approach roads were built to connect villages in all parts of the country with towns. The isolation of villages was broken. Metalling of roads which were heavily travelled, the PWD of the State Government made them fit to be used by buses and trucks so that dependence on the slow and cumbersome bullock cart as the sole means of rural transport ended. Tens of thousands of primary schools were opened in villages and thousands of secondary schools were opened in large villages so that increasing numbers of children, boys and girls, could go to primary and secondary schools. Adult literacy programmes were organized in order to eradicate illiteracy among adults. Primary health centres (mini hospitals) with six beds, one or more doctors, nurses and dispensers were opened at the community development block/*taluka* level, usually small or medium sized towns to provide treatment to the sick and disseminate principles of clean living so that incidence of disease among rural men, women and children was reduced. Construction or improvement of tens of thousands of drinking water wells, tanks and other water supply sources had the same object besides reducing the hardship of rural women in fetching water from distant wells and tanks. Thousands of veterinary dispensaries were opened for treatment of and prevention of diseases among livestock. The agricultural extension programme promoted use of improved seed, manure and/or chemical fertilizers and pesticides to increase yields of crops. As a result, production of cereals increased rapidly as also of other crops.

(ii) Discovery of Large Deposits of Crude Oil

The second growth pole was the discovery of large deposits of crude oil off the coasts of Mumbai and off-shore and on-shore Gujarat. To process the oil, petroleum refineries were opened near Mumbai, in coastal Gujarat and near centres of consumption of products. Technical assistance for exploration and development of the oil fields was given by the Soviet Union. However, construction of pipelines to centres of consumption usually cities and comparatively prosperous agricultural regions was done through India's own funds.

These developments had the effect of large increase in the use of motor vehicles for transport. Several plants were opened to manufacture motor vehicles—buses and trucks, passenger cars, 3-wheeler and 2-wheeler scooters and motor bicycles. The plants were located in the peri-urban areas of large cities—Mumbai, Kolkata, Chennai, Pune, Kanpur and Delhi. The availability of petroleum products within the country enabled India to survive the shocks in 1973 and 1979 given by the sharp increase in the prices of crude oil, made by the principal oil producing countries of the world. Technical assistance for establishing plants of motor vehicles was given on a strictly commercial basis by Germany, Britain, Japan and Italy. India could motorize its transport and produce petrochemical products ranging from polyester fibre to a variety of plastic goods.

(iii) High Yielding Dwarf Varieties of Wheat and Rice Crops

With availability and use of dwarf, high yielding varieties of the most widely consumed cereals—wheat and rice from the mid-1960s to the mid-1970s under conditions of assured and controlled moisture provided by an assured and dependable rainfall and/or irrigation, along with the use of recommended doses of chemical fertilizers/organic manure and pesticides gave two to three times the yields of the older varieties. Use of these varieties spread like wild fire in the wheat growing states of Punjab, Haryana, western U.P. and three districts of northern Rajasthan as well as in coastal Andhra Pradesh, coastal Tamil Nadu, south west Karnataka and parts of West Bengal in which rice is grown under conditions of assured moisture. As a result, India became self-sufficient in cereals by 1971. Output of cereals has been increasing steadily ever since so much so that by the mid and late 1990s, their output was about 200 mt., three and a half time the output of less than 60 mt. in the 1950s. Furthermore, their widespread use has created regions of agricultural prosperity in Punjab, Haryana, western Uttar Pradesh and other regions which are mentioned below. In these areas, high yield wheat is grown along with other crops. In Punjab, it is produced along with high yield rice; in Haryana, it is grown with medium staple cotton and oil seeds; in western U.P., it is grown with sugarcane and oil seeds.

In coastal Andhra Pradesh, especially the deltas of the Godavari and Krishna rivers, high yield rice is grown along with sugarcane. There are a large number of rice and sugar mills. In one district, flue cured tobacco used for making cigarettes is the principal crop which is both labour intensive and highly remunerative. In West Bengal as also in the delta of the Kaveri River in Tamil Nadu two or three crops of paddy are harvested. In south-west Karnataka high yield varieties of rice are grown along with high yield sugarcane. Here also there are a number of sugar and rice mills. In the area around Coimbatore which is irrigated by a canal from the Pykara River, high yield medium staple cotton is grown. There are a large number of textile mills and various industrial units producing machine tools for the mills and other industrial goods.

In western Maharashtra a large area is irrigated by a number of streams flowing from the Western Ghats to the Arabian Sea. High yield sugarcane with high sugar content is the principal crop. There are a number of sugar mills, and a number of industrial units produce a variety of machine tools for the mills. In Mumbai and Pune and the 170 km rail-*cum*-road strip, there are a very large number of industrial units which produce everything from textiles, garments, shoes and other leather, consumer durables, toiletries, pharmaceutical drugs and motor vehicles. In the area around Nasik are produced high yield grapes, sweet lime, oranges and a variety of vegetables. A large number of farmers and agricultural labourers are busy growing the crops and creating them for consumption in northern and western India and for export to countries of the Gulf primarily for consumption of Indians settled there.

In Coastal Gujarat farmers grow high yield oil seed and sorghum and millets. There are a very large number of industrial units manufacturing everything from cloth and garments to consumer durables such as air conditioners and refrigerators and a variety of machine tools. Because of the offshore and on-shore deposits of crude oil there are petroleum refineries and industrial units manufacturing petrochemical products such as polyester fibre for textiles and plastics for a variety of domestic goods.

In the area around Anand in central Gujarat large employment opportunities are available to wives of farmers and agricultural labourers in producing liquid milk for Mumbai and other cities in Gujarat. Amul dairy in Anand provides large employment in shipping milk to various cities and processing surplus milk to produce butter, cheese and baby food. It is the largest producer of these products in India. The farmers grow fodder crops for the animals; their wives and daughters look after one to three buffaloes to produce milk.

(iv) Information Technology Industries and Pharmaceutical Drug Industries

The expansion from the early 1970s of information technology industries, use of computer software for export and domestic use, e-mail and internet has contributed substantially to high growth rate of the Indian economy during the 1990s. Their export makes a valuable contribution to India's foreign exchange while its domestic use in industries increases efficiency and makes the products competitive in foreign markets.

Their use in modern service institutions has had two beneficial results. Nationalized banks and insurance corporations have become competitive with foreign institutions. Besides, they can mobilize large savings from households within the country and from non-resident Indians to finance economic growth within the country. The increase of growth of GDP from 3-4 per cent p.a. from the early 1960s to the end of the 1980s, to 5-7 per cent in the 1990s is due in large part to India's success in export of computer software.

Development of drugs based on original research, some of them on the principles of the ancient Ayurvedic system of medicine, that are effective in the treatment of the aged, as well as women and children have large sales within India and abroad. Two companies, one based in

Hyderabad and the other in Delhi, that have developed these drugs have a turnover of several hundred million dollars and are poised for rapid growth. There will be a rapid increase in use of these drugs especially in southern India and Sri Lanka because Ayurvedic medicines are more popular in southern India and Sri Lanka than in northern India. The likely future centres of production of these drugs are Vadodara in Gujarat in which there are two companies which already make highly popular Ayurvedic drugs, Lucknow where the Central Drug Research Institute in U.P. is located and Chennai or Thiruvananthapuram in southern India.

Since these two industries have and will continue to have major impact on economic growth, and various other components are discussed in a separate section of this chapter.

(v) Other Contributors to Economic Development

The country has been able to maintain a growth rate of 5-7 per cent per annum which was achieved in 1991, due to:

(a) *Favourable Economic Environment*: Prices of crude oil import which makes a large dent in India's foreign exchange resources were low. Bureaucratic controls on export of domestic producers and import of raw material was relaxed so that they could export products and import raw materials. The international environment has been unfavourable since early 2000. International prices of crude oil have been extremely high. Indian manufacturers face increasing competition in foreign markets. Foreign direct investment has been less than two billion, less than 0.25 per cent of the GDP. However, growth has been maintained due to the contribution made by information technology industries in earning foreign exchange. The bonds issued by nationalized banks such as the State Bank of India and the Bank of Baroda have mobilized savings of non-resident Indians. Continuance of these policies and privatization of loss making state enterprises such as Air India, Indian Airlines, steel and aluminium plants and others by finding strategic foreign partners will help India attain self-sustaining economic growth.

Since the information technology industries have experienced most rapid growth during the last two decades, the principal producers of services such as telecommunications have a strong influence on government policies. Such influence is bound to remain high during the next two decades.

(b) *Several Manufacturing Facilities to Serve Regional Markets*: Some companies which have commanding position in sale of their products have established several factories for serving regional markets. The outstanding examples at present are:

Indian Tobacco Co. which has a commanding position in the market for cigarettes and other tobacco products. It has factories in Hyderabad, Mangalore and Saharanpur to serve the markets of south, east and north India.

Hindustan Lever, which has a similar commanding position in the manufacture of soap and other toiletries, cooking oil and tea has similarly several factories to serve consumers in different markets. The principal reason for this is well known to students of geography. The cost of transporting raw materials is much less than that of transporting finished products. The trend could spread to manufacture of other products. One leading bicycle manufacturing company which has its main factory in Haryana has eight other factories in other regions of India and in neighbouring countries.

The Governments of Andhra Pradesh and Karnataka are aggressively promoting location of IT industries in cyber cities in Hyderabad and Bangalore. They are creating the infrastructures for these and other industries. The governments of Tamil Nadu, Maharashtra and Gujarat are also creating infrastructures and providing all facilities for location of IT and other industries within their states. The Government of West Bengal has successfully arrested the decline in industries in the Calcutta Metropolitan District and is now developing successfully a petroleum refining and petrochemical complex at Haldia. In the north, the Government of Haryana has successfully promoted location of industries including IT industries and offices of commercial business in the two satellite cities of Delhi-Gurgaon and Faridabad.

(vi) Effects of Technological Change on Human Development and Modernization

During the past two decades economists have emphasized the importance of increase in welfare of the people, as an indicator of development rather than only increase in per capita income. Technological advance has been considered a major change influencing human well-being.

In the 1950s, production of enough food was itself a problem. However, development of dwarf, very high yielding varieties of wheat and rice in the 1960s and the 1970s under conditions of assured and adequate water supply, provided by rainfall and/or irrigation meant that there could be enough food for all. The use of radio and television to an increasing extent by rural people meant that it became possible to disseminate information about a number of improved agricultural techniques which was earlier possible only with face-to-face communication. Thus, technological advance has been considered a major change influence in itself.

Statements on India of Human Development Reports provide a good commentary on India's economic and social progress as indicated by various indicators of economic development and social change. The Census Reports indicate the changes over a 10-year period between the latest census and its predecessor; the national sample surveys indicate changes over a five year (shorter) period, i.e. between the latest and the last survey. None of these makes any projections however. The HDR statements use official statistics of the Census, the NSS and other agencies and also make projections using the highly sophisticated model for India's economic and social progress developed by the statistical division of the United Nations. The statements on past progress and need for further progress provide a valuable guide to policy makers—from the Prime Minister and the Ministries of Finance to Education and Health to Information Technology and Telecommunications, on the policies to be pursued to maximize literacy, primary and secondary education, access to protective health and medical care and above all access to enough food and safe and adequate drinking water to all. The projections on probable progress provide a challenge to them to formulate policies so that these values can be achieved or exceeded. The following observations on the role of technology in India's economic and social development are based on the UN Human Development Report, 2001.

Role of Technology in India's Economic Development

The Human Development Report for 2001 focuses on the role of technology in India's economic development. The Report indicates that the value of export of computer software in 1999 was about $4 billion, having increased from $150 million in 1990. In the latter year, it contributed about 10 per cent of the total value of exports. One study estimates that they could reach $50 billion by 2008 and could contribute 30 per cent of total value of exports and 7.5 per cent of the GDP in that year (HDR, 2001, p.11). The number of IT professionals (computer programmers, engineers and scientists) needed to achieve this target would be 2.2 million, up from 180,000 in 1998 (*ibid*).

This would mean, however, enormous investment by companies and the Central and State Governments in training personnel and expanding infrastructures (such as dependable supplies of electricity and water, telecommunications and air communication etc.). It would be necessary also to ensure that the trained persons work in India and do not emigrate in droves to the USA, Western Europe and other countries. A most interesting suggestion, coming from a New York based agency, is that every professional (engineer or scientist) who migrates after being trained in India should pay to the Government a certain specified amount as compensation for the cost of his training which is estimated at between $15,000 and $20,000 to a maximum of two months salary (Human Development Report, 2001, p. 22). This would be only token compensation for the brain drain from a poor country.

Effect of Radio and Television Broadcasts

Radio and television broadcasts cannot of course provide medical care, or advice about family planning. But they can provide information to farmers about prices of their crops, and also about when to sow and harvest the crops, so that they can benefit the most from the vagaries of the monsoon and post-monsoon rains in different regions of India.

Radio and television can also advise farmers on the timing and amount of use of fertilizers and pesticides to maximize yields from their crops. Similarly, they can advise illiterate village women about how to keep their homes and children clean and thus avoid their families falling victim to communicable diseases. Their contribution in disaster relief has been demonstrated by two recent examples. Andhra Pradesh has an efficient system of telecommunication which enabled the district and lower level officials to provide food, blankets and other needs to the people marooned in floods caused by a cyclone in 2001. Medical teams with vaccine were flown in to inject people against communicable diseases. After the floods receded, building materials were quickly supplied to the people to rebuild their homes.

Similarly in the earthquake of 26 January, 2001 in Kutch, in which more than 20,000 people are estimated to have perished and extensive damage was caused to Bhuj and other towns and many villages of Kutch, the International Red Cross and Indian disaster relief agencies through use of these networks quickly organized disaster relief. The telecommunication network was quickly restored; the runway at Bhuj airport was repaired by the army to keep it airworthy to handle a continuing stream of aircraft bringing food, water, medical teams with vaccines and later building materials for rebuilding their homes to people rendered homeless as a result of the earthquake. The official machinery, which was in disarray for the first few weeks, started working normally thereafter.

Effect of Internet

Use of Internet reduces dependence on mainline telecommunications among rural people who are too poor to afford mainline phones. The Indian Institute of Technology, Madras (Chennai) has created in 1999, a low cost Internet connection system that requires a modem or inexpensive copper wires. The result is faster and cheaper communications ideal for providing access to low income communities in India and beyond (p. 23). An institute located in Pondicherry has set up information centres for local communications and Internet access using solar and electric power for wired and wireless communication. Farmers are getting information such as market prices, enabling them to negotiate better with intermediaries. Fisherman can download satellite images off the coast of Pondicherry and Tamil Nadu that indicate where fish shoals are. The catch of fish has increased greatly and an efficient system of roads enables fishermen to transport the catch to storage quickly and then to markets at maximized prices.

Effect of Education

India has within it great contrasts of education and technology. It has in Bangalore a world-class technology hub. At the same time, almost 40 per cent of the adults are illiterate and even those who are literate have completed only five years of school. Again, there is great contrast between states in access to electricity and telecommunications. In Maharashtra almost 60 per cent of the households have access to electricity; in Punjab and Karnataka the figure is 63 per cent. In U.P. however, it is only 20 per cent. In Maharashtra and Kerala, 43 per cent of the households have access to telephones; in Punjab, the figure is 47 per cent. But in U.P. the figure is 10 per cent (HDR, 2001, p.17). Figures on Internet connections have even wider inter-state variations. Maharashtra has 8.2 per 1000 persons; the corresponding figures for U.P. and Orissa are 0.12; a range of 64:1 (*ibid*). Maharashtra is the richest and most developed state in India while U.P. is one of the most backward and poorest. Of the 1.4 million Internet connections in India, 1.3 million are in four states (Maharashtra, Delhi, Karnataka and Tamil Nadu) (*ibid*). This shows the digital divide among states.

The Human Development Report brings out that literacy and education bring greater inclination to use modern high productivity techniques for raising agricultural output. Use of fertilizer to increase crop production has increased more than seven times between 1970 and 1999. The number of tractors in use per hectare of available land has increased 15 times during the same period (HDR, 2001, p.14). Educated farmers are more likely to use irrigation, improved seeds and chemical fertilizers to increase crop production than uneducated ones (HDR, 2001, p. 9).

The literacy rate has improved to 56.5 per cent. Population below poverty line has been estimated during 1994-1999 at 35.0 per cent; the latest estimate of the CSO however is 26 per cent in 1999-2000. As much as 88 per cent of the population is estimated to have access to improved water supplies in 1999, a major improvement over the position even a decade ago. However, as many as 31 per cent of the population does not have access to adequate sanitation, a result of squatters in urban and rural slums. On the other hand, India has major achievements in immunization of children against communicable diseases including tuberculosis. The per capita income has increased by 4.1 per cent p.a. The estimate of the CSO is of more than 5.4 per cent p.a. Electricity consumption per capita has increased three-fold from 130 KWH in 1980 to 384 KWH. in 1990.

Effect on Longevity of Life and Population

According to the latest estimate of the CSO life expectancy at birth has gone up from 50 years during 1970-75 to 56 years in 1995 to 62.3 years during 1995-2000.

The report gives a number of indices of technology achievement, human development and others. However, the point it emphasizes is that while India has made rapid progress in the 1990s it needs to make a major effort in the next 15 years to enable the rural and urban poor to increase their income and level of living.

India's population, 1027 million is projected to reach 1235 million by 2015. The rate of growth of population 1.9 per cent p.a. during 1991-2001 is expected to decline to an average of 1.3 per cent p.a., a rate which has been attained so far by only four states—Kerala, Goa, Tamil Nadu and Andhra Pradesh. Assumption of such a low rate of population growth is over-optimistic considering the fact that the rate in several large states ranged between 2 and 2.5 per cent during 1991-2001. However, the total GDP growth of 36 per cent appears realistic because during 1991 India's per capita income was Rs. 2248 calculated at 1999 purchasing power estimate; a big statistical improvement over the World Bank's method of estimating per capita income in normal US $.

Education and Use of IT Techniques in Improvement of Techniques of Production and Income by Farmers and Fishermen

Effective utilization of these techniques has made dissemination of information about offshore shoals of fish to fishermen, by an institute located in Pondicherry coast, to cast their nets in offshore areas where the shoals are located and thus greatly increase their catch. An efficient system of roads ensures that the catches can be taken quickly to the warehouse; further the fishermen can obtain the best prices for their catches. Farmers in green revolution areas can obtain the latest prices of their crops, thus maximizing their gains.

Software has been developed for conveying information to illiterate users with Internet technology; villagers can communicate with nearby villages about using new farming techniques and avoiding diseases.

Educated farmers, however, are more likely to use improved agricultural techniques than illiterate ones. This is proved by the Indian experience. Use of high productivity varieties of wheat, rice, sugarcane and groundnut is concentrated in states from Punjab in the north to Tamil Nadu and Kerala in the south to Maharashtra in the west. These states are richer than those in which such varieties are not used. It is increasing in Rajasthan and West Bengal with increase in literacy. On the other hand, in U.P. (except west U.P.) Bihar and Orissa both levels of literacy and use of high productivity techniques are very low. Again four states—Maharashtra, Punjab, Kerala and Karnataka with significantly higher percentage of households using electricity are richer than U.P., Bihar and Orissa where the percentage of such users is low. Use of electricity per capita has gone up almost three times between 1980 and 1990. Every one-unit increase in electricity use increases per capita income by more than two times.

Telephone users per 1000 population have increased four times during the 1990s because of increase in the growth rate of the national income. Despite this, waiting list for telephone connections has more than doubled in these states. Expenditure on education and health care remains abysmally low, however, despite all the tall talk about increasing it by finance ministers. Expenditure on education remained 3.2 per cent of GNP in both 1986-87 and 1996-97. Expenditure on health was less than 1 per cent of GNP in both periods.

(vii) Probable Effects of Rapid Growth of Information Technology Industries on Presentation of Phenomena of Interest to Geographers and Economists

The information technology industries—computer software, telecommunications, e-mail and internet have experienced very rapid growth during the last three decades and are expected to continue to experience similar rapid growth during the next two decades. Growth of these industries is making a major contribution to increasing gross domestic product and exports from India (HRD, 2001, p.11). The Secretary General of the United Nations, Mr. Kofi Annan has in his Millennium Report stated that: "the Indian software industry would increase eight-fold in the eight years—2000-2008 and could generate $85 billion by the latter year. Over 300 software companies are working in Bangalore alone. The turnover of the largest companies is in hundreds of million dollars" (*Times of India*, 5 April 2000, p. 11).

The object of this section is to put forward a few hypotheses in order to stimulate discussion on them. The section discusses the effect of these techniques on production of maps and monographs, on forecasting of weather and consequent effects on disaster relief and agricultural production, on district administration, and on rural and urban settlement patterns. Also discussed are market research and the need for participation of geographers in it.

Production of Maps and Monographs: Computer Graphics and Desk Top Printing

Computer graphics has become the most widely used technique for production of maps. Desktop printing is the most widely used technique for producing monographs which are not expected to have a large sale in their first printing. The cost of producing maps showing spatial distribution of various phenomena of interest to geographers—seasonal variations in temperature, incidence and amount of rainfall within the monsoon season and in the post-monsoon season in some states; regional variations in topography, soils, vegetation, density of population in different states and in districts within them; inter-state differences in levels of total and female literacy; birth, death and infant mortality rates; growth rate of population and per capita income—the list is large—are all being produced by computer graphics. The cost is much lower and the phenomena can be depicted as well or with greater accuracy than with manual methods. An indication of this is provided by the daily newspapers, and by the various reports issued by the Census Commissioner of India, and by the UNDP and the World Bank. The English language dailies often illustrate the various phenomena described on them with colour charts and graphs. It takes very little time for computerized data to be made available to readers. In the case of Population Census data the first profile containing these and other demographic and topographic data by States revealed by the Census 2001 (conducted in February) was published and made available in May 2001, within three months of conduct of the Census. The section was beautifully printed and contains a large number of Maps (including a Map of Districts), bar charts and pictograms so that the Census data are easily understood by members of Parliament and Legislatures of different states.

The international development agencies have followed this practice of presentation of their reports to make them easily understood by policy makers in member countries, or their secretaries.

These techniques have also led to the development of GIS (Geographic Information System) whereby comprehensive information of interest to geographers has been assembled for every place in a country.

Forecasting of Weather and Climate and Disaster Relief

These techniques have given the meteorologists a powerful tool for forecasting weather and climate with great accuracy. Using them, the Indian Meteorology Department has been forecasting with increasing accuracy the amount and distribution within the monsoon and the post-monsoon seasons of rainfall in different parts of the country. Rapid dissemination of this information through radio and television receivers enables farmers in rain-fed areas to adjust the timing of planting, weeding and harvesting of their monsoon season crops. Farmers in irrigated areas can adjust the amount and timing of irrigation of their crops because their requirements of moisture can be adjusted by farmers keeping the forecasts in view.

Disaster relief is also assisted. The Meteorology Department can forecast the time, intensity, direction of advance and the areas likely to be affected by cyclones that hit the coastal areas of the country during the monsoon or post-monsoon seasons and the areas likely to be affected by drought or floods.

The vulnerable populations—fishermen and farmers living in the coastal areas that would be flooded by the heavy rain brought by a cyclone can be evacuated ahead of time. The result has been an enormous saving of life and property. The large loss of life and property in the cyclone in Orissa, in January 2000 was due to the fact that the state and district administrations did not heed the warnings of the Meteorology Department about the cyclone and did not evacuate the vulnerable populations in time. The Government of Andhra Pradesh on the other hand took effective steps to rehabilitate the populations affected by the cyclone that hit the coastal area of the state a year later. As a result, there was minimum loss of life and property and the farmers could replant their crops soon after the cyclone.

Improvement in District Administration

When revenue records are computerized, as is being considered by some State Governments, the present dependence on *patwaries* (called *karnams* or *talaties* in some states) would be eliminated. Most of them are corrupt because they are paid so little. Furthermore, most of them are inefficient because they are educated only to primary or (8-grade) middle school. They would be replaced by young men, educated to higher secondary school levels that are proficient in the use of computers. They would live in relatively large villages and be provided bicycles or motor cycles to travel to five or more small villages within their jurisdiction to collect the information contained in the present land records. The computerized records would not only be permanent and easily accessible but the cost of storing them at the district or *taluka* headquarters would be much less than of the mountains of books that contain them at present.

With basic equipment—a telephone, a computer and a fax machine—provided in the office of every Collector, information on progress of various development programmes being implemented in a district could be provided to the concerned departments of the State Governments much faster and in much greater detail than is possible at present with dependence on the use of post, telegraph and telephones. One of the effects of use of these techniques is that modifications in policies and programmes, after recognizing problems in implementation could be done more rapidly than is possible at present.

Possible Effects on Inter-State Disparities in Economic Development

The principal centres of the information technology industries are all in states which have higher levels of economic development than the all India average. Bangalore in Karnataka is the most important of these industries at present. Other important centres are Chennai in Tamil Nadu, Hyderabad in Andhra Pradesh, Mumbai and Pune in Maharashtra, Ahmedabad in Gujarat, Gurgaon in Haryana and Noida in U.P. The last two are satellite cities of Delhi. Growth of these industries will in the foreseeable future also be concentrated in these centres so that the total domestic product of the states in which they are located will increase faster than in states without them.

Possible new centres are Kolkata in West Bengal and Kanpur or Lucknow in Uttar Pradesh. Development in Kolkata would be assisted by location of the Indian Statistical Institute in Barrackpur, a suburb of Kolkata, and in Kolkata itself of two Universities which have strong departments of science; one has a college of engineering. The possible development of Kanpur or Lucknow would be encouraged by location near an Institute of Technology in the former and of a good university in the latter.

Chandigarh in Punjab should also emerge as a centre. It has a University, a Regional Engineering College and a world-class teaching hospital. It would attract a large number of Punjabi computer software specialists who are now settled in the U.S.A. Another favourable factor is access to venture capital because of the strong entrepreneurial tradition among the punjabis. Furthermore it has a salubrious climate, and relatively low levels of pollution of air and water.

With the exception of Uttar Pradesh, all the states in which the IT centres are located or are expected to come up in the foreseeable future have higher per capita income than the all India averages (Table 11.1) so that inter-state disparities in economic development could increase with rapid growth of these industries.

Table 11.1: Per Capita Income of States (1997-98)

States	*Per Capita Income in 1997-98 (Rupees)*
Andhra Pradesh.	10,680
Assam	7,330
Bihar	4,664
Gujarat	16,291
Maharashtra	18,364
Orissa	6,767
Rajasthan	9,819
Tamil Nadu	12,989
Uttar Pradesh	7,293
Madhya Pradesh	8,114
Karnataka	11,583
Kerala	11,935

All States with higher Per Capita Income have developed I.T. Industry

Source: Statistical outline of India 2000-01, Tata Services Ltd., Bombay House, Mumbai-400001, p. 133.

Effect on the Settlement Pattern

The effect of these techniques on the rural and urban settlement patterns cannot be forecast with any degree of accuracy but it is likely that the long-term trend towards concentration of the rural population in large villages will be accentuated. There are several reasons for this.

The agricultural extension officers that advise farmers regarding adoption of high productivity techniques concentrate their attention on farmers, in large villages. These villages are easily approached by motorable roads; so that large farmers who market most of their produce live in them. Branches of cooperative societies and of land mortgage banks that provide short and medium-term credit for buying inputs of high productivity agriculture are located in them—stores that sell improved seed, chemical fertilizers, pesticides and medicines (tractors, pump sets driven by diesel oil or electricity) fuel for the machines and facilities for their repair and for spare parts. With the use of long distance telephones up-to-date information on prices of crops is available to farmers. Secondary schools for boys and girls and primary health centres that provide advice on preventive health and nutrition and treatment in case of sickness are located there. Farmers who live in them have better health and productivity and have access to education facilities for their children so that some of them can become white-collar workers. Agricultural labourers will live in or near them so that they will have the opportunity for employment on the farms, in the states mentioned above, or those which send crops to regional markets.

Probable Effects on the Rural and Urban Settlement Patterns

These effects are more difficult to foresee because of the great diversity in the present settlement pattern in different states of India. The variation in the rural pattern is all the way from most farm households living in their own compounds with a drinking water well, and a small patch growing vegetables and tapioca and the family's rice field in the back in Kerala, to most of the rural people living in relatively large villages with populations of 1000 or more in Punjab, Haryana, western U.P., northern Rajasthan, Gujarat and north-western Madhya Pradesh.

Information on weather and prices of crops can be broadcast to farmers in small villages as well as in large ones. Similarly, because of near universal rural electrification in several states, electrically operated pumps on irrigation wells and electrically operated machines for de-husking rice and wheat, shelling maize, pressing sugar cane to make *khandsari* or brown sugar for local consumption or processing oil seeds to make cooking oil for similar use can be done just as well in small villages as in large ones.

However, residents of relatively large villages have an advantage over those of small villages in a number of ways. Approach roads to them are better because the large farmers who are the principal sellers of crops are concentrated in them. The villages have the advantage in production of high value perishable foods—milk, vegetables, fruit and poultry products (chicken and eggs) for urban and local markets. Output and consumption of these foods is increasing rapidly and they are providing remunerative employment and income to those—small farmers and rural women—who would otherwise be unemployed. Residents of large villages have access to better roads to take their produce to markets. Offices of producers' cooperatives which supply essential inputs—chemical fertilizers and pesticides needed for production of crops, medicines for livestock and vaccines for birds are all located in relatively large villages. Another advantage for residents of large villages is that one or more public telephone booths and several private telephones are installed in relatively large villages. Their residents will, therefore, have access to telecommunication with relatives and friends living at long distances, unlike residents of small villages. Thus, in states and regions mentioned earlier, concentration of the rural population in relatively large villages will be accentuated.

The principal future effect on the urban settlement pattern is to accelerate spatial expansion of the large metropolitan cities in the peri-urban areas of which the information technology industries are located. This is because the infrastructure needed for location and growth of these industries—dependable (preferably captive) supplies of electricity and water, freedom from noise and dust pollution, enough space for expansion of the IT companies and suitable housing and various service facilities for their executives and employees can be located in the peri-urban areas of the cities. In Hyderabad, the industries are concentrated in Cyber city, about 30 km from the city in which all facilities for their location and growth have been provided by the Government of Andhra Pradesh. In Chennai, they are in the vicinity of the Institutes of Technology—at Guindy about 30 km north of the city. In Mumbai they are in the vicinity of the Institute of Technology in Pawai, about 30 km north of the city. This is because, most of the investors in these industries are graduates of the IITs. In Delhi, however, they are in Gurgaon and NOIDA, both of which are satellite cities 20-30 km from New Delhi.

(viii) Market Research

Geographers in the USA and several other western developed countries have participated since the 1960s in market research aimed at delineating the hinterland of large stores in the shopping malls of large cities that sell consumer goods such as processed foods, trendy clothes, shoes, and other leather goods, jewellery, medicines and other health care products and consumer durables ranging from TV receivers, refrigerators and air conditioners to motor bicycles and passenger cars. Manufacturers of these consumer goods also have their own market research agencies to determine the volume of goods that they would sell in different regions of a country such as the USA, Canada, countries of Europe or Latin America and Asia.

Market research is making rapid strides in India. One of the largest companies in India, Hindustan Lever, has its own market research agency to collect data needed for maximizing sale of its products. Polls of various kinds are being used by daily newspapers or magazines with large circulation to obtain opinions of residents of large metropolitan cities on various issues of current interest or to forecast results of elections to the state legislatures or the Parliament.

The demand for processed foods, ready to wear garments, factory made shoes and other accessories as well as of consumer durables ranging from fans to refrigerators, air conditioners, washing machines and motor vehicles is increasing rapidly in India. In addition to the middle and high income residents of cities, farmers with large and medium sized holdings in areas of agricultural prosperity such as Punjab, Haryana, western U.P., coastal Gujarat, areas producing sugarcane or vegetables and fruit in western Maharashtra, coastal Andhra Pradesh, coastal Tamil Nadu, the peri-urban areas of Coimbatore and the 170 km long strip between Bangalore and Mysore in Karnataka have become buyers of these products. The companies that make these products are anxious that the demand for their products be forecast with accuracy.

Developing countries can come under pressure from donor agencies, non-profit organizations, multinational agencies to adopt techniques that reduce environmental pollution. Dupont, a U.S. based manufacturer of chemicals and other products, holder of the patents on CFC substitutes, refused to license production of these substitutes to manufacturers in India and Korea where the high cost of importing (Dupont's) chemicals limited the widespread diffusion of an environmentally sound technology (p. 26).

Use of IT techniques cannot of course prevent political or bureaucratic inefficiency as a result of which about 60 million tonnes of food bought by the government rotted in the open when PDS could lift only one million tonnes and the storage capacity of the Food Corporation of India is only 20 million tonnes.

Geographers with basic knowledge of computer software should participate increasingly in market research. Every university located in States with IT industries should have one or more staff members who have specialized in market research. Their earnings would, besides enriching them, make a handsome contribution to the expenses of running the departments. A number of graduate students should be encouraged to specialize in market research. They will find remunerative employment after getting their degrees.

References

UNDP, *Human Development Report, 2001: Making New Technologies Work for Human Development*—Statement on India, 2001.

Perroux F., '*La Notion de Poles de Croissance*', Economic Appliquee, 1955, and L'Economic due xxe, Siecle PUF 1961.

Boudeville, J.R., '*Problem of Regional Economic Planning*', Edinburgh at the University Press.

Lewis, J.P., '*Quiet Crisis in India—Economic Development and American Policy*', the Brookings Institution, Washington, 1962.

12

Architects of Economic Growth

(a) The Bureaucrat (1950—1990)

The bureaucrats had become the most important person responsible for the successful functioning of several public sector enterprises and for management of the growing economy and thus for accelerating growth of GDP in India from 3-4 per cent per annum during the 30 years 1960-80 to 5-7 per cent per annum during the 1990s. In the subsequent increase in growth rate private entrepreneurs have made a significant contribution, however.

In the former period, the Government of India made large investments in establishing five large integrated steel mills, mills for converting bauxite into alumina and metallic aluminium, irrigation-*cum*-hydropower-*cum*-flood control projects, thermal power plants, a heavy machine tool factory, a factory for making light machine tools, two more factories for making machines for generating and transmission of electricity, factory for making diesel driven electric locomotives, wagons and coaches for the railways and a factory for making penicillin and other basic pharmaceutical drugs.

After the discovery of oil off the coasts of Mumbai and Gujarat, large investments were made in exploration and development of the oil fields, refining of crude oil into motor spirit, diesel oil, kerosene and liquefied natural gas for cooking. Large investments were made also for constructing pipelines from the refineries to metropolitan cities which were the principal consuming centres.

Quasi-independent public sector companies were established for managing each of these investments. Thus the Oil and Natural Gas Commission was established for exploration and development of the oil fields and the Indian Oil Corporation was established for establishing refineries, constructing pipelines for taking petroleum products and gas from the refineries to the metropolitan cities and rural areas of high consumption. It has the responsibility for managing the network of dealers of its products. Technical and financial assistance for establishing these factories was obtained from the Soviet Union, Germany, and Britain and to a much smaller extent from Canada. Technical assistance was obtained also from the United States and Switzerland.

After establishing the enterprises the efforts of the Government of India have been concentrated on reducing the loss of the steel mills and other loss making enterprises, by over carrying deficiencies of management and infrastructure. The petroleum related enterprises were generating large profits from the beginning and the light machine tools factories started making profits after a few years, as did the factories which made machines for generation of transmission and distribution of electricity. However, the steel mills and heavy machine tools factories are still making losses.

During this period, the bureaucrats had great power. The managers of the plants came to the secretaries and joint secretaries of the Ministries of Steel, Power, Petroleum and Railways for funds needed to reduce the loss of the enterprises or for expansion of capacity or for modernization of the plants making locomotives, wagons or coaches for the railways, the changes needed in pricing of various products etc. The ministers in-charge of these ministries relied on their senior bureaucrats for advice on sanctioning additional funds or for changes in policies.

(b) Intellectual or Visionary Entrepreneur

The information technology industries have been the fastest expanding industries during the last three decades and are expected to maintain such growth during the next two decades.

The founders of the best companies such as WIPRO, Infosys and HCL are outstanding computer engineers. The non-resident Indians who have made millions in Silicon Valley in the U.S.A. are young men who have become affluent as successful owners of IT companies. They now want to set up these companies in their home states—Punjab, Karnataka, Tamil Nadu, Maharashtra, Gujarat and Delhi. Some of them are offering to share the cost of running their *alma maters*—Institutes of Science and Technology; Schools of Management and of universities such as Delhi to ensure that they maintain high standards.

Groups of outstanding physicians and surgeons have established a chain of world-class hospitals in several India's metropolitan cities—Chennai, Hyderabad and Delhi. These hospitals provide state-of-the-art medical and surgical treatment while generating profits. They are now thinking of expanding the chain to other metropolitan cities. The heads of the pharmaceutical companies that have developed drugs based on original research are also outstanding students of pharmaceutical science who have had brilliant ideas to develop these drugs. The companies that manufacture highly effective Ayurvedic drugs are managed by entrepreneurs who are highly knowledgeable in pharmacy. Other companies which succeed in this rapid growth industry would also be established by such pharmaceuticals.

The intellectual entrepreneurs or businessmen are likely to remain the dominant players in the information revolution that is sweeping the world. Unless they develop new service products, multinationals will hire them.

An enterprising entrepreneur was one of the first to establish world-class hotels in several metropolitan cities in India. In collaboration with hotel chains, a group of enterprising young men have established restaurants serving north Indian and south Indian food in several cities in neighbouring countries of South, South East Asia, East Africa, in the countries of the Gulf, and in the U.S.A. and Britain. There are several such restaurants in London, besides those in other cities in which there are large Indian or Pakistani communities. Not only their own nationals but also millions of Americans and British citizens visit these. Tandoori chicken and mutton curry and *nan, idli, dosa* are favourite exotic foods in these communities. The list can be increased.

The Tatas have set up world-class hotels in several metropolitan cities in India and in places visited by large numbers of foreign tourists. Their hotels were established in collaboration with foreign chains in some of the American and British cities.

Some of the Indian businessmen who have become multi-billionaires in Britain are offering to take over India's sinking public sector enterprises such as the air lines. One group has already bought India's largest company whose activities range from mining of coal to manufacture of liquor.

(c) Efficient Managers

Rapid and accelerating economic growth is dependent upon efficient managers. All the big industrial houses realize this. The Tatas were the first to realize this truth. Although the head of Tatas was always a relative of the founding family, the directors and managers of different enterprises in the group are people belonging to various communities and provinces.

They are chosen for the top posts on the basis of outstanding performance in various positions in the company that they have held since they joined it. The result of this policy has been that every company floated by the Tatas has become a major profit centre over the long-term. Any company that does not make the growth is sold off. Other leading companies Reliance, Godrej, Kirloskar and Bajaj Auto are following the same policy. Although the chairman continues to belong to the founding family and the heads of various enterprises controlled by the company are the most efficient managers. Multinationals such as Hindustan Lever and Indian Tobacco Company doing business in India for decades are following the same policy.

The heads of the biggest companies are sending their sons to the best business schools in the U.S.A. so that they know the essentials of good management and make profit-making new investments.

The best managers are paid high salaries and have perquisites such as a car and a furnished house both paid for by the company. Even after deduction of income tax they live extremely well. They too ensure that their sons attend the best business schools so that they become efficient managers. However, if the manager fails to deliver high and increasing profits through adverse market conditions, he may be summarily dismissed. Thus a trained and talented man may find himself out of a job in mid-career, unless he is picked up for a management position in another company.

Thus the job of an efficient manager carries high rewards and trust. If he is not successful and lucky he may end up using his skill to float an enterprise of his own and if he is really good, he must be successful in it. Otherwise he becomes a management consultant with a consulting firm or sets up his own agency to advise small but growing industrial enterprises.

Thus, almost all efficient managers are affluent through most of their working life and also after retirement. Indeed the habit of hard work is so strong among them that their periods of complete retirement are brief.

13

Sustainable Economic Development

(A) Development and Environment Preservation

Self-sustaining development means development that does not lead to environmental deterioration or depletion of natural resources of soil, water, vegetation or minerals. Consider two examples. The grasses in the pasture lands of semi-desert or desert areas of Rajasthan were self-re-generating as long as the number of livestock was not too large, so that grazing during the dry season was followed by restoration of the grass in the monsoon season. The thin cover of thorn forest in these areas checked wind erosion and allowed the pastures to regenerate themselves. Leaves of certain trees served as food for sheep and goats. However, increase in livestock numbers now exhausts the grass a few months after the rains so that migration of herds to pasture lands of eastern Rajasthan has become an annual phenomenon. Thousands of livestock die and the pastures are impoverished in years of drought, which come once or twice in three years.

Second, the use of new farm technologies for production of crops—consider production of wheat and rice in the areas with assured and regulated supplies of water provided by rainfall and/or irrigation sources, mainly surface wells fitted with electric pumps in Punjab. Yields per hectare of both crops are high with application of heavy doses of chemical fertilizers and pesticides. However, there have been increasingly frequent disturbing reports about a steep fall in the ground water table in some areas and increasing areas suffering from salinity as well as harmful effects on the health of the population due to use of chemical fertilizer to achieve high fertility from land.

Change in the Cropping Pattern

In Punjab, paddy is followed by wheat; in Haryana winter wheat is followed by cotton or oil seed; in western U.P. wheat is followed by oil seed. In U.P. farmers also grow sugarcane, which occupies the cropped area for almost a year or even more. These have become the normal cropping patterns. Earlier, in all these areas, wheat used to be followed by summer fallow or a fodder crop in the monsoon season. The latter provided food for livestock which were used for farm work. They provided also manure and fuel; the females provided milk which together with milk products (ghee, curds and butter) forms an important component of the food of the people. Besides certain fodder crops enriched the soil by fixing nitrogen from the air.

Apparently, the new cropping pattern is not self-sustaining and will need to be changed either by reversion to the old self-sustaining pattern or by evolving a new pattern. The farmers' income would not be lower if they reverted to the old pattern of wheat, rice or sugarcane followed by a period of fallow or growing fodder crops. The yield of wheat would increase and the livestock would enrich the soil. Crop production by the farmers and of milk, butter, cheese and *ghee* by livestock would also have a ready market in the cities. Farmers with small holdings could grow vegetables and produce milk for urban markets. They could also take up poultry keeping, to produce chicken and eggs for which there is a very large demand in Delhi and other cities in the region. Their income would not be lower than in the present cropping pattern which reduces fertility of the soil and water tables.

(B) Reducing Growth Rate of Population

Rapid growth of population is viewed as a problem which must be solved if sustainable economic development is to be achieved. Kerala and Goa where rates of increase of population are little more than replacement rates are considered ideals to be achieved by the other states within the next two decades. Here it is forgotten by the theorists that population is also a resource which produces up to a period its own means of subsistence.

The danger of too rapid growth of population was emphasized by the Census Commissioner of 1951. He wrote in his report that with all the known means of increasing food production, India could not sustain a population of more than 500 million, which at the 1941-51 growth rate of population of 12.5 per cent per decade would be reached by 1969-70. Thereafter, Malthusian checks, famine and pestilence would apply. The population in 1951 was 361 million. The population in 2001 is expected to exceed 1 billion—almost three times, the number in 1951. Production of cereals at the end of the 1990s was about 200 million tonnes, three and one-third times the production of about 60 million tonnes in the mid-1950s. Per capita consumption of cloth has doubled. In other words, the average Indian is somewhat better fed and better clothed now than he was in 1951.

Reducing growth rate of population is the basis of the national population policy which was adopted by the Government of India in January 2001. The chances of reducing it from the estimated current rate of increase of 1.9 per cent per annum are much greater now than ever before because birth rates in several large and relatively developed states—Tamil Nadu, Karnataka, Andhra Pradesh, Maharashtra and Gujarat are falling already. A recent study in a backward area of Rajasthan, a state with one of the highest rate of population growth shows that family planning, the very mention of which was anathema to rural women in 1961, is so acceptable now that an auxiliary nurse midwife whose main business is to advise on family planning is stationed permanently in a large village. A variety of contraceptives are being used by men and women and it is reported that 100 'operations' are performed (on women) every month. The principal reason for this change is that the survival rate of children is much higher now than in 1961. Women have access to clean water for bathing and drinking and to a private medical practitioner in a neighbouring village and a well-equipped hospital at the district headquarter, about five km from the village. They and their children are much cleaner and better nourished than they were in 1961. In case of any sickness they can go to the physician for ordinary ailments and to the hospital for serious sickness. Their children, most of the young boys and a few girls are cleaner because they go to school where the teachers insist that they come to school after a bath using soap and hair oil and in a uniform which is washed at least once in two days. In 1961 most of the girls never went to school because they were busy taking care of their younger siblings while the mothers worked in the fields. Now the mothers have less work in the fields because their fields are ploughed by tractors and there are machines for dehusking wheat and shelling sorghum and millets. Oilseeds grown in the village are sold to dealers in the market except for small quantities required for local consumption.

Most of the women and men interviewed by the researchers[1] said that they want no more than three children of which one must be a son; in 1961 this question could not be asked at all. Although the number of children borne by the women is higher than two or three (the state-wise average was 4.6 live births per woman in the 1980s) the desire for fewer children would be reflected in smaller number of live births in the state during the next decade which would in turn be reflected in a fall in the rate of growth of population in the forthcoming population censuses.

The field experience in this study only confirms the experience of Kerala and Goa in India and of countries in which there has been rapid decline in growth of population in the last two to three decades and shows that:

(i) With increase in literacy and female literacy in particular and decline in infant, child and maternal mortality, the rate of population growth declines. The principal reason for this is that with increase in survival rate of children, there is less desire among women to have more children.

(ii) Success in achieving a rapid decline in growth of population is through greater investment, in providing adequate and clean drinking water, facilities for primary health care and education to avoid common diseases and facilities for medical care in case of sickness and for education of both boys and girls.

(C) Political Development: Pluralist or Competitive Democracy

India selected the system of parliamentary democracy for governance. This means that different political parties compete for control of the government. The legislators are those selected by the people to represent them in the state legislatures and the national parliament. The Party which has the maximum number of legislators in these bodies forms the government and carries out development and other programmes indicated by it in its election manifesto. The opposition parties and independent members routinely ask the government to explain why it has adopted the economic, fiscal or political policies selected by it and why they should not be altered in the interest of the poor, for more rapid economic growth and for better relations with neighbouring and other countries. The government answers these questions and modifies those, criticism of which is justified. As soon as a party loses its majority, after an election or earlier at times it goes out of office and is succeeded by a party or a coalition of parties which can muster a majority of seats.

Although the majority of the electorate is poor and illiterate they have exercised their vote with ultimate care. They consider their vote a valuable gift of independence. Twelve elections have been fought since the Constitution of India was enforced in 1950, without too much violence. The thirteenth government which came to power in 2004 since independence was formed by a non-Congress Party coalition which finished its five year term. It is significant that it followed the same economic and fiscal policies that were introduced by the government formed by the Congress Party in 1991 in order to avert the balance of payments crisis that faced the country in that year. Certain important features of its foreign policy, i.e. relations with the neighbouring and other countries were not too different from those policies initiated by Pandit Nehru in 1952 or earlier. Thus, there is both continuity and change in policies and programmes in India's Parliamentary system of government.

A major weakness of our political development is increase in inefficiency and corruption among officials and workers in municipal, state and even some national services. It has affected also the legislators and ministers in many state governments.

Corruption has seeped into the system so much that Indians expect every politician and civil servant to be corrupt. It is rampant in all political parties and the electorate uses the only instrument it has—the vote—to unseat any party in power in the subsequent election; only the visibly non-corrupt governments (results of recent Gujarat state election is one such example) have been given a second chance. Corruption has also led to inefficiency in administration.

(D) Inefficiency and Corruption

(i) The Situation in the British Period

The British Government placed great emphasis on efficiency in all branches of public services and honesty among top ranking members of the All India and provincial civil, judicial and medical services.

The members of the Indian and the Provincial Civil Services who were responsible for maintaining law and order in the rural areas and the cities were expected to be efficient and honest. They were expected to deal competently with crisis situations such as communal riots or floods in the area of their responsibility.

They were paid handsomely and had besides perquisites, which enabled them to have a comfortable life style. Their pensions were also high enough to enable them to live comfortably in retirement. Officers who showed exceptional efficiency were knighted or given some Indian titles. Similar honours were conferred on wealthy businessmen and big landlords especially if they had taken some steps for benefit of the public or helped the British to recruit men for the armed forces. This practice ensured their loyalty to the government and gave them an incentive to do some work such as financing maintenance of a charitable hospital or a secondary school or college.

Highly successful lawyers were promoted as judges of the High Courts. One of them ended his career as Chief Justice of the Supreme Court of India.

Doctors in the provincial medical service were paid salaries which enabled them to have a comfortable life style. In addition, they were allowed private practice without prejudice to their duties in the hospitals to which they were attached. The same was true of members of the subordinate medical service who manned mini-hospitals or dispensaries in large villages. The British realized that they could augment their income by private practice so they allowed it. The professors and lecturers in colleges of humanities and sciences, medicine, engineering and other services were also paid well enough not to need to augment their incomes by private work. They too were honoured if they made major contributions to increasing efficiency in their service or by their research.

India had inherited such services from the British. The Prime Minister, Pandit Nehru, the Home Minister, Sardar Patel, the Finance Minister and the Defence Minister relied on their advice in formulation and implementation of their policies. Integration of princely states with the Indian Union, the most important achievement of Sardar Patel was achieved with assistance from highly competent civil servants. He used also their experience in restoring peace and order in Punjab, Delhi and western Uttar Pradesh after the communal riots of 1947-48 during which tens of thousands died and hundreds of thousands were injured.

Pandit Nehru was his own Foreign Minister. But the top officers in his ministry were those who had worked in the political affairs department of the British Government or were senior ICS officers. Pandit Nehru appointed several of them as Ambassadors or High Commissioners in European countries and others in which India had established its embassies and high commissions.

The Finance Minister of India during 1950-58 Mr. C.D. Deshmukh, a distinguished civil servant himself appointed the most competent and experienced officers in important posts in his ministry and as Governor of the Reserve Bank of India. Furthermore, the Governors, if not working already in the bank had to be of such calibre as would enjoy the confidence of the deputy governors and other senior officers of the bank.

This policy continues till today. The governor is an eminent economist or an experienced banker. He does carry out the policies initiated by the

Finance Minister but at the same time warns him against the dangers of any measures taken in response to political demands. The governor being India's representative in the IMF, the World Bank and other international financial institutions has to enjoy also the confidence of these organizations.

The Defence Minister similarly followed implicitly the advice of the secretaries of defence and the Chief of the three armed forces in all areas relating to the defense of the country. Going against their advice led to disastrous results as evidenced by the ignominious defeat of the Indian forces by the Chinese in October-November 1962.

(ii) The Situation after Independence

The emoluments of the ICS, the Indian Police Service and other all India services were reduced in practice after independence. Although their nominal salaries remained the same its purchasing power declined steeply due to inflation during Second World War. However, besides the emoluments, a highly subsidized bungalow in New Delhi and three to four servants provided free were enough to enable them to have a comfortable life style. Their pensions were also adequate to enable them to maintain the same life style after retirement. Many became directors of large companies, which gave them additional income.

(iii) Deterioration—1962 to-date

The ICS (Indian Civil Service) and other services established by the British were succeeded after independence by the Indian Administrative Service, the Indian Foreign Service, the Indian Police Service and other central services which followed their predecessors of the British period. With this change, the emoluments and other perquisites of the officers suffered a drastic decline. However, even in the 1950s, the emoluments were high enough to attract the best graduates of Indian universities. The members of the IAS had to work under ministers who did not put implicit faith in their advice. The position is so bad now that in several states most of the IAS officers prefer to work in the Central Government and the secretariats of states to working as Collectors or Commissioners. Today, a Collector who does not bend the rules to satisfy a minister or an influential MLA may find himself transferred to a difficult district. In many states such as Uttar Pradesh, the average duration of a stay of the Collector in a district is less than six months, instead of the prescribed two to three years. How any Collector can establish effective contact with the rural people is hard to imagine.

The overbearing attitude of Chief Ministers and most important ministers in government of several large states has led to a progressive decline in the quality and efficiency of the civil services. Today (2002) the situation is so bad that the best graduates of Indian universities prefer to become doctors, engineers, or employees of nationalized or foreign banks, officers in Indian companies such as the Tatas and Reliance or of multinationals such as Hindustan Lever or the Indian Tobacco Company to joining the IAS. The salaries and emoluments are far higher in the companies than in the IAS. Security of service is as much as in the IAS and outstanding work is rewarded by quick promotions. Accepting a teaching or research position in good universities such as Delhi, Jawaharlal Nehru, and Chennai is also preferred to joining the IAS or other services. There is security of service for a lecturer or a professor in these universities, so that one can raise one's family without being disturbed by the whims of the ministers. Most good professors spend a year or more teaching in American or Australian Universities, where they get high salaries. At the other extreme, a collector who incurs the displeasure of the Chief Minister or even an influential local MLA for not bending the rules to suit his interests may find himself transferred to a most undesirable district in the state in which he is working.

The Union Public Service Commission reports routinely in its annual reports about decline in the quality of the candidates that appear in the annual examinations for selection of recruits for these services. Today the top-level advisers of the Prime Minister are those drawn from various fields including politics. They are not from the Indian Administrative Service. The Home Minister still depends upon the advice of the bureaucrats recruited from the Indian Administrative Service. At the other extreme the position in the Defence Ministry is so bad that the chiefs of the armed forces routinely protest about advancement to top position in the services of people who are junior to those whose claims have been unjustly overlooked. They complain also that the defence minister relies more on the advice of the defence secretary, a civilian, than to them.

Successive Railway Ministers have routinely announced opening of new railway lines which are uneconomic, neglecting the expenditures for maintenance of the railway track, supply of wagons, and conversion of single track railways to double track and appropriate maintenance of those already constructed. The accidents resulting from such neglect are routinely put down to human error. The policy is then changed and a belated and inadequate effort is put into essential maintenance.

(iv) Main Causes of Deterioration

One of the main causes of corruption in the political executives is that the practice of duly recording contributions to the election expenses of political parties by companies was abandoned in 1969 for political expediency and has not been restored. The result is that moneys for fighting elections are obtained from various sources—companies, big businessmen and even smugglers and other criminals. After having financed the elections of various parties and of the ministers these criminals have no hesitation in continuing their criminal activities. The Chief Minister of one large state has been in and out of jail during the last 3 years because there are proved charges of corruption against him. However, when in jail he runs the administration through his wife who has been elected as the Chief Minister. His following among the poor people of the state is so large that every time he is sent to jail his followers start riots.

A former Chief Minister of another large state has been convicted of massive corruption. However her political following is so large that every time her case came up for trial in the courts, her followers started a riot which was curbed with some difficulty.

Both the Chief Ministers are secure in their positions;[2] there is no strong movement for their resignation. On the other hand there is great instability among the chief ministers of U.P. which is one of the most inefficiently administered states in India.

Corruption in some departments of the Central Government, such as Income Tax and Excise, and of State Governments, such as sales tax is so widespread that all officers from the Inspectors to the Assistant Commissioners or even many Commissioners are presumed to be corrupt. The lowest officers in these departments can line their pockets without any fear of being persecuted by their superiors. The position is worse among employees of the municipal bodies and state electricity boards which supply electricity to both urban and rural areas. Under-payment or non-payment of municipal taxes or not attending to their duties for days together by the lowest staff such as sanitation workers is common. They do it because they have the protection of influential councillors. Many councillors connive with the staff to permit encroachment on municipal lands by the slum dwellers. Theft of electricity by the slum dwellers as also by high income households, by farmers who use electric motors on surface wells is so great that most of the state electricity boards incur large losses every year. As a result, privatization of transmission and distribution of electricity is being actively considered by the Central Government. The argument is that the companies which take over the responsibility for transmission and distribution of electricity will curb theft in order to earn an adequate return on their investment. Privatization of other municipal services such as water supply and waste disposal is also being advocated for the same reason.

Competent, well-paid, well-trained and uncorrupted administrative and technical services are essential for efficiency in government and avoidance of serious errors of policy and programme formulation and implementation.

(v) Movement for Change

The Indian electorate can tolerate a degree of corruption but would not tolerate when it goes beyond a limit. The government headed by Mr. Rajiv Gandhi (1984-89) was forced to resign because there were credible charges of corruption against it. It was followed by two unstable coalitions. The government headed by Mr. P.V. Narsimha Rao which lasted for five years, 1991-96, made sweeping changes in economic and fiscal policies as a result of which growth of GDP went up from 3-4 per cent per annum to 5-7 per cent p.a. India's balance of payments deficit was wiped out and has not been negative since then. But he lost the election in 1996 because there were credible charges of corruption against him and some of his ministers. They are being tried in courts and some of them have been convicted by a special judge.

The present government (NDA) which followed two unstable coalitions expects to complete its five-year tenure of office, because the Prime Minister and several other senior ministers in the cabinet are known to be scrupulously honest and efficient.

A determined Election Commissioner decided about six years ago to ensure that there was minimum of violence in the election process. As a result, there has been little violence in the three elections to Parliament and significant reduction in violence in elections to many states legislatures held since 1996.

(vi) Ground Swell for Efficiency

The desire of the Indian electorate for honesty in government has been mentioned above. There is a similar keen desire for efficiency at the state level. Among the most popular chief ministers today are of Andhra Pradesh, Karnataka and Delhi. They may not all be honest but they are making determined efforts for economic development of their states. The Chief Ministers of Andhra Pradesh, Tamil Nadu and Karnataka are in competition to provide the most suitable infrastructure for information technology industries which are experiencing such rapid growth in India that major exports of computer software services to the U.S.A. and Europe make a major contribution to Indian export earnings. The Chief Minister of Haryana similarly, is making all out efforts to attract information technology and various consumer durable industries and offices of multinationals to the two satellite towns of Delhi—Gurgaon and Faridabad.

The Chief Ministers of Maharashtra and Gujarat are doing their best to preserve the primacy of their states in industry. Besides there are no credible charges of corruption against any of these chief ministers. The Chief Minister of Andhra Pradesh, a computer buff has established a practice of receiving information everyday about events in the districts from all collectors. As a result of his system of communications, government could provide relief and ensure rehabilitation of the thousands of people who were affected by floods during a cyclone earlier this year (2000) within a week. As a result loss of life and property was reduced to the minimum. On the other hand, the Government of Orissa couldn't provide such relief or arrange rehabilitation of the cyclone-hit people for several months; thousands died and many thousands remained homeless for months.

The Chief Minister of Punjab, a farmer himself, has persuaded or literally forced the Central Government to pay prices for wheat and rice which would provide to the farmers in his state an adequate income besides an adequate return on their investment. Due to the joint efforts of the Chief Ministers of Punjab and Haryana the environment of Chandigarh is attractive enough for it to be a most suitable location for two most rapidly growing industries—information technology and manufacture of pharmaceutical drugs.

The Chief Minister of West Bengal during 1970-1990, a wealthy barrister before he joined politics, carried out land reforms, viz. abolition of *zamindari* which had been resisted by the zamindars for three decades after independence. His government, led by the Communist Party of India has been in office for almost three decades and is secure. The principal reason for this is that the peasants vote for him because the government has conferred on them full and heritable rights in lands that they cultivate. Output of rice, the main food crop has doubled after the reform and that of jute; the main cash crop has also increased. The government brought peace to the industry sector of Calcutta (Kolkata) and Howrah which had been so badly affected by the activity of militant trade unions, that most of the leading industrialists shifted their factories to Maharashtra or Tamil Nadu. Although the industries have not come back, despite the strenuous efforts of his government to woo the industrialists, the flight of capital from Kolkata and Howrah has stopped. Most important, the civil servants can do their job efficiently without fear of incurring the wrath of the chief ministers or other ministers.

Respect for efficiency and honesty of senior officers is being slowly restored after three decades of decline in it. Increase in their emoluments and other perquisites, so that they can have a comfortable lifestyle without resort to corruption, is a matter of time. The electorate realizes that a certain degree of corruption among the ministers is inescapable. But there is a keen desire for honesty and efficiency among government officers. The elections in Punjab earlier this year (2001) replaced an unpopular government which was perceived as dishonest with a Congress Chief Minister whose main election issue was corruption in Badal led Akali Dal Government. The electorate of Tamil Nadu has similarly dismissed a corrupt and inefficient government and replaced it with one chief minister who is not scrupulously honest but is efficient and is assisting rapid economic development in the state.[3]

(E) Accessibility of Government

The government was accessible to the common people in some ways during British rule. The Collector, the district officer regularly toured his district in the cool season and listened to the grievances of the peasants in order to redress them. He was accessible also to the big landlords and businessmen and professionals such as physicians and surgeons and conferred honors on them in order to retain their loyalty. Such accessibility had been greatly reduced for some years after independence, but it has been restored after the inauguration of the Community Development Programme. The Block Development Officers toured their CD blocks regularly listened to the demands of the rural people and urged them to contribute their labour and locally available materials for construction of much needed facilities such as approach roads, improving water supply sources and construction of buildings for primary and secondary schools. They conveyed also to the State Governments any complaints that the rural people had about functioning of the government. However, there is not enough contact between the collector and the rural people. The collectors are so busy with other duties that they do not have the time to visit most of the villages in their districts.

In the army, similarly the British captain of a regiment participated regularly in the games of the soldiers and had tea with them after the games. Once a month he dined with them. This contact created a bond between the officers and the men which induced the men to obey the orders of the captain implicitly even if it meant dying in battle. The men who had fought valiantly during a battle were given monetary rewards and widows of those who had died were given a pension for life which was enough to meet their living expenses. Their sons were given first preference in joining army. Such contact has been greatly reduced after independence because Indian officers do not establish the *bon home* with their men that the British officers did.

Government should be accessible to the people through their elected representatives. Every legislator (member of the state assembly or Parliament) is visited regularly by his constituents who present to him grievances and seek his intervention with local officials to remove them and if not to request the government to redress them. The legislators convey the demands to the ministers and try to ensure that these are met.

There is less contact between the government and the people in the urban areas particularly in large metropolitan cities. The population of the cities is too large for the municipal committees to try to listen to the needs and problems of the people, particularly the poor. The government becomes accessible to the people only in a crisis such as outbreak of an epidemic disease or if there is a serious shortage of water, electricity or food grains, sugar, kerosene which are distributed through the public distribution system. However, in order to avoid such crisis, it is essential to establish regular contact between the government and the people of metropolitan cities.

This can be done through neighbourhood welfare associations, whose presidents and secretaries should have monthly meetings with officials and engineers that are responsible for providing electricity and water, public transport (such as buses), removal of solid and liquid wastes and other municipal services. In these meetings they should convey to the officials their difficulties so that they can be quickly removed.

(F) Respect for Human Rights

The Indian administration has not been responsive to human rights for a long time. The British administrators, although trained in the liberal traditions of Oxford and Cambridge thought nothing of throwing thousands of freedom fighters in jails. Death or serious injury in police custody was also overlooked many a time. The position is not much better today. The law and order situation in states like Bihar and the Telengana regions of Andhra Pradesh is chaotic. Burning of villages of the scheduled castes and murder of their leaders by armed gangs of high castes is common. In Telengana villages, similarly burning of villages of the scheduled castes and killing of particularly oppressive landlords by the gangs of the scheduled castes are common. Murder or kidnapping of leaders of one gang of criminals by members of a rival gang is routine in Mumbai and the police is powerless to stop it.

The British maintained law and order at all costs. This is no longer possible now as mentioned above. For the situation to improve, it is essential first that all those against whom there are charges of any serious crime, such as murder, or rape should be debarred from contesting elections to the state legislatures or Parliament or from holding any other elective office. Second, any police officer against whom there are charges of causing death or serious injury to any person in judicial custody or overlooking such a death should be immediately suspended and then tried like any other criminal. Officers and legislators against whom there are such charges must resign because of unrelenting criticism against their continuance in the government. They should be allowed to resume their official positions only after they have been acquitted by the courts. A government like that of Orissa, in which hundreds died due to lack of food or shelter for weeks after the cyclone in 1998 due to its inefficiency, should be dismissed by the President. These and similar other steps should be taken as a matter of course so that the State Governments have greater respect for human rights.

(G) An Independent Judiciary

The judiciary was not independent during the British period. Despite promises to the contrary the courts assisted in implementation of policies of the administration. During the Quit India Movement of 1942, thousands including the top most leaders of the Congress Party were sent to jail without trial and remained there till the duration of Second World War.

Independence of the judiciary is a basic principal of the Constitution of India. All citizens of India have a right to fair trial, if accused of any crime. This position continued till the Emergency which lasted between 1974 and 1977. Hundreds were put in jails without trial. Torture of those in jails was common. Most of those guilty of such crimes were not convicted after the emergency ended. However, after the emergency the Supreme Court and the High Courts in most of the important states have regained their independence. The courts routinely blame the governments for wilful neglect or inefficiency in performance of some of their essential functions. In Delhi, public interest petitions are filed by concerned citizens to the Supreme Court or the High Court for the failure of the state electricity or water supply boards to guarantee uninterrupted supplies of electricity and water. The Supreme Court or the High Courts pass strictures against them and order them to take action to improve performance.

Earlier this year the Supreme Court ordered the Delhi Transport Authority to remove all two-wheeler, three-wheeler and four-wheeler vehicles which were more than eight years old from Delhi's roads in order to reduce pollution of air in Delhi. These vehicles have gone off the roads despite two strikes by the owners or operators of these. Pollution of air in Delhi is visibly less. During the two month (October-November 2000) the Supreme Court has passed an order to raise the height of the Sardar Sarovar Dam by five metres and asked the states to ensure resettlement of the persons whose homes will be submerged without delay. Madhya Pradesh and other states are taking action accordingly. Through another order, the court has asked the governments of Karnataka and Tamil Nadu to desist from freeing about 50 TADA accused sheltered by forest brigand Veerappan in exchange for release of the actor Rajkumar. The states have complied. Meanwhile, Rajkumar has been released. Regaining of its independence by the Supreme Court and High Courts in several other states is a most hopeful development in the process of India's development of a vibrant democracy.

Notes

1. Three senior researchers and Kamla Nath, wife of the author visited the three villages of Sawai Madhopur district in January 2000 to capture the economic and social changes studied by the author in 1961 when he was posted as Collector of the district.
2. She was displaced by her opponents but came back to power in spite of charges against her still to be proved or disproved.
3. Somehow the presumably corrupt Chief Minister has returned to power again in 2003.

14

Goals and Strategies of Development 2000-2020

I. Goals

There should be no major change in the most important goals of development, viz. eradication of poverty, illiteracy and disease and reducing to the extent possible the imbalances that have developed among regions and various economic groups of society.

During the last 50 years the rate of growth of gross domestic product has increased progressively from an average of 3-4 per cent per annum during 1960-80 to 5-7 per cent per annum in the 1990s. After allowing for increase in population of about 2 per cent per annum, this means an increase in GDP per capita from 1-2 per cent per annum to 3-4 per cent per annum. Economic policies should be so designed that the latter rate is maintained and if possible increased in the next two decades[1] emphasis should be on poverty elimination rather than raising the GDP. Increase in GDP will not ensure improvement of the poor sections. The goals of development mentioned above cannot be achieved if this condition is not fulfilled.

The principal regional imbalance is in employment and income of the farmers and agricultural labourers in the nearly 35 per cent of the cropland that has assured and controlled water supply provided by an adequate and dependable rainfall and/or irrigation. These areas contribute most of the output of food grains (wheat and rice), sugar, cotton, jute, tea, coffee and spices. Both farmers and agricultural labourers have employment for most of the year and their incomes and levels of living are far higher than those in the areas which do not have these advantages. The latter, which contribute almost 65 per cent of the cropland, contribute much less than this percentage to agricultural output. Despite all the measures the regional imbalance between income and employment for farmers and agricultural workers in the areas having assured water supply provided by dependable rainfall and those which do not have this advantage shall remain. This should be accepted and the measures mentioned earlier in this section should be taken to provide productive work in such areas. Most of the poor are concentrated in the following areas:

(i) The hilly, forested areas inhabited mainly by tribal people in Madhya Pradesh, in Jharkhand region of Bihar, inland Orissa and small areas in West Bengal, the Telengana region of Andhra Pradesh, Maharashtra, Gujarat and Rajasthan.

(ii) The mountainous areas of Uttrakhand, Himachal Pradesh and parts of Jammu and Kashmir and some of the hill states of the north east.

(iii) The drought-prone areas of peninsular U.P. (south west U.P.), Madhya Pradesh, Saurashtra and Kutch in Gujarat, a large part of Maharashtra, the Telengana region of Andhra Pradesh and inland areas of Karnataka and Tamil Nadu.

(iv) The desert and semi-desert areas of western Rajasthan.

(v) The plains of central and eastern U.P., Bihar, parts of West Bengal and coastal Orissa.

The Jharkhand area of Bihar and the adjoining areas of West Bengal, inland Orissa and Madhya Pradesh are rich in mineral, power and forest resources. There are a number of large industrial units, owned principally by the Government of India but also by private entrepreneurs. Tribal youth could be educated and trained to work in the industrial units as skilled, semi-skilled or white-collar workers. A major effort must be made in all the areas mentioned to increase agricultural output by adoption of suitable improved agricultural practices. Soil conservation works must be undertaken to prevent loss of fertility by wind and water erosion. Re-forestation to restore the greatly depleted forest resource would provide the tribal and non-tribal people with fuel, fodder, medicinal herbs and food.

In the other areas mentioned above, agricultural output could be increased slowly by evolving varieties of seeds of food grains (rice and coarse grains) and oil seeds that give higher yields than those sown by the farmers at present. In parts of U.P. and Bihar large areas of inherently fertile soil get covered every year by deposits of coarse sand, boulders and silt by monsoon floods. The fertility of land can be restored by flood control and reclamation of land by suitable measures financed by the State and Central Governments. A beginning should be made by reforestation on the hill slopes that are continually eroded in the monsoon because of lack of forest cover.

The present government of West Bengal has improved the productivity of such lands by controlled measures and by providing loans and subsidies to farmers for installation of electric motors on irrigation wells.

Food-for-work programmes must be undertaken in all these areas from time to time to avert starvation in years when the rains fail. These programmes can be used also as an educational tool. Balanced food (cereals, pulses, sugar, cooking oil and powdered milk) should be given to the workers along with instructions on the principles of nutrition and child care to reduce the incidence of epidemic diseases among the recipients. The Food Corporation of India has surplus food grains and their problem is one of maintenance of the stored grains. The maintenance cost is more than its total value. So, it will be better to distribute these food grains to the poor section at subsidized rates and not to sell it to foreign countries at prices lower than the cost, as the government has decided to do. Or government can start the food-for-work programme to dispose of the surplus grains. In this way food prices can be raised to some satisfactory level and the continuing scenario of the suicides of farmers can be averted. The Government of India and of various states have implemented successfully for almost 50 years programmes aimed at assuring employment and reasonable earnings to handloom weavers and handicraft workers. These programmes will need to be continued. Emphasis in the programmes for assistance to handicraft workers should be on those who manufacture goods, a proportion of which is exported. Carpet weaving around Mirzapur, the manufacture of decorative brassware in Moradabad and weaving of silk saris and other garments for festive occasions in a suburb of Varanasi in U.P., in Kanchipuram in Tamil Nadu and in various other temple towns in the south provide examples. Use of child labour in carpet weaving should be banned so that the products have a large export market. Furthermore, the workers should be given higher wages and trained to use modern high productivity looms and modern designs to make the products more acceptable in both domestic and foreign markets. Government should provide market facilities to the organized sector and the entry of multinationals should be checked in the household and small-scale industries, as our small-scale industries cannot stand before MNCs in the market.

In most of the handicraft industries, the Governments of India and of the states have encouraged formation of cooperatives which procure raw materials, provide training to workers to improve productivity, modernize designs and market products. Experiences of cooperatives have been disappointing in India. There is huge corruption among the cooperatives. If we have to continue with cooperatives, transparency must be ensured.

Role of Producers' Cooperatives

Milk producers' cooperatives organized by the National Dairy Development Board on the pattern of Amul in Gujarat are supplying most of the milk used in metropolitan cities—Mumbai, Delhi, Hyderabad, Ludhiana, Chandigarh and cities in Gujarat. They provide year round employment to men and wives of milk producers most of whom are small farmers with bare subsistence holdings and contribute a significant proportion to their income. Government has made a deal with Denmark to import milk, which will be sold in India at a price lower than the cost of the Indian milk production. It will result in the destruction of Indian dairying. Hence this trend must be checked.

Producers' cooperatives have proved to be the best organizations for providing fruit, vegetables and poultry products for the cities. In the areas of production, they organize supplies of fertilizers and pesticides to the growers needed to increase yield among fruit and vegetables and vaccines to poultry farmers to immunize the birds against diseases. They also organize shipment of products to markets in order to obtain the best prices for the producers. The cooperatives in areas around Nasik in Maharashtra, which supply onions and other vegetables, crate them for supply to Indian cities and for export to countries of the Gulf, are rich and have constructed large storage facilities in order to supply the markets throughout the year.

A large proportion of the country's sugar is produced by sugarcane growers' cooperatives in valleys irrigated by small streams in Maharashtra and rivers in Andhra Pradesh and south Karnataka. In Maharashtra, these cooperatives also own sugar mills. Their members are affluent enough to dominate the politics of Maharashtra. Producers' Cooperatives should be organized wherever possible.

Role of Non-governmental Organizations/Civil Society

Non-governmental organizations such as *Sewa* in Ahmedabad, which has implemented successfully an employment generation programme for poor women for some decades, should be provided financial assistance to encourage them to expand their activities. There is a need for some statistical data of the performance of *Sewa*. There are several other such organizations in different parts of the country. They should be given funds to expand their activities. Other non-governmental organizations have been active in preventing crime and violence against women. They should also be assisted, after due evaluation of their motives and sources of finance. Financial assistance by foreign governments should be scrutinized in order to ensure that their motivation is genuine.

Increased Importance of Business and Industry

Whereas agriculture contributed more than half of the GDP in the 1950s, 75 per cent of the output was produced in industries and modern services by the mid-1990s. The latter proportion will increase progressively in the next two decades. This is because while agriculture output would increase by a maximum of 3-4 per cent per annum, output in industries and modern services would increase 6-8 per cent per annum or faster.

Consistent with this trend is the increased influence of organizations of industrialists or associations of modern service providers which have a strong influence on policies of the present government. The Federation of Indian Chambers of Commerce and Industry, the Confederation of Indian Industries, chambers of business and industries in several states, associations of tourist operators and of hotel owners are examples. These associations have a strong influence on the present government's policies for encouraging growth of industries and services. This influence is bound to grow. While the reform of economic policies suggested by the World Bank and IMF must be implemented by the government to improve modern service and competitiveness of modern industries, the interests of the consumers has to be guarded.

The organizations of affluent farmers which produce most of the wheat, rice, sugarcane, high quality cotton and groundnut have a strong influence on procurement prices fixed by the Government of India. They are so strong in pressing for protection of their incomes that government has to placate them regardless of the effect that they have had on the consumers' cost of living. This cannot continue for too long, however. The government succumbing to the pressure of farmers' lobbies is being widely criticized. It is unlikely that the body will have a lasting impact on government policies, this criticism will increase and the government will have to pay economic prices in the interest of the consumers.

Since the information technology industries have experienced most rapid growth during the last two decades, the principal producers of services such as telecommunications have a strong influence on government policies. Such influence is bound to remain high during the next two decades. The government should guard the interest of small and marginal farmers. After GATT, farmers cannot compete with the farming of big business companies and of MNCs of developed countries which are all getting very high subsidies from their respective governments.

The heads of the most progressive information technology companies make their agreements for export of IT services in the USA and Western Europe first and ask for approval of the government later, if necessary.

Corruption

One negative social change is increase in monetary corruption by bureaucrats, who deal with the public—whether in the departments that provide electricity, water and other services or medical care in hospitals and health centres opened by the government in cities, and in the dispensaries and primary health centres in block/*taluka* headquarter towns. This must be reduced to the maximum extent—Government hospitals are the only medical care facilities that are open to the rural and urban poor. Private charitable organizations cannot be expected to assume this role. They can provide at most a small percentage of the needs. Many of the development programmes mentioned earlier are not implemented successfully because most of the funds provided for them are in fact pocketed by the MPs or MLAs of the areas and the district and lower level officials responsible for implementation of these programmes. *Panchayati Raj* institutions which should ensure proper utilization of funds are weak and are not allowed to become stronger. As a result, the poor are frustrated and lose confidence in the ability of the government to provide them with needed assistance. Finally, land reforms which confer ownership rights in land on actual tillers have been introduced in most parts of the country, mostly on paper and have not been implemented in practice.

It is only in crises such as an outbreak of an epidemic disease in a city or area that governments mobilize efforts to step in. However, even in crises like floods caused by excessive monsoon rains in Assam, parts of West Bengal, Bihar or U.P. and coastal areas of Orissa, Andhra Pradesh, and Tamil Nadu when millions lose their homes and are stranded for weeks, hundreds die and thousands of cattle die, funds for relief work sanctioned by the Central Government are not utilized quickly for rehabilitation of the affected people. Furthermore, there is much leakage in utilization of funds. It is only in the relatively rich areas mentioned in Section II that these organizations are strong enough to ensure proper utilization of these funds. Thus the imbalance between the relatively developed and the poor and backward regions increases.

Accordingly, a most urgent task is to mobilize public opinion in both rural and urban areas to check corruption so that the effects of government programmes effectively reach the most deserving.

II. Self-Sustaining Economic Growth: The Prospect 2000-2020

If despite adverse foreign economic conditions, the country can maintain a GDP growth rate of 5-6 per cent per annum for several years in the current decade, it will be considered to have reached self-sustaining economic growth. The principal influences contributing to it will be:

(a) Information Technology Industries

Further growth of information technology industries for export and use in manufacturing industries and modern services will contribute to India's foreign exchange earnings, while use of these techniques in manufacturing industries within India will improve the quality of the products, reduce their prices and make them more competitive in international markets. The growth of pharmaceutical drug industries based on original research, some based on principles of Ayurveda (the ancient Indian system of medicine), also will make a significant contribution to increase export earnings if the drugs are effective in the treatment of diseases of the aged, or of women and children. There is a very large demand for such drugs in the developed countries and also in India.

(b) Public Sector Enterprises

A more important influence will be reduction in losses of public sector enterprises which are loss making such as steel plants, domestic and international airlines and hotels. The government has an active programme of finding strategic partners who will take over shares in these enterprises and make them profitable by better management and infusion of much needed funds to buy additional machines and spare parts and offering surplus staff voluntary retirement packages. There is strong opposition to such dis-investment at present but it is bound to reduce progressively. On the other hand profit making public enterprises should be given additional funds to enable them to grow for domestic and international markets. Two groups of hotel operators—the Taj and the Oberois—are already strong enough to open profit making hotels in various cities and places of tourist interest in India. They have established also, in collaboration with international hotel operators or by themselves profit making hotels in the U.S.A. and in developing countries of South Asia and Africa.

(c) Banking and Insurance

A number of nationalized banks such as the State Bank of India, the Punjab National Bank and the Bank of Baroda have already become profit making. They will progressively reduce their non-performing assets (bad debts) and staff and reduce costs by closing down branches in villages and small towns which are running at a loss.

The bonds of various derivation issued by these banks are making a major contribution to mobilizing small savings for economic growth. Similarly, the Unit Trust of India has become profit making after a period. Since the dividends earned by investing in these units are tax exempt up to a certain limit, they will make a major contribution to mobilizing domestic savings, which can be used for financing infrastructures. Efficiency could be increased progressively so that they can mobilize more funds. Life Insurance Corporation should be encouraged to enter areas like health insurance by itself or in partnership with well-established companies abroad. The consumer's interests will be served and part of the large profits in this area will accrue to a domestic company. Similarly the General Insurance Corporation should in collaboration with reputed foreign companies enter areas such as marine insurance, which it has avoided so far.

The voluntary retirement packages being offered by the banks and which have proved very popular have two benefits. Productivity per worker employed in the banks will increase so that they become more efficient and can compete with foreign banks, which are making large profits. The employees who retire are generally efficient managers and those with good knowledge of banking. These will start their own new banking financial institutions such as chit funds to mobilize savings of the poor. They could also with the help of the loans given by the banks start successful industrial enterprises.

The dollar bonds of the State Bank of India are mobilizing savings of non-resident Indians. The bonds of various duration issued by it and other banks, are making a major contribution to mobilizing small savings for economic growth.

(d) Infrastructure Development

The Maharashtra and Gujarat Governments which are among the most developed states in India have already constructed 4 and 6-lane expressways on stretches of roads along which traffic is heavy. The two governments have also developed small ports which are being used for developing 'special enterprise zones (SEZs) in which multinationals and non-resident Indians who have industrial or trading enterprises abroad can establish manufacturing facilities. The Mittals, an Indian group based in Britain, which has acquired control of a large number of steel plants round the world and made them profitable by improving management should be encouraged to take over management of loss making steel plants so that their losses can be progressively eliminated and they become profit making.

(e) Agricultural Production and Growth

Agricultural output could continue to increase by 3-4 per cent per annum. Cereal production can be increased in rain-fed areas in which potentially fertile lands are rendered infertile because they are covered every year by coarse sand and boulders brought down by monsoon floods. This can be avoided by afforestation on the hill slopes and reclamation of lands in the plains by farmers with financial assistance from the State Governments. Punjab Sikhs have developed highly productive farms which produce rice and wheat by reclaiming some of these areas in the sub-mountainous area of western U.P. The small holders of the lands should be provided loans for reclamation of land, buying livestock and improved seed for cultivation. The Government of West Bengal has reclaimed large areas of such lands by land reforms to make actual farmers owner of the lands and controlling floods through check dams and giving loans to farmers to buy improved seed and bullocks, if needed. The Government of U.P. and of Bihar can do the same. The new states of Uttrakhand and Jharkhand in which there are large numbers of educated and skilled people could do the same, thus ending the food deficit of these states.

Encouraging production of milk, vegetables and poultry and eggs in areas which produce most of the cereals in the country will make a further contribution to increase in agriculture output. Production of fruit and vegetables can be increased also in areas which already produce these by giving loans to the producers' co-operatives to establish cold storage facilities, arranging marketing of products and for establishing facilities for processing fruit and vegetables.

(f) Education and Skill Formation

Education and skill formation among men and young women will enable the tribal youth of Jharkhand to take up jobs of white-collar workers and skilled workers in the numerous industrial units which are at present held by outsiders. The list could be extended but the thrust of the argument is clear from the above notes.

Conclusion

The management of loss making public sector enterprises such as the steel plants should be entrusted to non-resident Indian groups like the Mittals, which has a proven record of making loss making steel mills profitable by using their capital and expertise. The loss making modern service enterprises such as Air India, Indian Airlines and hotels should be entrusted to Indian multinationals or partners in Indian and foreign companies which have a proven record of turning around loss making enterprises like the Tata Singapore Airlines consortium. The management of loss making public sector hotels could be entrusted to the Taj and Oberoi groups of hotel operators which are operating hotels in various cities and places of tourist interest in India and in collaboration with foreign multinationals in various cities in Britain and the U.S.A.

On the other hand, profit making public sector enterprises such as Hindustan Machine Tools and Bharat Heavy Electricals should be given all facilities especially allowing expansion in their operations within India and in neighbouring countries as far as possible.

All these steps and related others will contribute to India attaining self-sustaining economic growth. Reference has been made already to increasing production of cereals in the irrigated lands which are inherently fertile but are rendered unproductive by deposits of coarse sand and boulders in the monsoon. Two examples have been given to illustrate this fact.

Increase in production of protective foods—milk, vegetables, fruit, chicken and eggs and meat—will contribute to further increase in agricultural production. Producers' cooperatives or individual small holders which produce and market these products successfully should be enabled to expand their operations.

Industrial production can be increased by undertaking some of the steps mentioned above. The rapid growth of IT and pharmaceutical drug industries should be given all facilities to expand their operations. The country has been able to maintain a growth rate in GDP of 5-6 per cent per annum despite adverse foreign conditions such as steep increase in prices of crude oil and its inability to reduce its fiscal deficit. The increase has been possible despite meagre foreign aid or foreign direct investment.

Note

1. Post Script (2003): Tenth Five Year Plan's goal to achieve 7-8 per cent p.a. increase in GDP during the plan period has been announced by the Prime Minister; Mr. Jalan (Governor RBI) has confirmed that such a growth rate will be achieved during the plan. Mukesh Ambani of Reliance has forecast an increase in GDP of 15 per cent p.a. during 2020 onwards.

There might have been some excuse for keeping its functions or methods of work undefined back in 1950, when there was no experience with planning and nobody had any idea how the Commission would have to go about its business; there is and has been no justification for keeping it undefined all these years. There were not a few people in the secretariat who thought the setting up of the Commission was a political stunt, designed to serve as a weapon in the forthcoming (1951) election campaign. There is no doubt that the First Plan did serve a political purpose. In fact the timing of the Commission's last minute urgency and hectic speed of preparation of the First Plan were all done with political objectives. The political fortune of the Congress Party was a cause of concern to at least some of the Members of the Planning Commission. Besides the ministers, the Prime Minister, C.D. Deshmukh, G.L. Nanda and Patil were active politicians of the Congress Party and not a little unconcerned with the political impact of the Plan. It must also be remembered that the Congress was not so politically supreme in 1950, as it appeared in 1956 (and later for a long time); it was not by any means certain that it would dominate the polls. The way it swept them was unexpected, perhaps by most Congressmen themselves.

In 1951 Jawaharlal Nehru, the Prime Minister, was less certain of his position, both in the country and within the Congress Party. He was by no means unquestioned king of India. The electorate had not yet given its verdict. The boss of the Congress party had been Sardar Patel, and Panditji was an individual with only a following of some personal admirers and friends. He was always a mass hero, and it was his dominant stature as a mass hero, and the utter lack of courage and stature in the rival group that enabled him to capture the party and the country in 1951. But also to a young and sensitive mind, he was then in many ways a much more inspiring personality.

Few expected that the Commission would be a permanent body. Most Secretariat people with Secretariat minds thought that it would be a temporary affair, and would be wound up, like other commissions, after it had submitted its report and formulated the Plan. In fact I can't forget the stirrings, the uncertainties in the minds of our Research Officers, when the signatures were being affixed to the Draft Outline. Many of us felt that we would lose our jobs, and this is a serious matter any day in India.[2] Mr. Nanda timorously asked Pandit Nehru, "Panditji, the staff of the Commission is quite worried about their future. They are afraid that since the Plan has been prepared, the Planning Commission would be wound up. Panditji replied almost angrily "What nonsense! Planning is a continuous process. The first plan will be followed by a Second Plan, which will be followed by a Third Plan, a Fourth Plan and so on and you can assure the staff that they should have no fears about their career prospects".

Panditji's word "planning is a continuous process: there is no question of the Commission being wound up" which he said to the assembled officers and staff of the commission on July 7, 1951 are still vivid and clear in my mind. How serious the perturbation was can be seen by the fact that the question was put by Nanda himself. Perhaps another side light to this was that even the Deputy Chairman of the Commission didn't know about its future and had either not had the occasion or the courage to discuss it with the Prime Minister. This aspect of working of the teams under the leadership of the Prime Minister (whether it is the Planning Commission or the Cabinet) should not be lost sight of when evaluating the Nehru age. These words of the Prime Minister set at rest any suspicions about the immediate winding up of the Commission. But they did nothing to get either the cabinet to give better shape and clearer direction to its powers and functions, nor did the Commission ever take upon itself the task of assessing its functions, defining the scope or methods of its working or even caring to examine what it was or wasn't doing.

Work on formulation of the First Five Year Plan 1951-56, started in right earnest only after J.J. Anjaria, an economist, who had been working as a Professor in Economics in Bombay joined as Head of the Economics Division. He was a very able economist and also one of the finest men under whom I have worked.[3]

The first draft of the First Five Year Plan was prepared in December 1951, after 18 months of work in the Commission. Pandit Nehru used to attend most of the important meetings of the Commission. I remember that when a paper outlining the economic projections for 1951-56 to 1975 was prepared by the Economic Division, Pandit Nehru came and spent an hour reading it in pin-drop silence. After reading it, he raised a number of questions which were answered to his satisfaction, by Mr. Anjaria and Mr. Deshmukh. I was greatly impressed with Pandit Nehru's strong interest in planning. Although he knew little economics, he had considered it his duty to understand the future of the economy, as outlined in the papers. He had been greatly impressed by the economic planning system of the USSR, which was directed under a Communist Party regime, however.

Because of the importance that Pandit Nehru attached to the views of the Planning Commission, no project or programme could be implemented by any Ministry without the approval of the Commission. If the

Commission wanted any changes in any part of the project or programme, they would have to be made before the project or programme was approved by his Cabinet.

This influence of the Planning Commission was succinctly expressed in a humorous remark which was popular among senior officials of the ministries; "there are three policy making and deliberating bodies within the Government of India—the *Lok Sabha* (the Lower House of Parliament), the *Rajya Sabha* (the Upper House of Parliament) and the Tarlok *Sabha* (the Planning Commission)". The latter designation also expressed the resentment of the senior most civil servants of the influence on policy making of Sardar Tarlok Singh, who was Secretary to the Planning Commission, but junior to them in the ICS.

The Plan was generally received favourably by the press. It was considered realistic because of its emphasis on agriculture and rural development and because the modest investment on it could be mobilized easily. However, the irrepressible cartoonist, Mr. Shankar Pillai, a personal friend and admirer and a critic of Pandit Nehru, had on the cover of his weekly journal, a cartoon which showed a famished Indian groaning under the weight of two thick volumes of the Plan.

Planning was by no means a novel idea in 1950. As early as 1935 the National Planning Committee (NPC) was formed with Nehru as Chairman and it did produce a large number of reports which are remarkable, mostly for the compiling capacity without any analytical thought of K.T. Shah then for anything else. There doesn't seem to be any indication that many on the panels in this committee took their job seriously. And what came out was a series of essays on different aspects of the Indian economy. All the ideas which were agitating the Indian intelligentsia in the 1930s duly found their place in the NPC volumes. Its contribution is merely one of being the first in the picture.

The Bombay Plan was an immensely superior document. Put together by businessmen, it was well thought out, ambitious yet not beyond the reach of possibility and coherent. It was the kind of thinking on planning which, alas has been too much in absence in the Planning Commission and Government during all these years. Courageous yet calculated, diversified yet coherent, it inspired the nation to a bold vision demanding sacrifices of hard work and intense endeavour yet giving hope of fulfilment. We have come closer to it in the Second Plan but unfortunately in the First we seemed to have missed most of its virtues.

The British Government had taken up the idea of development. A post-war reconstruction plan had been formulated. A large number of policy committees had been appointed for framing policies for development after the war (post-war construction it was called even during the war). Most departments had their Post-War Reconstruction Plans by the end of the War and it is these really, which laid the ground-work of the First Plan. Some of the Reports of the Committees or individuals appointed for Planning at this time are unequalled for their excellence of analysis and suggesting most realistic and suitable lines of advice. The Memorandum of Forest Policy by the late I.G. Patel is unequalled by anything produced on the subject since. The cabinet had been seized of the need to coordinate[4] these reconstruction Plans, and already in 1949 Dr. Gian Chand made a comprehensive review of the development programmes in operation in the Centre and the States.

In spite of what had gone before, the task which the Commission faced was a momentous one. The country had never a Plan and wanted it very much. The Bombay Plan, bold and inspiring had remained a vision and any possibility of giving content to its ideas, much less executing them had been shattered by the partition. Moreover, it was a business magnates' plan and this had its distinct drawbacks. The post-war reconstruction plans had been insipid and bureaucratic and in spite of the excellence of many of the ideas had never caught the imagination of the people. To most they were unknown. *The country wanted a 'Plan'!*

The Men Who Composed the Commission

Assembling outstanding or even suitable men together is not Panditji's forte. Anybody has to look at the composition of the Cabinets to understand the significance of this. But in assembling the original Planning Commission, he did extraordinarily well and it is a pity and a misfortune of the country that the gaps caused by their departures were allowed to continue.

Deshmukh, Krishnamachari, Nanda, Mehta, Patil, the original members (though not perhaps the best possible), were an outstanding team by any standard. They were able men, distinguished in one way or the other. The Deputy Chairman, Mr. Gulzari Lal Nanda, was a highly successful labour leader of Ahmedabad; Mr. C.D. Deshmukh, an ICS officer, was the member-in-charge of Finance and Economic Affairs, Sir V.T. Krishnamachari, who had headed the Finance Commission, after retiring from a long tenure of service as the Dewan (Prime Minister) of two princely states—Baroda and Jaipur, had been put-charge of development of natural resources, which included development of irrigation, power and mineral resources. Mr. G.L. Mehta, who had retired from a long tenure as a top executive of the Scindia Steam Navigation Co. which operated ships between various Indian ports, had been given the portfolio of industries. Mr. R.K. Patil, who had resigned his post as a member of the ICS in 1943 at the height of the Quit India Movement launched by Gandhiji in 1942, and had become an ardent Congressman, had the responsibility of development of agriculture.

Besides they were able to get along and function something like a team, (which has never been easy since). Despite the differences in their background and views on different economic and social issues, the personal relations between the members were cordial and expressions of strong differences in views by one member from another were made and received in good humour. I remember that in one meeting on land reforms, an issue on which Sir, V.T. Krishnamachari and Mr. R.K. Patil had strong differences of views, VTK remarked, "Patil you want to bring about revolution with *pan, supari* (betel nut, which is chewed by a large proportion of India's population) and rose water". The implication was that a revolutionary change like radical land reforms would not be made peacefully. The remark was made in good humour and received without offence. Similarly in their discussions with the ministers and top officials of the State Governments, the members would express their reservations about the advisability or otherwise of particular projects or programmes strongly but then leave the state governments to take their own decisions. I remember that in one meeting VTK and Mr. C.D. Deshmukh expressed very strong reservations about some aspects of the Hirakud Project—a large irrigation-*cum*-power-*cum*-flood control project—being constructed in Orissa to the Chief Secretary of the State and asked him to convey them to the Orissa Cabinet. But they did not urge him to ask the Cabinet to change its decisions in the light of their criticism! VTK and Mr. Deshmukh were right and the programmes on which they had expressed their reservations failed.

The Commission was not so lucky in the choice of officers. It got some outstanding men in the first haul: Tarlok Singh, Anjaria, and Nagaraja Rao and among the young men Raj. But that was all. Its will to attract the best available minds seems to have finished there. The Commission showed a singular lack of imagination, sense of purpose, and vision of its proper role and task when it ceased to obtain the officers it needed. Apart from a Chief of the Economic Division who was obviously needed to analyse the economic trend in the country for them to access the financial resources of the state, and their development plans, the Commission has had no really clear idea of what kinds of officers it needed.

At the end of the First Five Year Plan, the author observes that due to the planning exercise, the prospect for policy change was very bright indeed. It would probably be possible to achieve the targets set in the Plan in about seven to eight years. But all the same the effort would be very much worthwhile. The targets have given a momentum and direction to the economy. Take production: industrial production has increased 40 per cent during the period of the Plan and is about 50 per cent in excess of the Plan beginning; in the six years before the Plan it was more or less stagnant. Agricultural production, in spite of ups and downs, has a steady upward trend under current and in 1956-57 prices. It was at an all time high with food grains at 68.6 million tonnes (compared with about 55 million tonnes in 1951) and cotton at about 48 million tonnes compared with 28 million tonnes in 1950-51. The stratagem stagnation in the economy has been broken and a steady upward movement has started. National income has risen. There is a shortage of technical personnel in spite of increasing facilities for education and training. Social overheads like transport and communications network have greatly expanded; I think railways—their total assets must have increased by something like 33 per cent during these years and will more than double during the next few years and it is not confined to government and its expenditure. The countryside has begun to move—look at the pressure on the transport system, the postal system—even the banking system—there is no slack season any more. Look at the way the fertilizer consumption has risen for instance or the fast growing demand for seeds, if supplies can be had. Hard core development will be delayed, partly because we want to do the things ourselves, and not give everything completely to foreign interests or even commercial interests, however, much money will be wasted; we have neither the experience nor the technical personnel. The policy, attempted in Rourkela, failed and the government has progressively moved in the direction of setting up new plants with foreign assistance—Bhilai, Durgapur, the Bhopal factory. But still the trend is towards doing things ourselves to the extent possible. Justifiable, also sound and even speedy in the long run, but initial progress is slow. Bhakra-Nangal for instance, may be the French firm could have done it faster, cheaper. But now we shall be able to construct many Bhakras—provided provincial feelings don't prevent transport of personnel from one part of the country to the other—Nagarjunasagar Dam for instance. Cottage industries will be delayed and much money will be wasted. The NES will not be delayed in its mechanical expansion but bringing in the full fruits of the NES will be delayed considerably because integration of the administrative machinery in the NES will take time.

Also the idea of annual planning should be given much more importance. At the beginning of each financial year, while we are preparing the budget, we should give greater attention to formulation of precise targets of achievements in view of the availability of material, trained manpower, administrative personnel, and financial allocations. It is the lack of such detailed work in an overall manner that is responsible for the difficulties. Every year distinction between the essential and the desirables should be made. Don't cut on heavy industries; the private sector's capacity to contribute to industrial expansion and on measures to improve agriculture production. Have a better re-appraisal of your capacities. We haven't yet brought the small investor into the picture: and national savings certificate alone won't do it. It is with increasing facilities for private small investors to invest in private undertakings; something like a minimum guaranteed dividend if a person invests in an approved scheduled company. There is not enough inter-ministerial coordination in the field of planning. For instance a standing coordinating committee of Secretaries/Joint Secretaries under the auspices of the Planning Commission is an urgent necessity. Such a committee, meeting every month can resolve problems needing inter-ministerial attention and can hammer out the plans for the succeeding year. There is need for much more detailed work and inter-ministerial coordination than does exist. This standing committee should also have a number of sub-committees, e.g. in financial matters.

2001

Indian planning exercise has been burdened with imbibing contradictory ideologies. The targets and contents of the Plans have to be changed frequently in response to external and natural factors as well as by ideological orientation of the planners (*see* Noble and Dutt, 1978 p. 210)[5].

The 1960s saw nationalization of banks, and air travel, setting up of government owned and managed hotels. In the 1970-90s the stress was on reducing losses of the public enterprises, investment in roads, water supply and setting up facilities for training of doctors and engineers etc.

In the 1990s the policy of running industries under the public sector and control over expansion of the private sector had demonstrated that the government has played its role in initiating agricultural and rural development and industrial development as also providing electricity and water supply to cities and to villages, running banks and other economic services, insurance companies, airlines and tourist hotels. Under the impact of the use of dwarf varieties of wheat and rice cultivation with assured water supply there has been a revolutionary increase in their production. Although there has been no similar increase in production of other major crops—sugarcane, cotton and millets, their production has been increasing steadily with slow but steady improvements in varieties and their adoption by the farmers. Today the principal deficit, met by imports, is in the case of cooking oil because production of oil seeds has not kept pace with increase in demand. There has been no famine during all these decades, although local scarcities, particularly in the hilly and forested areas, of Central and Eastern India inhabited by the tribal population are unavoidable because of poor communications.

Although the stock of doctors, trained engineers, scientists and other professionals is not enough, the government has set up and continues to expand such training facilities. It has tried to provide facilities for universal literacy, primary and secondary education and lower and middle level skill development. It has set up primary health centres in and around rural areas and multi-facility hospitals in towns and cities. Its various rural development and welfare schemes, though not run in the most efficient manner, have benefited millions of people. Massive amounts put through small industries development schemes and revolving loans to small collectives has encouraged entrepreneurship development in small towns and villages.

However, the country was put through severe strains because of a system of controls through a licensing system and policy of giving subsidies to export oriented industries in order to maintain a favourable balance of payments position and to qualify for large international loans needed to achieve targets of social and infrastructure development. But the amount of loan repayment obligations and unfavourable balance of payments position had made the country's repayment position precarious. Although the life and general insurance companies remained profitable, the losses of nationalized banks mounted because they were forced to open branches in villages and lend to non-credit-worthy borrowers, under the slogan of *Gharibi Hatao* (Remove Poverty). Although some industries set up under the public sector made profit, a number of them continued to incur losses into crores of rupees.

By 1991, when the country was faced with a balance of payments crisis, all these policies were reversed in order to get bridging loans from the IMF and the World Bank. Under its new policy of liberalization and globalization, it is felt that most of the industries and services are best run by private entrepreneurs and government should concentrate on assisting increase in production of cereals and cotton along with producers' cooperatives of sugar, milk, vegetables and fruit and finally, focus on alleviating poverty by food for work and other programmes. Private entrepreneurs should provide jobs by aggressively improving their products and services such as information technology to make them internationally competitive. This is the essence of the Structural Adjustment Programmes advocated by the IMF and the World Bank. India had to follow this formula from 1991 with consequent increase in growth rate of GDP from 3-4 per cent per annum to 5-6 per cent per annum wiping out its foreign exchange deficit and reducing government's fiscal deficits. It has been able to maintain the latter rate, despite an unfavourable international economic environment. Steep rise in prices of crude oil, three-fourths of the country's requirements of which are met by imports, make a large dent in the country's foreign exchange earnings. India's exports of manufactured consumer goods, consumer durables and machine tools face stiff competition from rapidly developing countries and those from western developed countries.

In the 1990s planning has been reduced to outlining policies and programmes by adopting which Government ensures that balance of payments remains positive and India does not land in the situation in which it found itself in 1991 when foreign exchange reserves were exhausted and India had to abolish most of the export and import controls, under the dictates of the IMF and the World Bank in order to get a loan from the IMF and aid for projects being financed by the Bank. The country still persists in making Five Year Plans and fixing targets of achievement in different sectors. The Plans serve also as an envelope for coordinating the development plans of different states and Union territories; but the Plans have to be modified continually keeping in view the fiscal and balance of payments situation in the country and the international situation, particularly prices for India's imports and prospects for exports. The fiscal deficit must be within respectable limits and the foreign exchange resources must be on the increase so that the country can finance the investments envisaged in the Plans. But Five Year Plans had reached its limits of usefulness.

Emphasis henceforth would be on making monetary and fiscal policies every year, providing funds for implementation of the plans. The latter must concentrate on expansion of infrastructures—improvement of inter-state highways, ports, electric supplies for cities and rural areas, water supplies for drinking and irrigation etc. Development of industries and provision of modern services is left to the leaders of business and industry; the plans should only facilitate their investments.

The policy is to enable private industrialists to improve the quality of their products in order to make them internationally competitive. Increased exports of products such as garments, leather goods, consumer durables ranging from furnishing for home and office to chasses for buses and trucks and a variety of other goods and finally, rapidly expanding exports of computer software have enabled India to have a positive balance of payments. There is now a consensus that most of the industries and infrastructure such as distribution and transmission of electricity and water supply, telecommunications etc. are better managed by companies than by the government. Denationalization of the banks that have started making profits is also being considered actively; certain areas of insurance have been thrown open to foreign insurance companies in order to provide competition to the domestic life and general insurance corporations.

Economic and developmental policies are formulated by the Prime Minister, Finance Minister and other influential ministers in consultation with the commerce and industries associations. The Reserve Bank has acquired much greater influence than it had earlier. Fiscal, monetary and developmental policies are now made by the Ministry of Finance in consultation with the Chambers of Commerce and Industry and planning is reduced to incorporating the results in various Plans. The Plans still serve as instruments of fixing targets for increasing production of products ranging from food grains to consumer durables and coordinating the plan of the Centre and State Governments.

But planning has lost the glamour that it had earlier. Also, it is felt now that in the rapidly changing economic and political situation in the world, five years is too long a period to be useful for projecting trends of investment or its allocation between different sectors of the economy.

To conclude, the fascination with Five Year Plans and with nationalization of means of production is over. It is now believed that monetary and fiscal policies and targets of investment by the government and the private sector should be made annually keeping in view the domestic and international economic situation. The Planning Commission no longer has the influence that it had in the 1950s and the 1960s. The Tenth Plan 2000-2007 has fixed targets to be achieved of various sectors of the economy. However, the targets will be continually modified keeping in view the progress in different sectors of the economy. Furthermore the earlier policy of monetary assistance to cottage, small scale and big industries has to change into providing an enabling environment for their growth and expansion. Earlier the All India Handloom and Handicrafts Boards had concentrated on protection of employment for handloom weavers, and craftsmen. Now these boards must concentrate on assisting handloom weavers to modernize designs and improve quality of festive garments produced by them so as to have large and expanding markets for their products for the affluent and in the export markets. Earlier the institutes of technology and management were established by the Government, now the IT professionals, trainees of these institutes, settled abroad are offering to upgrade these institutions with suitable financial contribution. The physicians and surgeons settled abroad are eager to come home to establish world class hospitals providing standard treatment. The Escorts Hospital in Delhi is an example. Development of industries and provision of modern services is left to the leaders of business and industry; the plans should only facilitate their investments.

Following India's lead, most of the developing countries of South and South East Asia and Africa also prepared five year plans. Many of them still persist with preparation of five-year plans. But in them also plans have met a similar fate that it has in India. The era of five-year plans has gone.

Notes

1. The author joined the Planning Commission in April 1950; he along with Dr. K.N. Raj was about the fifth officer to join the Commission.
2. It was particularly serious for me in those days, when neither I nor my parents had any savings and jobs were not plentiful as they are today.
3. Since I was a Geographer in an Economic Division, he did not quite know what to do with me. Therefore, he left me to do the studies that I wanted to.
4. The need for coordination is felt by a body in proportion to its habits of confused thinking and unsystematic action and was undoubtedly felt much more acutely by the Indian Government than by the British. This need is the best excuse for multiplying staff and most fruitful way of confusing things further all-around. Today, coordination and the ways of achieving it are India's contribution to the English language and governmental practice.
5. "Any evaluation of Indian national planning activity must take into account the conflicting bases upon which that activity was founded. The initial emphasis upon agriculture and village self-sufficiency reflected Gandhian principles of useful labour and the intrinsic value of the individual. Later emphases upon capital intensive and large-scale industrial developments mirror the growing strength of the collective good over the individual good and the substitution of Russian Marxist model for indigenous approaches. The recent attempts to strike a balance between the two approaches in the Fourth and Fifth Five-Year Plans result in part from a gradual weakening of the position of the Soviet-style Marxist planning and a strengthening of the

15

Role of Economic Planning: Retrospect and Prospect

Planning Commission and Its Usefulness

In the concluding chapter we give the author's observations on the functioning of the Planning Commission at two points of time. One in 1956, after he had spent six years in the Planning Commission and the First Five Year Plan's implementation results could be observed. The second was written in 2001, fifty years after the setting up of the Planning Commission.

1956

The Planning Commission set up early in 1950[1] was one of the biggest pieces of news which was exercising the intellect and intelligentsia of the country. It obtained very wide publicity and people expected great things from it. There were misgivings and doubts also, especially among the better informed and more thinking. The place, which the Planning Commission found in the resignation letter of John Mathai, had only stimulated and heightened these misgivings. Actually there was much force in Mathai's criticism of the Commission's setting up. The terms of reference of the Commission were so broad and general, and its relationship with the Central and State Governments were so undefined that any person with an analytical or precise mind would have raised his voice strongly against the setting up of such a body in this fashion. The ghost of John Mathai has haunted the Commission throughout its existence, and it is this very lack of definition of its powers, functions and way of working that have been practically responsible for the ineffective state to which the Commission has been reduced.

position of indigenous ingenuity. Although in some instances the Soviet approach has continued to influence events in India such as the recent nationalization of banking and coal mining; the failure of nationalization efforts in the wheat trade lends support to the posture of pragmatic realism adopted by the Indian planners. Dutt asserts that the most effective strategy in retrospect would have been a decided emphasis upon an agriculturally-based economy for the first fifteen years or so of the planning period. Industrialization schemes related to improving agricultural production and village self-sufficiency would have been more useful than the heavy emphasis upon urban-based industrial activity. Probably, after strengthening the agricultural base, an industrial emphasis would have been more meaningful and appropriate to the Indian conditions.

The process of planning in India has also been deficient in that objectives have usually been overstated and, consequently, difficult to achieve, and the entire nature of the planning environment was not adequately assessed to systematically relate cause and effect relationships. The primary example of this latter condition was the failure by Indian planners to recognize until the mid-1960s the vital importance of population control upon the success of the entire planning efforts."

Reference

Dutt, Ashok, K. Dutt and Frank Casta: "Ideological Orientation of the National Planning Process in India" in *Indian Urbanization and Planning*. Tata MacGaw Hill, New Delhi, 1978, pp. 199-211.

Index